Getting What
You Deserve

Mary:
Here's hoping you'll
soon be able to hit
the links

Bob

DALE GOLDHAWK

Getting What You Deserve

The Adventures of
Goldhawk Fights Back

THE DUNDURN GROUP
TORONTO

Copy-Editor: Michael Hodge
Design: Jennifer Scott
Printer: Transcontinental

National Library of Canada Cataloguing in Publication
Goldhawk, Dale
Getting what you deserve : the adventures of Goldhawk fights back / Dale Goldhawk.

ISBN 1-55002-467-1

1. Goldhawk, Dale. 2. Consumer protection—Canada. I. Title.

HC120.C63G64 2003   381.3'4'092   C2003-904874-8

1   2   3   4   5   07   06   05   04   03

Canada

THE CANADA COUNCIL | LE CONSEIL DES ARTS
FOR THE ARTS | DU CANADA
SINCE 1957 | DEPUIS 1957

ONTARIO ARTS COUNCIL
CONSEIL DES ARTS DE L'ONTARIO

We acknowledge the support of the **Canada Council for the Arts** and the **Ontario Arts Council** for our publishing program. We also acknowledge the financial support of the **Government of Canada** through the **Book Publishing Industry Development Program** and **The Association for the Export of Canadian Books**, and the **Government of Ontario** through the **Ontario Book Publishers Tax Credit** program, and the **Ontario Media Development Corporation's Ontario Book Initiative.**

Care has been taken to trace the ownership of copyright material used in this book. The author and the publisher welcome any information enabling them to rectify any references or credit in subsequent editions.

J. Kirk Howard, President

Printed and bound in Canada.⊕
Printed on recycled paper.
www.dundurn.com

Dundurn Press
8 Market Street
Suite 200
Toronto, Ontario, Canada
M5E 1M6

Dundurn Press
2250 Military Road
Tonawanda NY
U.S.A. 14150

To Jill, Emma, and Nick,
the joys of my life; my reason for being.

And to Alphonse and Pauline
who shine brightly inside me, even now.

Acknowledgements

Goldhawk Fights Back has always been a team effort. My deep thanks go to Senior Producer Laurie Few, and Producers Marlene McArdle, Stacey Johnson, Jennifer Sheriff, Brian Woodcock, John Soroka, and Heinz Avigdor at CTV. And from CBC, where it all began, my thanks to Senior Producer Trudie Richards (now Professor Richards, Faculty Co-op Advisor, Public Relations at Mount St. Vincent University in Halifax) and Producers Susan Nightingale, Marie Capuccetti, Rob Roy, Malcolm Hamilton, and Ann Seymour.

Table of Contents

Prologue

August 28, 2001

I was trying to gird up for battle one more time. I even put on a suit. Lashed a tie around my neck, loose as a noose. I looked at my Florsheims, but I yanked-on my cowboy boots. I was ready for anything.

Season number ten was about to begin. It was hard to believe I had survived nine years at CTV — solving problems, chasing bad guys, and fighting for change. That was our mantra. When anybody asked us for a job description, we would chant the mantra.

Some of the younger members of my team had trouble in the beginning believing we could do it. I knew we could. I had done it before. And I was just stubborn enough to think we could do it forever.

In nine years, 250,000 Canadians came to us with their problems. Looking for help. Asking for advice. Blowing the whistle. Wanting us to hold a government or a company or some slippery Oil Can Harry accountable. Those 250,000 Canadians touched our lives. Deeply. They gave us their trust. They let us into their lives. They knew they could share their vulnerabilities with us. We worked hard to never let them down. Sometimes we did. Sometimes we had no choice. When we couldn't win, it made us a little crazy. We told ourselves that anything that didn't kill us made us stronger. Crazier, but stronger.

Exactly 390 episodes of *Goldhawk Fights Back* appeared on CTV. More than nineteen hours of injustice, unfairness, tragedy, and loss. In the end, the good guys usually won. Just like the old westerns. But this was real.

So was the money, we found out. We never planned to keep track of how much we got back or won for those who came to us for help. That seemed crass. And not all problems can be solved with money, anyway. One year, near the end, when we had some extra help for a few months, we did take a calculator and add up the cash — settlements, pensions, refunds, awards. In 1999 alone, we helped put $3.2 million back into the pockets of Canadians. We also helped put several people in jail, we tried to get one out, we helped some people die with dignity, we annoyed politicians and guys in way-too-expensive suits, we triggered changes in laws and government regulations, we equalized unfair battles, and we chased a phony reverend through traffic down a mountain highway and all the way out of the country. And we laughed. A lot. We were fond of saying we helped people get what they deserve.

We were like the plumber you get late at night when the overflowing toilet won't stop pouring water into your basement office. We hammered away at last-ditch solutions. Our clients usually came to us when nothing else worked, when the situation had become hopeless. We almost never opened a case where the solution looked like a slam dunk. An old friend joked I had become the St. Jude of Canadian journalism. St. Jude is the patron saint of hopeless causes. My father knew that. When I was a kid, I remember he kept a St. Christopher statuette stuck to the dashboard for safety and a St. Jude medallion tucked away in his wallet for hope. You never knew. It couldn't hurt.

I walked out the back door and pressed the button to unlock the Beater. *Click.* The beloved Beater. A Cougar, the last of its line. Now extinct. It was backed into the garage, ready for action. I pressed the garage door opener on the sun visor. Fired up the 4.6 litre, fully blown, dual-exhaust V8. It gave a throaty response. Geez, I loved that sound. The Cougar leapt out the door and was soon gone from the neighbourhood.

That was one of the things I liked about Pierre Trudeau. He taught me that move. Once, in 1979, I was chasing him for the brief time he was out of power during his sixteen-year gig as prime minister. Canadians were in the Joe Clark "hiccup of history" government and my assignment editor, who obviously never cared about weekends, sent me and my long-suffering sidekick Don Purser to Montreal Friday night. Mission: Find Trudeau over the weekend. Engage him in conversation. Right. No problem.

We lived in the car outside his sister's place for twenty-four hours. We knew he was in there with his sons. It was just a matter of time. At hour twenty-five, the garage door opened just in time to spit out a speeding Volvo station wagon. The Trudeau kids were in the back, peeking out at us. Trudeau was scrunched down in the passenger seat. Mountie at the wheel. We gave chase. But the Volvo was soon gone from the neighbourhood.

I punched the gas and merged with the traffic on Highway 401. I was headed for the compound. Agincourt. CTV headquarters. I always thought about management as I sped toward the building I had taken to calling "the Font of all Human Knowledge." I don't know why. I guess because it's the dumbest description I could make up.

That was the thing about management types. They always triggered strong emotion. Some had their heads in the clouds, some had their heads up their own asses. Some had none at all.

At *Goldhawk Fights Back*, we said one thing to our long-suffering, sometimes hapless news supervisors and editors at CTV: "Please, don't help us. Just let us do it. Tell us when we're wrong, we'll take it under consideration. Dump us when you can't stand us anymore. Just don't help us."

How many times had I danced that dance? Sung that hymn? The assignment editor had always treated us with benign neglect. I loved it. Ignored but not hated. It was the best we could expect. But every once in a while, some news biggie would put the thumbscrews to the assignment editor. He would shape up by offering to help us. We went nuts. Help us? Are you crazy?

Getting the system to move for our clients, playing all sides in delicate negotiations, keeping an ultra-low profile in our investigations — all this required much more than gross motor skills. I had a nightmare one night: The GFB team was performing delicate heart surgery on the side of the road, when the assignment editor drove up in his coffee wagon. He was keeping the donor heart alive in his bun oven.

And don't get me wrong. That assignment editor was an old room-mate of mine. We cut our teeth as cub reporters at the *Telegram*, the *Toronto Star*'s worst nightmare in the newspaper wars of the late sixties in Toronto. I loved that guy. Just don't help us, I pleaded. Let us rise or fall on our own. Give us the rope. We'll hang ourselves. We used a lot of gallows humour on the team. Hardly anybody in the entire network escaped (what we called) our charming wit. We were often told that someday we would be kicked out of the network. Downsized. Neutralized. Sanitized. Euthanized. I reminded everybody that the first guy out on the street gets the best spot.

Humour was always our best weapon at the network. We also used it as a shield. And a tranquilizer. God knows not much else worked. Only a handful of people understood and valued what we did. News Boss Henry Kowalski, and after him News Boss Robert Hurst. CTV Superboss Ivan Fecan understood, too. He had been in the news trenches as a young man. And he had been the guy who invented *Goldhawk Fights Back* in 1981, when he was my boss at CBC TV. Eerily, we even look alike.

All most people knew was that *Goldhawk Fights Back* cost too much money, raised too much hell, spent too much time on the line with lawyers, had a disrespectful attitude, cost too much money, wouldn't take much editorial guidance, didn't fit the corporate mould, and cost too much money.

But I still think John Cassaday liked us. After a fashion. Cassaday was CTV president when I was hired. We all lived together happily in the CTV office tower in the Eaton Centre. It was an open-concept office with a huge hole cut in the floor between the executive level and the lower, editorial level. My office was right under Cassaday's. He would lean over once in while to yell at us, usually me, to shut up. He apparently couldn't hear himself think. It was tough to do presidential stuff with all that shouting on the phone going on in the background. Cassaday called *Goldhawk Fights Back* the "Commercial Removal Department." It was a misnomer. As far as I knew — and I'm sure I would have been the first one to find out — we never triggered the removal of a commercial.

Sure, there was that Ford thing. Ford of Canada threatened to remove $7 million worth of advertising. But it never happened. What did happen was that Ford, pursued by *Goldhawk Fights Back* to recall faulty ignition switches that set vehicles on fire, did issue a recall, the biggest ever for its Canadian operation. That happened after I chased a now-past president of Ford into a linen closet at a large hotel during a shareholders' meeting. But there was no commercial removal.

Cassaday did have a point when he talked about the way the TV crews dressed — the sound men and the cameramen. He said they dressed like gardeners. I thought some of them didn't dress as well as gardeners, but I may not be the best judge. A lot of people thought I dressed like a guy who had spent too long at the Calgary Stampede. To further annoy any suits, I always needed a haircut. When Don Ferguson of the CBC's *Royal Canadian Air Farce* used to play me in skits, he wore a grey fright wig. It wasn't far off.

I came down out of warp drive in time to make the exit at McCowan. It loomed large ahead. The compound. It sits at the end of a street named for the local affiliate, Channel Nine Drive. It's a dead end street. I leaned out the window and used my electronic card to open the security gate and drove to where I could find a place to beach the Beater — at the back of a crowded lot large enough to park a 747.

I had lots of time to think while I trekked toward the door. It was as if large chunks of my life were passing through my brain. Flashing before me. For the last few weeks, CTV, as it had done many times in the past, had been playing coy with my contract. They had once again passed the deadline for notifying me of their intention (or not) to engage in negotiations for a new contract for *Goldhawk Fights Back*. It was the same little game of footsie we had played almost every year since 1992.

I was in regular contact with CTV's Vice-President of News, Dennis McIntosh. Sure, money was tight, he said to me constantly. But things should be fine for next year, he said, if we lop off the plans I had to replace a staff member who was leaving the team. That would have brought us down to a two-person operation, from a four-person team in the good old days. I winced about that, but said OK. Dennis assured me things were fine. My budget, he said, would be flat. But it would be there. No problem.

But I still did not have the official notice that CTV intended to enter into negotiations for a new contract. That irritated me. All the navel gazing I had been doing was triggered by that irritation. And the irritation led to a nagging worry. Maybe they were going to ambush me at the last minute and kill *Goldhawk Fights Back* on the spot. Nah, I thought. Every year I said that.

But maybe this was the year. Maybe I had finally pissed off too many people at the network level. Chasing bad guys and solving problems in the real world was a cinch compared to this. Out there, it was fight or die. Inside the network lived the stony silence of management. You never knew what they thought. Even after they talked, you wondered what they meant.

As I put my card into another security slot by the back door a new thought struck me. What if my hair had finally caught up with me? Say what you will about television, hard-driving newsrooms, and investigative journalism, sooner or later, no matter how hard you fight it, it all comes down to hair.

I was just about the only on-air guy at the network with grey hair. Long grey hair. The only one left. Ken Ernhoffer had neat, mercilessly trimmed silver-grey hair, and he had been turfed out by CTV in 1999, almost two years ago to the very day (August 26, 1999). And Ken, the former CTV Moscow Bureau Chief, was a hell of a lot nicer than I was. He wore better suits.

There were greyhairs at the network. It's just that they were hidden. Lloyd Robertson was forced to go in for his periodic dip in the dye vat. His hair colour vacillated from a kind of purply-grey to an odd shade of henna. And then there was Craig Oliver, CTV's legendary Ottawa Bureau Chief. He used to have little tufts of whitish hair in the back, and then one day he showed up with strange henna-coloured hair. Sort of like Lloyd's. I ran into him at the Ottawa Bureau, on my way to chase somebody on the Hill, and I had a tough time averting my eyes from the top of his head. It occurred to me then that this henna colour, not found in nature, was also the colour Dennis McIntosh had been sporting over his grey. What was it, the power colour? The way to get ahead at CTV?

I was grinning to myself as I walked down the long hallway by the control room called Megamaster. Power colour. I got out my card again to unlock security door number two. Then I thought about my old friend Mike Duffy. Wait a minute. Has he got any hair at all on his huge, fact-packed, melon head? Yeah, a little bit of white, neatly trimmed. Must be room, then, for my bushy grey. I had to stop it. My daydreaming was producing a facial expression that seemed to suggest I was having a good day. Bad idea to wear a happy face in the dour, shiny hallways of Agincourt.

I stuck my card into security door number three, the final airlock leading to the newsroom. News weenies were scampering everywhere, as usual. Other, more senior weenies were hunched over keyboards. Pecking. Here and there, attempts were being made to commit some serious journalism. I looked around for Dennis. We had a 9 a.m. appointment. I walked out a side door to check his little office. He wasn't there. His office always brought a smile to my face. It had been a CFTO star dressing room. Then it became the green room for *Canada AM*. Now it was Dennis's room. The desk was crammed over into the corner and Dennis sat with his back to the door. Anybody could sneak up on him. When you stuck your head in the door the first thing you saw was the still-functional dressing room hair-sink.

I went back into the newsroom and spotted Dennis in a far corner, talking to his deputy weenies. One had a painted smile on her face. The other stared at me as if I had an arrow sticking out of my back. Uh oh.

"Dennis. Ready for me?" I called out.

"Let's go to my office," he said, taking off across the room. I followed. I walked in and sank into the leather couch.

"Well, the news isn't good."

"The news is never good."

Dennis grabbed a single piece of paper from his desk. It was a "Dear Goldhawk" letter. "Please be advised that CTV shall not be renewing..."

"What?" was all I could manage. Then, "Why?"

"It's a money thing," said Dennis.

"You could have warned me this was coming."

"The decision was just made."

Oh great, I thought. Always good to be hit right between the eyes with a nice, fresh decision. Those stale ones really hurt.

"There's a process, Dale," Dennis was saying. "When you leave the building now, your card will work on all the doors then be deleted from the computer as you clear the back door. You all right?"

"Fine," I said. I made the long walk down the shiny hallways, watched from behind by two security guards tailing me at a tasteful distance. I used my card to unlock the exterior door and then tossed it in a handy garbage can full of cigarette butts and coffee cups. I climbed into the Beater and was soon gone from the neighbourhood.

1.

Step One

It was a Monday in mid-October, 1992. I was stuck in rush hour traffic in Toronto on the Don Valley Parkway at 7:30 a.m. Of course I was stuck. This was Toronto. Everybody was stuck in traffic.

The leaves were turning. I got a good chance to look at them. Nice reds and yellows. Red and yellow tail lights, too. Inside my head it was all black and blue. I was in culture shock. The night before, I had flown back to Toronto from Montreal, after I did my usual national radio phone-in show. Now I was heading back to TV Land, going downtown again after years with CBC Radio, most recently as the voice behind *Cross Country Checkup*. I lived in Toronto, but I had to fly to Montreal every weekend because that's where CCCU was produced for the network. For the next month, wrapping up one job and launching into another, I would work seven days a week — weekdays at CTV and weekends at CBC Montreal.

I hated to leave *Checkup*. I loved that show, even though several of my way-too-earnest acquaintances in the trade called it "Cross Country Upchuck." As a species, we journalists can be a snide, snotty bunch. One of my friends in the biz could not understand how I could, as he used to say, "listen to complete drivel in wide-eyed wonder." I thought many of my callers were a whole lot smarter than some of the pundits and smartasses they listened to on the radio, read in the newspapers, and watched on television.

Behind the wheel, killing time, wearing my first tie in four years, I was thinking ahead — something all of us in broadcasting should try once in a while. What kind of adjustments would I have to make in my new life as ombudsman for CTV *National News*? By the way, is that title pompous, or what? Could anybody even say it? Then I thought, as I inched ahead a car length or so and hit the brakes again, maybe it was the same job, with the volume turned way up.

At CBC Radio, I tried to give a forum to Canadians; I defended their right to free speech. Now I was going to do that again, and also step out of the studio to even-up the sides in unfair battles. To be sure, it was a populist approach to journalism, one that required the proper kind of attitude. I was always sure about attitude: skeptical, not cynical; serious, not about myself, but about the work; and suspicious enough to understand that news is what they don't want you to know — everything else is advertising.

I wheeled up in front of 42 Charles Street, the world headquarters of the CTV Television Network. It was a bit of a dump — one of those nondescript brick blockhouses, built to last forever in the 1950s. There was no place to park. I finally found a spot on the B2 level of a seedy, leaking underground garage a block and a half away. Convenient. The offices of *Goldhawk Fights Back*, I was told with some pride, would be on the top floor of the CTV building. When the elevator opened on the ninth floor, I thought I had pressed the wrong button. It was a warehouse — a huge, open storage area where CTV's broken desks, disembowelled computers, and three-legged chairs had come to die.

There in the middle of it all stood Laurie Few, my CTV producer — my only staff. The sardonic Cheshire cat grin on her face told me I was in the right place. We spent several hours assembling an office. It looked like something out of a Mickey Rooney movie: By the end of the day, the neighborhood kids had pulled enough junk together to put on a play.

Everybody in Canada knew I was coming. CTV was broadcasting the World Series that fall. The Blue Jays were steaming. People were glued to their sets right across Canada. Almost every time CTV took a break from the game, there I was: *Goldhawk Fights Back*, coming soon to a CTV affiliate near you. Joe Carter would blast one out of the park and then there I was, darting down fire escapes, lurking in back alleys, always with a furtive expression. I was hard at work, dammit, and I meant business. In one scene, I was seen comforting a suffering patient in a hospital bed. I was relieved the CTV promotion department didn't have me act out all the beatitudes.

The *Goldhawk Fights Back* promos stuck like glue. Everybody had seen them. Everybody knew that Goldhawk was coming to CTV to pick a fight or something. People would stop me on the street while the World Series was still on and say they just loved what I did. When I explained, with some consternation, that I hadn't done anything yet, they just nodded happily and sympathetically. Poor guy. He must be working too hard.

Then the phone started to ring. We heard from Canadians anywhere and everywhere across the country. It was a trickle for a day or two, and then a deluge. We were soon overwhelmed, performing our own brand of problem-solving triage on hundreds of callers. People would leave messages and we would spend hours taking off the messages the next day. Our greatest angst in those days was how far behind we were on the phones. We opened files on dozens and dozens of cases where we thought we might be able to make a difference.

Karen King called us from the Halifax area, where she had been fighting a one-woman battle to get heard. But she was a single mom who lived on the wrong side of the tracks in the small village of Beaverbank. Actually, Karen also lived on the wrong side of the highway that went through town.

Every day she walked her son to kindergarten, shadowing him safely across the busy highway to the elementary school. Karen had an option: She could have subjected her son to a long school bus ride twice a day just to get him the three blocks he was from school. She didn't have the heart. And she didn't have a car, as most other parents in the village did.

I watched as most parents who lived on the other side of the highway drove up to the school and dropped off their kids. To them, crossing the highway was not an issue, not even on their radar. But to Karen, watching every penny, living the life of poverty, cars and the safety they could provide was for other kids and other families.

When Karen raised the issue in Beaverbank, before she called us and before we went to visit her, nobody really paid much attention. Her neighbours paid the usual lip service. Yes, it was a good idea to have a crosswalk on the highway, but no they didn't really have any time to engage in a fight to get it. Besides, as we were told by many residents of Beaverbank, nobody wanted to rock the boat. It was a small place where everybody knew everybody and complaining en masse in public just wasn't done. So much for the good life available to families lucky enough to live in small communities.

Karen King complained to local councillors, to her MP, and to her MPP. She went up one side of bureaucrats and down the other. She even phoned the premier's office. Everybody treated her equally. They listened. Some nodded heads. They all ignored her.

Getting a crosswalk meant money. It would cost $700 to paint lines on the road and $4,000 a year to hire a crosswalk guard. Halifax County Councillor Dave Merrigan was one of Karen King's prime targets.

"She's driving me nuts," he told us. "Besides, she's really the only one complaining about this. This is not a controversy. Her kid can take the school bus if she's worried."

Well, other parents were worried. So were school officials. They were just very low-key about it, that's all. Let Karen do all the heavy lifting. As for Merrigan, he seemed more riled up by Karen King's attitude than by any questions involving child safety around the school in Beaverbank.

When we went to town, he did consent to an interview to explore whether anything could be done. It was a long, heated conversation on the shoulder of the busy highway, and in the end I did seem to get some kind of concession or mild promise of action from Merrigan.

"I haven't found anybody who thinks the crosswalk is a bad idea. You're not saying that, are you?" I asked an irritated Merrigan.

"No, I'm not," he replied. "But I would suggest to you that there are lots of things we might want here in Beaverbank we can't get."

"Can't afford it?"

"No."

"Okay," I said, looking for some kind of commitment, even concern about the traffic that whizzed past us as we talked. "Assuming that the Department of Transport says this is a good place to put a crosswalk and parents here volunteer to work the crosswalk, would you paint the lines on the road? Could there, under those circumstances, be a cross-walk here?"

"Absolutely," he said, way too fast. "Who could disagree with that?"

"You tell me," I said.

"There's no way," replied Merrigan. It was a loose, unspecific, shaky promise as weak as any tea Aunt Nelly ever drank. But it was all I had.

I called the *Goldhawk Fights Back* Used Furniture Depot back in Toronto to report my limited success. Laurie Few and I agreed we would have to watch this file for several months to make sure a crosswalk was installed for Karen King and her timid neighbours and friends. Where are we as a society, if we can't even shell out a few bucks to keep our children safe from traffic?

It was a lukewarm, wishy-washy beginning for *GFB* on CTV. We hadn't really been able to do much of anything. Karen King put her faith in us and we were unable to deliver.

Already, I was wondering about this latest career move. My return to a life on the road, a life I had survived many years earlier in my career, was a hard reality bite. It would take some adjusting.

Few thought I should have a field producer on this first shoot. So she found me one and sent him along with me. When we had checked into the hotel the night before the shoot and made contact with the local CTV Bureau cameraman, I asked the producer if he would like to join me for a drink in the lobby bar.

"I don't drink, he said. "I have this sickness."

"You mean you're an alcoholic?"

"I'm sick with this condition."

"What kind of condition?"

"It's terminal."

"You mean you're gonna die?"

"Well, eventually. Right now, I can watch you drink, if you like."

"No thanks," I said. "You sound like an old girlfriend I once knew."

The next day, right in the middle of the raucous interview with Merrigan, the producer yelled, "Cut!"

"This interview is degenerating into an argument," he announced. I couldn't believe it. I was having a tough enough time with Merrigan as it was. The councillor already thought we were all peckerheads. Now the producer was proving it by pouring cold water on a good, hot debate. I looked at the cameraman, my old friend Gordon Danielson, moved my index finger in the customary circular motion, and we rolled again.

After the interview was over and Merrigan had left us on the side of the road, the crew and I held a seminar on yelling "Cut."

"Gord already knows my rule about the camera stopping from long years of experience, but I am willing to repeat it," I said, looking at the field producer, the reporter, and the sound guy. Gord started to grin. He knew what was coming.

"The camera stops when a) I say 'Stop the camera,' or b) long after I'm dead or unconscious, when all physical activity in the vicinity has ceased," I explained.

The policy was almost a 100 percent success. During the next nine years, *Goldhawk Fights Back* would shoot about a thousand hours of videotape. In all that time, only one cameraman put down his camera after a vividly-worded threat delivered by an angry, big-fisted farmer. I thought Marty McSorley's dad was going to pound me into the ground like a tent peg. Maybe the cameraman had the right idea, but I still gave him hell later — after McSorley let us live.

Glued to my cellphone in the airport departure lounge in Halifax, Laurie and I talked about the success we were having with Janet Watson's case. Janet was only thirty-eight, but a severe on-the-job back injury in Toronto meant she could not work at all. Six doctors, from general practitioners to neurosurgeons, had said she was unfit for work.

But the Workers' Compensation Board in Ontario said their doctors declared her healthy. Janet had been surviving on $1,200 a month from the board, when the board changed her status. Her disability pension was cut down to $187.71 a month for what the board called a "loss of enjoyment of life" pension. At that point, Janet had lost all her independence and was relying on help from friends and relatives just to eat.

She sure couldn't work. She couldn't stand the back pain. She couldn't even stand up for very long without help.

We took the case back to the board and it changed its mind. Janet was put back on full pension while new doctors evaluated her condition. The full pension stayed with Janet until she was able to gradually do some work, several months after she had come to us for help.

Clifford and Donald Ross of Webb, Saskatchewan, didn't want our help at all. At least for themselves. They wanted us to fight for better-quality, less-dangerous diesel fuel being sold to thousands of Saskatchewan farmers. Both Donald and Clifford knew how bad it could get. They both bought contaminated diesel fuel from a wholesaler. At first, it made their tractors run roughly. Then two of them caught fire. Damage was in the thousands of dollars. Several of Donald and Clifton's neighbours in Northern Saskatchewan had the same problem. The Cliftons took the matter into their own hands and sued the wholesaler.

In the heat of that battle, they discovered that Saskatchewan was only one of two provinces in Canada that did not have its own fuel standards. That's where the Cliftons wanted us to come in. Convince the government to pass a fuel standards law.

As we were leaving the farmhouse, Donald said, "Will ye be stayin' fer dinner?" I said no, and we headed out on the long drive back to Saskatoon. I don't know what random big-city gene made me say no. After that, I always said yes, even though at times in some remote parts of the country I was not always sure what I was eating.

The next day, we went to Justice Minister Bob Mitchell. We caught up with him in the halls of the legislature in Regina. Mitchell said those fuel standards could easily be enshrined in law.

"The first time I heard about it is when you guys called," Mitchell said. "Fuel quality is vitally important to Saskatchewan farms. We'll look into it. It ought not to be hard to get some fuel standards. We'll take a look at the federal guidelines and see if we can adapt them for Saskatchewan."

"There oughta be a law?" I asked.

"Yeah," he said. "There oughta be a law."

While I had been hanging around in the hallways of the Saskatchewan legislature, waiting for Mitchell, I had time to think once again about Agnes Schwarz. Worry about her, really. Agnes came to us hoping we could help her stay alive. Agnes, who lived at the time in Eastern Ontario, was only forty-nine. But she had lived a lifetime of abuse and hardship. Agnes married twice. Both husbands were abusive. She was first married at seventeen. She bore two sons. Her husband beat her regularly. Finally, she could take it no longer. She packed up her two little sons and ran away from her husband, with only seventy-six cents in her pocket.

Those sons were grown now, and doing well in university. But Agnes faced a new threat from an obsessive, drug-addicted boyfriend. She had told him to get lost. He wouldn't. He chased her everywhere. Broke into her home. Attacked her. Tried to kill her. Restraining orders, to him, were meaningless. Agnes only slept well when he was in jail. Sometimes, Agnes put him there herself by complaining to police.

By November 23, 1992, the boyfriend had been out of jail for six days, and Agnes was convinced he was on his way to her home in Cobourg, Ontario.

"He told me before he went to jail, 'When I get out of jail, bitch, you're mine. If I can't have you, you die.' He's just biding his time. I know it. I can sit here and tell you, it's going happen," Agnes whispered. "But I believe, 100 percent, that wherever or whenever he gets me, I'm not going to die. I'm going to survive."

We spent a lot of time sharing all the facts of this case with the Cobourg Police Department. The officers and Chief D.K. McDougall were determined they would protect Agnes. Everyone waited. Day by day. Finally, Cobourg Police were told the boyfriend had already been arrested by another police force for a break-and-enter charge. He had been on his way back to Cobourg and needed some cash. The boyfriend went back to jail. Agnes was safe, at least for awhile.

There had been no safe refuge for thirty-three-year-old Ann Pirko, the mother of two young boys. No police force could help her. She was raped and murdered in Brampton, Ontario, on March 20, 1990. She was killed by a violent sex offender out on bail after attacking a woman in Saskatchewan.

Ontario's Criminal Injuries Compensation Board, in correct bureaucratic fashion, paid $4,000 for Ann Pirko's funeral. It could not compensate the little boys or their father because Ann Pirko had not been working outside the home at the time of her death. She was a student. Unemployed. So the government could not, officially, compensate the family for any loss of income.

"So, if you're not earning anything, you're not worth anything," said Doug Roche, Ann Pirko's brother.

He came to us for help. We went to the board only to find the policy about not working was a flexible one. The board promised that, since we had brought this to its attention, it would deliberate once again. It did, awarding the family $58,000. Appreciable, for a societal benefit. Not much of anything for a mom, a wife, and a sister.

Lynda Cameron would have paid any price for a little peace for her nineteen-year-old son, Robert. He suffered from a deep and distressing mental illness that defied treatment. Lynda was worried he would hurt someone. His rash, sometimes violent behaviour frightened everybody around him. Robert's illness had already destroyed Lynda's marriage. Lynda was left to manage — mainly to find a safe and secure spot for Robert to be treated.

She had become, of necessity, an expert in mental health facilities. She knew the Whitby Psychiatric hospital just east of Toronto had the kind of secure treatment centre where Robert could stay, and maybe find a treatment some day that would alleviate his combined manic depression and schizophrenia. The kind of madness that compelled him to walk out into busy traffic, believing God would protect him.

But Whitby Psychiatric was full. We put Robert's case before the officials there one more time. Impressed by a closer look at his file, realizing his extreme need, they made room. Robert had found a home where people would know how to care for him. Lynda cried when she heard the news. We felt her relief, her sadness, and her regret.

We were really starting to develop a rhythm with the *Goldhawk Fights Back* operation. We were on the road every week, turning in one item a week to the desk to be aired on *CTV National News* that night. The item was always accompanied by a debrief with Lloyd Robertson at the big anchor desk.

I always enjoyed my time with Lloyd. Lloyd was a quick study. He would understand the gist of the story immediately and in a few seconds we would work out how I would, in conversation, reveal a few additional facts or last-minute events to round-out the story. We taped the debrief at 9 p.m. CTV news editors and producers always played it ultra-safe — no live debriefs unless it was some kind of national emergency. The debrief was the brainchild of News VP Henry Kowalski. He wanted something that would set the GFB items aside from the rest of the newscast.

But it was one thing to be loved up on executive row and quite another to survive on the floor of the jungle — in the network news room. It was a place of soaring egos, faded hopes, grinding cynicism, raging hormones, and ruinous jealousy. Fresh in from Carpetland my mere presence set off a symphony of moaning, whining, bleating, and farting. They couldn't figure out what the hell I was supposed to be doing. Was this news, or an episode of Dick Tracy? What's a news guy doing helping people, anyway? Aren't we all supposed to be impartial observers of the human condition?

There were two major battles to be won: assignment and script approval. One we won, one we fought tooth and nail for nine years. The basic internal machinery of news operations goes like this: News bosses send out news reporters on stories chosen by the news bosses. That's how it always worked in the past. GFB turned that notion on its ear. I was assigned, I was fond of saying, by our viewers, our clients, who came to us for help. We removed the news boss as middleman. We were, if there ever was such a beast in a news operation, self-assigning. That had some news noses out of joint from the beginning.

Then there was the script — I always wrote it chronologically, from beginning to end, so the solution, the help, the final moment of satisfaction, the police arrest, was at the end, as in real life.

Television news stories were usually written on the inverted pyramid style. The most important facts were first, the least important facts last. Our style never fit the editors' notion of what news stories were supposed to look like and how they should unfold.

Besides, the editors and writers on the floor didn't like the attitude. It was too aggressive, too in-your-face, too much crusading Goldhawk. I never gave in. So they switched tactics. Since they couldn't change the style, they started sniffing suspiciously at every word. They would surgically remove a "but." Or substitute an "a" for "the." Throw in a couple of commas. The editors could then go home and sleep soundly. They had screwed with the script, therefore they had done their jobs.

At least once a month, a script would need to be vetted by a lawyer. Sometimes tough truths had to be told and the editors and show producers were always the first to hit the panic button. Then I would review the script, word for word, with in-house lawyers, or, on the bigger cases, outside legal counsel.

I would come back into the newsroom with a script vetted by a lawyer. It wasn't exactly like Moses coming down from the Mount loaded with stone tablets, but it was the next best thing. "Screw with this script at your peril. You can't change a thing." I would then leave the newsroom smiling. I never minded a legal vet. It made my life easier.

Leaving the newsroom was always the best strategy. Few and I spent as little time there as possible, preferring the outside world and our own little offices, which were moved several times, but never located at network headquarters. Once away from Agincourt, we could think again and concentrate on our ever-growing list of clients. That was the true glory and satisfaction of our jobs. That was why we worked sixty- and seventy-hour weeks. The newsroom is just purgatory. You never have to stay there forever.

When sixty-six-year-old Marilyn Heffernan called us, all she wanted was a bus shelter. Not even a new one. She would have been happy if they had just fixed the old one that got knocked down by a truck in her neighborhood more than two years before.

"Winter is coming once again and we seniors don't want to be without our bus shelter. None of us have cars. We depend on the bus and that shelter," she said.

Marilyn had called and yelled at all the bureaucrats she could find in the Borough of East York. Nothing. No real ripple of action. Just a few scattered lame excuses.

"You know, we can go on and on and on until kingdom come talking like bureaucrats. There's an expression for it, and you've probably heard it: B.S. baffles brains," she told me.

I went right to the top of the borough power structure, Mayor Dave Johnson. He told us that, as an amazing coincidence, that bus shelter was scheduled to be installed by the end of the week. It was Tuesday. Great.

We went out to look at the corner where it would go, on our way to see Marilyn Heffernan. On the corner was a bus shelter. I thought I was hallucinating. I got down on all fours and spotted the concrete dust in little piles around the lag bolts that had been drilled into the sidewalk to hold the shelter in place. The wind hadn't even had time to blow the dust away. Another amazing coincidence was that the shelter popped up before we had a chance to shoot an empty, shelter-free corner.

As useless as Marilyn Heffernan found the East York bureaucrats, we found a bureaucratic gem the next week in Timmins, Ontario. Joe Torlone was a welfare officer. He came to the rescue when we called. There was no hesitation, no usual bureaucratic mumbling, foot-shuffling, and regulation-quoting. All we wanted were a few emergency welfare dollars and maybe a word or two of comfort and encouragement for a young family living in poverty. Steve and Karita Suhonen and their young children, Rebekah, Jessica, Joshua, Tristin, and Carrie had absolutely no money for Christmas. They had no money for food.

Steve and Karita were going to Northern College down the road in South Porcupine, getting 80s and 90s in their accounting courses. They were planning for a better, independent, successful life for them all. But as students, the whole family lived on student loan money. And they were between cheques. Flat busted.

Joe Torlone made it work. When we told him all about the situation, he was able to offer the Suhonens a few hundred dollars to tide them over through Christmas. And the day we visited the Suhonens, the local church group came to the door as we were leaving, with food for the family. Joe and the church had the ability to give. No small thing. That was bothering Karita the most when she first talked to me.

"I was depressed. When you don't have anything, when you can't do for others like you usually do, that's the hardest part about Christmas."

On the way out of town, I went up to Joe Torlone and told him he was a great guy, especially for a bureaucrat. What the hell. It was Christmas.

2. ___

Beating the Bureaucrats

It's always a real trick getting a straight answer out of a bureaucrat — if the bureaucrat will even deign to speak to a mere mortal. They are way too busy running the country/province/city/town/village/settlement area to talk to the likes of us.

A civil servant need never be civil, when pressured they snivel, with issues they swivel. Sure, we all know that there are great public servants out there who really do believe that they are in business to serve the public, but they are the quiet ones, the ones who just do their jobs, the ones we never complain about. We are talking here about the ones, who by their own actions or lack of action, stick out like sore thumbs.

Early in 1994 we went to Tofield, a tiny town somewhat close to Edmonton, but just far enough away to be in the middle of nowhere. I walked the tracks where nineteen-year-old Rachael and twenty-five-year-old Robert Durack died suddenly and violently in their compact car. They were run down by a high-speed train they probably never saw until it was too late.

They were married on July 3, 1993. Fifteen days later they were dead. The Duracks had been picnicking at a bird sanctuary near Tofield and were on their way back home to Edmonton, when they drove over a level railway crossing. A VIA Rail passenger train coming from the east, traveling at 126 kilometres an hour, hit them as they drove across the tracks. They died instantly.

The rail crossing located, officially, at mile 224.74 of the Canadian National Wainright subdivision was already well-known to the local RCMP and to Transport Canada. Six months earlier, officials from

Tofield, Beaver County, CN Rail, Alberta Transportation and Utilities, and Transport Canada had visited mile 224.74 and concluded that a sharp curve and a hill just before the crossing meant nobody could ever see a train coming soon enough to avoid it.

Twenty trains went through there every day and two hundred cars used the crossing every day. The group recommended that signals and a crossing barrier be installed at the crossing. The estimated cost was $136,700 — 80 percent of which would be picked up by Transport Canada, if Transport Canada decided to accept the recommendation. Government wheels grind slowly. The work, if approved, couldn't even begin until the next year, 1994. The group made its recommendation in February of 1993.

Cheryl Heintz, Robert Durack's sister, made it her business to get the government up off its ass and approve the crossing right away. And while she was at it, she wanted to know exactly how the approval process worked in the first place. In a letter to *Goldhawk Fights Back* she wrote:

> The families feel that this accident could have been prevented if those in authority would have followed the recommendation that RCMP Sergeant Syd Perkins made up to Beaver County last December that lights should have been put up at this dangerous cross-ing. We were told that this was the third accident at this crossing in a month and a half but Robert and Rachael's was the first fatal one. After the funeral serv-ice, both families traveled from Wadena Saskatchewan to Edmonton, Alberta to collect Robert and Rachael's personal belongings. We decided to stop in Tofield and view the accident site.
>
> We drove up to the stop sign at the tracks and because of the high mounds of earth on either side, and high grass, there is no possible way to see if a train is coming. We proceeded to cross the tracks and it was not until we were actually on the tracks that we were able to see if a train was coming. Not only is there an obstruction before the tracks but the tracks run on an

angle and curve around a hill so by the time a train comes around the curve there is very little time to react, especially if the train is traveling at 126 kilometres an hour. We were all in shock again. We just shook our heads and said: "they didn't stand a chance." At that point, we knew something had to be done.

RCMP Sgt. Perkins had been the first to blow the official whistle on the site. In December of 1992, Perkins had written a letter to the County of Beaver, but it would be another two months beyond that before that group of investigators would visit the site. Perkins wrote to Beaver County officials, "The danger exists primarily because of the curve in the tracks on the east side which blinds the view from that direction. When a vehicle comes to a stop, the driver can view approaching trains from the west. However, trains coming from the east can only be seen as they round the curve."

Later, when I met Perkins, we walked the tracks where the accident happened. Perkins told me he had been saying there would be a tragedy here soon, if something was not done. He shook his head sadly at the fact that he had been right.

Cameraman Bill Purchase, sound man Wendell Tenove, and I stayed at the tracks as Perkins drove off. We were waiting for a train from the east so we could show how little warning a driver would get. It was very cold. And snowing.

Finally the train blew through. It was all over in seconds. The train appeared and then disappeared into clouds of swirling snow. Despite the fact that we knew roughly when it was coming, it flew around the curve so fast, we almost missed the shot. We shuddered at the thought of being inside a puny little vehicle seconds away from death.

We had spent five months on the telephone with Transport Canada bureaucrats and seemed to be getting nowhere fast. Many documents changed hands.

We spent a lot of time on the phone with the man in charge, Colin J. Churcher, Director General of Railway Safety. He told us that all such requests are ranked for importance and urgency, that Transport Canada only had, at that time, a $9 million budget for all rail crossing improvements in Canada that year. But he also said that sometimes the process — a process never really explained to us — could be shortcut. That's what he said on October 8, 1993.

On February 21, 1994, he called to tell us the rail crossing lights and gates had been approved. Maybe our attention had helped short-cut this process. Maybe not. We wanted an interview with Churcher. He said yes.

Then a few days later, we got the usual flak call. The Transport Canada flak department (Public Affairs) had taken over the file and Churcher — the man we wanted to interview — had obviously been removed from public scrutiny, and a public affairs officer, somebody trained to take any flak for the government, would be available for an interview.

That always drove me nuts. Public affairs officers are paid-mouth-pieces. They are the monkeys, not the organ grinders. They do not make the decisions. They do not know the details I want to know as a journalist. They come in on the file after the fact, in an effort to keep the government's ass well-covered.

In Ottawa, we set up for our interview with the flak. It was better than no interview at all. In walked the interview subject. Her name was Cindy Burnside. She was young, blonde, attractive, and very bright-eyed. I winced. How could I be tough on her? Everybody would think I was picking on her.

I decided to try my best, but soon realized that Burnside really had nothing to say. Her central message was rail safety. Nothing else mat-tered. It was the only thing worth saying. Forget the accident. Forget this single level crossing, the only thing that mattered was rail safety. Period. As the interview progressed, I silently lamented the fact I would get no useful information here because Colin Churcher either chose not to speak or, more likely, was told not to speak. So the inter-view degenerated into an argument. It was all I had left.

"Doesn't Colin Churcher have a responsibility to speak publicly, he being a civil servant?" I asked Cindy.

"I think we've gone over that a few times," said Cindy, starting to lose her polite good humour.

"We don't have an answer yet, that's why we're going over it."

"You have an answer."

"No, I don't."

"For this particular interview, I am the designated spokesperson."

"Why?"

"We're here to discuss railway safety."

"Now you're obfuscating. Why don't you just answer my question?"

"I would be happy to..."

"Why is Colin Churcher not available? You can tell me right now."

"But we're here to talk about railway safety."

"It's a little difficult to talk about railway safety when the Director General of Railway Safety is not available for an interview, wouldn't you agree?"

"No, I wouldn't agree at all."

Cindy Burnside stuck to her message. She endured the flak. The government was apparently saved. During the interview, we were sitting face to face, in chairs. Cindy's legs were crossed and the toe of one of her high heels was only a few inches from my shin. As the interview got hotter and heavier, Cindy started kicking me in the shin, unseen by the camera which was focussed in on a close-up. She would punctuate her words with a kick. Some were kind of hard.

After the interview, I laughed about it. She was apparently unaware that she had been kicking me. But I bet she was thinking about it. My rude behaviour on this story secured for *Goldhawk Fights Back* a partial ban. No one in Transport Canada would be available for an interview anytime, anywhere. We were only allowed to communicate with the bureaucrats by fax.

The directive wore off a few months later. The government machine has a short attention span. If it had a shorter reaction time, Rachael and Robert Durack might still be alive.

Sandy Blott, from Oak Lake, Manitoba, got my attention right away. She wanted to talk to me about the life of her husband, Jack Blott. He was seventy-one and held captive in the Brandon Mental Health Centre, inside a ward with a lock on the door. He was a prisoner. He wanted to go home to his wife Sandy.

When Sandy was allowed to visit, Jack would cry, cling to her, and plead to be taken home to their quiet little retirement cottage. The bureaucrats had told Sandy that was not going to happen.

A few months earlier, Jack had been in hospital, fighting cancer. Then he went home and developed some memory problems. Jack's doctors had prescribed some medication, but it was clear Jack was going through the early symptoms of Alzheimer's disease. He was in denial, greatly stressed about his lack of memory and his worsening speech problems.

Sandy thought it would be a good idea to get Jack into the Brandon Mental Health Centre where his medication could be checked and adjusted, if necessary, and then Jack could come back to his beloved cottage. Once in the hospital, however, Jack was declared mentally incompetent by a doctor, which automatically triggered the involvement of the Public Trustee's office in Manitoba.

What followed was a blizzard of bureaucratic involvement that pushed Sandy out of the picture. The bureaucracy moved swiftly, seizing control of Jack and Sandy's bank accounts and making medical decisions about Jack's care with little or token input from Sandy. Sandy felt she had kept Jack alive through his earlier battle with cancer — she was not going to desert the front lines now.

I don't know how many hours over the next few months I spent on the telephone with the Manitoba public trustee and the administrator of the Brandon Mental Health Centre. Confidentiality was always an issue. We talked in bureaucratic parables. I was told, frequently, of what would happen "in cases similar to Mr. Blott's, since I cannot speak to you of Mr. Blott himself."

Bureaucratic confidentiality is reassuring to all of us concerned about privacy issues, but it was a maddening handicap in our efforts to get a gentle man, confused and tortured by Alzheimer's disease, out of a locked mental health ward. Doctors and bureaucrats made a big deal out of the Alzheimer's issue. He could be dangerous. Unpredictable. He might run amok and hurt somebody.

The bureaucratic cognoscenti seemed to have a poor grasp of the true nature of Alzheimer's disease. Jack was essentially not dangerous as he slowly sank into a deep pit of total memory and personality loss. He was on his way to becoming a nonfunctioning person. Both Jack and Sandy wanted all the time together they could grab before that end came.

Gradually, I think the public trustee and the hospital grew tired of the battle. We were wearing them down. They were starting to worry about how this might look to the rest of Canada. Finally one day, as if out of the blue, the hospital suggested that Jack could go home for a trial period. That was it. The wall was crumbling.

I remember every step we climbed at the front entrance of the Brandon Mental Heath Centre the day we went to get Jack out. I was there, with Sandy and two of her neighbourhood friends, just for moral and numerical support. We walked in. The administrator was expecting us.

With few words, he took us to the locked ward. Inside, dozens of people were milling about in the hallways. Many of them followed us as we went into Jack's four-bed room. Jack had been expecting us. He shook my hand as Sandy reminded him who I was. Jack's smile broadened as he squeezed my hand harder. Off we went, heading for the bolted door to the ward. A nurse unlocked it and stood aside. Jack walked up to the doorway but would not go beyond.

"It's okay, Jack," said Sandy. "You can go. You're free." Jack looked for a long moment at Sandy and then turned to me. I nodded. Jack, with Sandy and I each on an arm, helped him through the door. He stepped high over the door jamb, as if stepping over a huge obstacle. Just then, one of Sandy's neighbours let out a stifled scream. A look of horror spread across her face.

"Goldhawk," she whispered, "one of those men following us down the hall just pinched me."

"Well," I said, "just keep smiling and keep walking."

We had a quiet, happy party back at the cottage. The whole neighbourhood was there. Jack was home, sitting out on the porch, listening to the birds, breathing deeply on the fresh breezes blowing off Oak Lake. Jack died a year later on June 14, 1994. He was seventy-two. He died at home. Sandy sent me the death notice and a note: "Dear Goldhawk: thank you for giving my wonderful husband back to me for another year. Thank you for coming into our lives and making them better. You made it possible for my husband to return to the place he loved so much."

We went into battle for many clients who had psychological and emotional demons they were trying to slay — a lot of those cases involved victims who had been abused earlier in life. I remember Theresa. She lived a hellish life of poverty and frustration in Thompson, Manitoba, a remote mining town $500 in airfare away from Winnipeg.

Theresa was suffering from multiple personality disorder, a bizarre psychological condition where many personalities live inside the same mind. The personality splits, say the experts, as a coping mechanism. Theresa was a victim of childhood abuse. Now, as an adult, when a strong-minded person was needed to fight a threat, one emerged. If a gentle, timid personality was needed, one came out.

Theresa felt, and psychiatrists agreed, that she was host to twenty-four separate personalities. They usually had no memory of each other, nor did they have much conscious control of the emergence of a personality. Each had a name.

Theresa, the main personality we usually talked to, suffered from long bouts of memory loss during which other characters were ruling her body, telling her where to go, what to say, what to do. Just before she had come to us for help, Theresa had spent fifty-four days in hospital, being treated for depression — not multiple personality disorder. She just couldn't get the help she needed. Three times before that hospital stay, she had tried to commit suicide. Her life was a mess.

Theresa's complaint to us: She couldn't get any direct treatment, any therapy that would deal with her MPD. She wanted to get better for her children and her husband.

Health bureaucracies are like anthills. Everybody is very busy, rushing somewhere on a secret mission. The existence of interloping mere mortals, trying to find out what — if anything — is going on, is barely acknowledged and minimally tolerated.

However, having no choice, we pressed on. Part of the trick here was to find some champions, locate those people in power in the bureaucracy who did give a damn. They were always there. You just had to find them. In Theresa's case, that's exactly what happened.

We found Deputy Minister of Health Frank Maynard and, in Winnipeg, a therapist well-versed in MPD, Pam Gayhan. The government paid to fly Theresa to see Pam on a regular basis, and tried to line her up with a psychiatrist, as well. At one point, in the months-long journey to get her what she needed, Theresa was even advising the Deputy Minister of Health on issues related to mental health — a therapy in itself for Theresa.

Sometimes it takes more than therapy. A woman I will identify only as Andrea, not her real name, came to me about her son, whom I will call John. I apologize for all the mumbo-jumbo, but I cannot use the names of the people involved in this story, as ordered by an Ontario judge. If you bear with me, you will see the need for the secrecy — the need to protect innocent victims.

In 1985, John said he had been sexually assaulted when he was nine by his hockey coach, who was also a teacher. This was no isolated incident. This teacher for years had been volunteering as a Cub Scout leader and had coached many young boys on hockey, baseball, and basketball teams. He confessed to police that's how he found his victims.

The teacher was convicted of indecent exposure in 1985. In 1991, he was convicted of sexually assaulting a six-year-old boy. In 1993, he pleaded guilty to sexually assaulting eleven boys. Court records show he committed new sexual assaults while on probation and he committed new sexual assaults while out on bail facing the 1993 charges. Only at the end of the long string of convictions was this teacher removed from schools and transferred to a new job at the board of education headquarters.

We tracked down the teacher, intent on putting his picture on television, just in case there were other victims out there who had not come forward.

"I am going to try and ask you a few questions," I said to the teacher as we approached his car, in the process of backing out of his garage.

"I have no comment," he said.

"Here's your chance to say something to the families of all those children you sexually assaulted," I added.

"Listen," he said, as he drove off, away from our camera, "I'm sorry for what happened." Later, the teacher was convicted on five sexual offences and sentenced to three years in prison.

Where was the school board in all this? That's what John's mother Andrea wanted to know. We did, too. The elected board officials and the bureaucrats circled the wagons. Their basic excuse for keeping the teacher in a school after he had been convicted of sexual offences against young boys was twofold: They didn't think it was that serious and they didn't realize the judge had ordered that the teacher be kept away from kids. I had this argument with the director of education:

"So he was allowed to stay in the school, on probation, after he had been convicted of sexually assaulting a twelve-year-old boy. That was okay?" I asked.

"After his 1991 conviction he was allowed, and this was done with the judgment of the staff," said the official.

"Can't you make a ruling that would say that anyone convicted of a sexual offence against a child should not be working in a school? Can't you at least say that?"

"I believe that's what the policy leads to."

"Anyone convicted of any sexual offence against a child is not allowed to work in one of your schools."

"That's what we're saying."

"Even thought that wasn't the case in the past, that's over."

"It is."

"When will that be written down as policy?"

"It is."

"Well, it isn't here in the documents you have given me."

"No, you don't have it."

"Will it be issued soon?"

"We will provide it to you."

A few days later, I actually got the amended document, after my tooth-pulling exercise with the director. Why a school board would even have to think twice about this kind of policy and why a school board would have no such policy is beyond me.

Of course, just having a policy does not always cut the mustard. You also need a policy that makes sense. Or am I being too picky? Brian Kavelman of Petersburg, Ontario, didn't think so. He came to us back in February of 1996 because he needed a power wheelchair. Brian suffered from osteogenesis imperfecta, a degenerative bone disease. Brian could break a rib by coughing. He broke his arm throwing a tennis ball. He broke his collarbone attempting to walk on crutches.

Brian was obviously unable to work; he stayed home with his two sons while his wife worked. The manual wheelchair Brian had did not allow him, by himself, to get up and down the ramp outside his house. Put another way, Brian was a prisoner in his own home without a power wheelchair.

Brian hoped that the Assistive Devices Branch of the Ministry of Health would pay about $5,500 toward the chair. His wife's private insurance from her employer would pay the rest of the cost for this $8,400 power wheelchair. Brian applied once. He was turned down. He tried again. He was turned down again. His "Dear Brian" letter from the Ministry of Health read, "Based on the documentation submitted, it is our understanding that the eligibility criteria for the equipment have not been met. Equipment prescribed must be basic and essential for mobility within the home and not a substitute for other transportation methods or to meet lifestyle preferences."

So going outside was now a lifestyle preference for Ontario's disabled. Clearly, the bureaucrats were not understanding Brian's plight. Either that, or the government policy at work here was just too boneheaded for words. Brian launched a third appeal and called us.

Immediately, we started annoying the government about the appeal. Finally, Brian won. The government went to great pains explaining how our involvement had nothing to do with the final approval. In explaining the approval, another bureaucrat said, "We have to recognize the client has to get from his home to whatever mode of transportation they're going to use to get them to whatever activity, and in this case, it was very clear on reassessment that activity had to be assisted by power mobility."

Huh? All I know is that Brian promised me, when he got his new power chair, that he would never use it to "meet lifestyle preferences." I said that was probably a wise choice.

We got to know a lot about wheelchairs at *Goldhawk Fights Back*. We soon learned how vital they were to the lives of people who needed them to do the one thing the rest of us take for granted: move. I soon learned never to describe people as being "confined to a wheelchair." Wheelchairs mean freedom, not confinement. Wheelchairs mean that Brian Kavelman can go outside, breathe some fresh air, and watch his sons play baseball.

When I met fifty-year-old Christine Stirman in Vancouver, she hadn't been outside her house in four years. Christine had amyotrophic lateral sclerosis (ALS), better known as Lou Gehrig's Disease, named after the baseball player who first brought the terminal illness into public view.

Christine, surrounded by her family — her grown kids and her loving husband, Wayne — had chosen to die at home. I remember her as a wonderfully buoyant, beautiful woman, who always smiled and had a brightness in her eye that shone through her terrible illness. ALS attacks your body; it leaves your mind clear to fight the growing paralysis.

Husband Wayne came to us for what initially seemed a modest request. The family was poor, Wayne was out of work, and any services they could get at home came at the generosity of the British Columbia government — both the Health Ministry and the Ministry of Social Services. The latter ministry had suddenly one day disallowed Christine's massage therapy. It may sound like a small thing — a therapist would massage Christine's ailing, degenerating limbs. But the Social Services Ministry, examining the supplied therapy, got hung-up on the nature of the service being supplied. Was it "chronic" or "acute," asked the government. "It's terminal," replied Wayne. The government said no "because the client has an ongoing condition and isn't eligible for extended therapy benefits."

In other words, since Christine was not going to get better, the therapy could not be supplied. Never mind that Christine was dying at home, saving the health system countless thousands of dollars. The added irony: the massage therapy relieved a lot of pain for Christine; it helped relieve chronic back pain and increased her circulation. And when Christine couldn't get the massage therapy, her resulting downturn put her in that expensive hospital bed, where doctors treated her problems created by that lack of therapy.

We went to Social Services and the massage therapy was quickly reinstated. But that was not the end of our involvement. Wayne called us a few months later with a bigger problem. Christine spent most of her waking hours in a special wheelchair. As her condition worsened, she needed a different kind of chair. Two years earlier, the family had applied for a new chair. It had finally been approved. But now, Christine, who continued to degenerate, needed a newer chair again. The one that had been delayed for two long years was now outdated. The government had approved the funding, more than $25,000, but it was for the wrong chair.

Wayne and Christine's physiotherapist had found the right chair for Christine and it was even cheaper — $23,000. But the government was digging-in its heels. This sudden change of wheelchair requirements seemed to baffle a government that apparently could not act in a time frame of any less than two years.

Once again, we got on the telephones and the officials we talked to seemed to get it. Yes, they conceded, it was taking a long time. Time was a commodity that Christine did not have. The right chair came within a few days, on November 30, 1999.

A few days after that, Christine left her house and headed for the mall, guiding her electric wheelchair with slight movements of her head, the only part of her body she could now move. She went Christmas shopping. Her husband Wayne could not stop smiling that day. Christine finally had the chair she needed.

But it would never kill the family's pain, said Wayne. "What we want and what we need are two different things. Know what I want? I want her to get out of the chair and throw her arms around me. I want to take her fishing."

ALS is a rapidly progressive neuromuscular disease. It attacks the neurological pathways that the body uses to send messages from the brain to its muscles. The result is muscle weakening and wasting; eventually, the patient is left totally paralyzed. ALS is not contagious, but can be hereditary. Christine's father had ALS. Then her brother. Then Christine.

Debbie Brinkman had no family to help her fight the rules. She had always been proud of her singular independence, having been on her own since she was eighteen. A single mother of two young children, Debbie dropped into a downward spiral in her life when she was laid off from her job as a receptionist in Guelph, Ontario.

First, she was on unemployment benefits. When the benefits dried up, she went on welfare. Every dollar had to be counted. Every can of food. Then one day, just before Christmas, welfare suddenly cut her off.

The Social Services Department in the County of Wellington decided that Debbie had not supplied enough information about the absent father of one of her children. This was not an easy topic for Debbie, but she told the bureaucrats all she knew. There are few personal secrets a welfare client is allowed to keep. Debbie admitted that the child in question was the result of a one-night stand at a party in Hamilton. Debbie only had a first name, and it could have been a false name at that. The father was never in the picture. She had no idea where he was. She had never had any contact with him beyond that one now-embarrassing night.

When she couldn't supply much information, the social workers categorically decided she was not telling the truth. With no proof, not even a lukewarm clue, the powers-that-be arbitrarily decided Debbie was lying. So her monthly cheque of $580 disappeared instantly.

We went directly to the welfare administrator, who admitted that deducing Debbie's guilt was a "subjective" exercise, but insisted his department could usually tell when somebody is lying. The administrator did promise he would review Debbie's case. He reported back in days that Debbie should not have been immediately deprived of money. He put her back on welfare, at a reduced rate of $494 a month. The $86 a month deduction was left in place because of Debbie's missing one-time lover.

Eleanor Sande of Montreal gave birth to her second son, Olivier, in February of 1996. The joyful occasion was mixed with sadness. Olivier had Down's syndrome. Eleanor eventually filled out several federal and provincial government forms declaring her son's disability. The bureaucracy responded by declaring her perfectly healthy six-year-old son mentally handicapped.

Not content to just mix up the names of Eleanor Sande's and Jean Leger's sons, it went on to make matters worse. The government sent out a disability cheque to the wrong son and then came out of a deep sleep and recognized its own error. At that point, the government demanded the cheque be returned, accusing the couple of making a false declaration.

Eleanor and Jan knew what to do. They went to their MP. One day, on the telephone with one of the MP's staff, the helpful assistant said that the registration of the birth of immigrant babies in Quebec had been delayed. Obviously, after reading the file Eleanor had sent to the MP, the assistant was just not getting it. Eleanor remembered some of that conversation for me:

"So I said, 'How does that affect us?' And he said, 'Because your husband is French.' I said, 'No.' He said, 'Because you're American.' I said, 'No.'"

"Well, how did they come up with those assumptions?" I asked.

"I don't know."

"So they thought your husband was from France, so you must be an American?"

"I guess. And on top of it, 'Monsieur,' I said, 'my baby was not born in March or April. He was born in February, so you're wrong on all three counts.'"

Needless to say, we quickly got the matter straightened out. God only knows what kind of monster this official error would have become over the years if left alive. Eleanor sent us a note thanking us for the public apology they got from the *Regie des Rentes*. "What a relief," she wrote, "We can put this to rest and get on with the healing and celebration of life."

It's pretty easy to enter the wrong information into a computer. With one misguided keystroke, a government clerk can screw up the life of some long-suffering citizen. So it was with real estate salesman John Stewart.

John knew a good deal when he saw one. He bought a used, one-year-old Chrysler Intrepid for $14,000. It was a low-mileage car to boot. John did his due diligence. To protect himself, he got a "Used Vehicle Information Package" from the Ontario Ministry of Transportation. That document stated that there were no liens registered against the car. It was free and clear.

John drove away, confident and happy about the good deal he had made. All went well for a year and a half. Then one day the bailiff showed up at his door, seized the car, and towed it to a locked-up vehicle compound in Milton, Ontario. The bailiff told John there was an $18,000 lien on the car. John could get the car back by paying an additional $18,000 to buy the car he thought he had already bought for $14,000.

John came to us for help, desperate to get his car back and get back to the business of selling real estate. We discovered that basically two things had gone wrong for John: First, the bad guy who sold him the car lied about the lien. Second, the Ministry of Transportation failed to warn John that the car was not the bad guy's car to sell. It still belonged to the bank. How could the government screw up? In many ways, actually.

Here's how it screwed up with this car: Back when the car was new, the original dealership called in the Vehicle Identification Number, the number from the little plate located on the dashboard of every vehicle near the windshield. When the dealership read the sixteen-character letter and numeral VIN to the clerk over the telephone, the clerk got one wrong. The clerk typed an "R" instead of a "T." So now, the Ministry of Transportation would not be able to access the right information about that vehicle because the VIN was wrong.

Obviously, the bank that loaned the money to our bad guy to buy the car in the first place had the right number and registered it accurately. It doesn't take much imagination to figure out that the bad guy probably knew the MTO had registered the wrong number by studying the ownership papers on the Intrepid. That meant the bad guy knew he could sell the car and the lien would never show.

The Ministry of Transportation admitted the mistake. Ministry spokesperson Anne McLaughlin told me, "In this case, it just appears to be a fluke. It really was. Something just of a fluke."

The wrong information about John's car was just one of twenty million transactions recorded by the government. I wonder how many others contain wrong information as well? In this case, the government made good and paid off the lien on the car, since it had been, after all, the government's fault that John had bought it.

Together, we went to the pound to pick up John's car, the CTV crew in tow. Later, after John watched how his problem had become public information from coast to coast, he wrote, "I was quite impressed with the presentation of the recovery of my car, which I watched on Friday evening. However, I don't think I am Hollywood material."

It's fair to say that John Stewart did everything right when he bought his car privately. He could have done one more thing that would have protected him from this bad deal: Check the VIN on the dashboard of the car against the VIN typed out on the vehicle ownership papers. If the seller of a vehicle complains you are being paranoid, explain that you are just protecting your own interests. Then tell the seller about John Stewart.

When Kim Kitchen worked as a waitress at a restaurant in Regina, she was sexually harassed by the boss. The harassment moved from verbal to physical. Then, the wife of the boss fired Kim. As Kim told me, "Emotionally and financially, it was a disaster."

Kim just couldn't shake the experience. "I lost my house, my car, because of bankruptcy. I went from being a bubbly, outgoing, in-the-middle-of-everything kind of person to not wanting to leave my house, not wanting to find a job."

Kim decided to move to Vancouver to start a new life. She also decided to fight back. She filed a complaint with the Saskatchewan Human Rights Commission. That took two years, but finally the Human Rights Commission determined that the restaurant owner should pay Kim $12,000 in lost wages and damages.

But nothing happened. Human Rights Commissions across Canada can make these determinations, usually years after an event, but the HRCs have no teeth. Anybody can pretty well ignore what they say.

The next step for Kim in Vancouver was to request, from the Saskatchewan Justice Ministry, a board of inquiry. It would have more teeth and could order the restaurant boss to pay, if it found in favour of Kim. All John Nilson, the justice minister, had to do was make one phone call and appoint a lawyer to look into the case. Over the next nine months, Kim made at least thirty calls to the ministry, but nothing happened. The ministry and the minister were apparently just too busy.

We called, and within five days a lawyer had been assigned to study Kim's case. She was on her way to getting justice in her long fight.

We went to the legislature looking for an explanation from John Nilson. He was unavailable. Out of sight. We never found him. In the minister's office, we did find Heather Nord, who suggested to us that the matter was just not important enough for the minister to be involved:

"Perhaps it's not a story that needs to go on air," suggested Nord.

"Trust me to make that determination," I replied.

"Trust us to tell you when we've given you an answer that we hope is sufficient."

"So no one in the ministry can talk to us about the policy involved here? Let's get that straight."

"Well, I'm not saying that at all," said Nord, ending the conversation with me being made none the wiser by the government.

I don't suppose it's the government's role to make me any wiser, but in too many cases governments keep us all in the dark. Sometimes they can't be bothered. Sometimes the bureaucrats get the notion they always know best and no input from pedestrians is needed or wanted.

Linda Densmore from Brookfield, Nova Scotia, was the proud owner of a pickup truck. It was a crew cab. Three could ride in front and two in back. Linda came to us when she realized she could not use her crew cab, only two years old at the time, to drive school kids to extracurricular events. It's fair to say that in Brookfield, in rural Nova Scotia, a lot of people drive pickups. But pickups, said government regulations, could not be used by parents to drive other people's kids to events — a community-based practice that is essential, especially in small towns.

Here's how ridiculous it was: Linda said to me, "The lady down the road who works all day, she has to go without supper to get her kids to soccer, and I drive right by her house with two empty seats but I can't take her kids."

The rule said that all vans, multi-passenger vehicles, mini-vans, and sports utility vehicles with a seating capacity of ten or less are allowed. The vehicle must be a 1994 model or later. Also, any car (of any age) can be used. But pickups were a no-no. So Uncle Bert down the road can take kids to a hockey game in his twenty-three-year-old Cadillac with the bumpers dragging on the ground, while Linda and many mothers like her can do nothing to help their neighbours.

It's not as if Linda hadn't tried to change the rules. She had complained to the school board, all levels of government, taken up petitions, and talked for hours on the telephone, all in vain. When Linda told us what was happening, we thought it was a dumb enough rule that it deserved to be defeated.

And who made up these regulations? Where was the Ministry of Silly Rules? It was the Nova Scotia Utility and Review Board, Public Passenger Division. Not all their rules were silly, but this one sure took the cake.

The first thing we did was ask ourselves "What's the difference between a sport utility vehicle and a pickup truck?" Were the safety standards any different? No. Linda checked out her own truck, and was told by General Motors that the safety standards for SUVs and pickups were the same.

We got the same information from Robin Myers, the Chief of Standards and Regulations for Road Safety and Motor Vehicle Regulations at Transport Canada. Myers ventured a guess that Nova Scotia must have been basing its regulations on something other than safety. *And what might that be?* we wondered.

Linda Densmore sent all the literature on safety regulations to D.W. White, the manager of the NSURB, PPD. White wrote back and said there would be no changes in the regulations. When we contacted White, he told us the regulations were changed in 1995 to include such vehicles as sports utility vehicles mainly because so many people were driving them. Apparently nobody thought anything about pickups.

White admitted to us that he had not had a chance to review the material Linda had sent him, although he had found enough time to write her a letter to tell her he would do nothing to change the regulations.

After our conversation, White apparently did read the material Linda had sent, but then called Linda to once again insist he was not changing the regulations. White said to Linda that safety was suddenly not the issue now. He told her changing that regulation was just not a priority and that if Linda wanted the change to be made she should lobby the government.

We lobbied, too. We talked to Brook Taylor, Member of the Legislative Assembly for Colchester–Musquodoboit, the Liberal Transportation Critic. He said the rules were preposterous and that White was just not using common sense. Taylor said the NSURB, PPD was unaccountable and unanswerable to anybody.

"It's a terrible system," added Taylor. "I know members on both sides of the House disagree with it." Taylor also told us there is always a shortage of volunteer drivers for school events. This rule only made that situation worse.

For the next several months we kept poking and prodding wherever and whenever we could, and suddenly one day, out popped a new rule. Michelle McKinnon, a spokesperson for the Nova Scotia Justice Department, was dispatched to bring the happy news to our waiting camera. "Now the regulations will be changed, will be amended to include trucks, 1994 model year or later," she announced. Meanwhile, David White, the public servant who makes public policy, had nothing to say publicly.

"Some people are more comfortable about going on camera than others," explained McKinnon.

"It isn't a matter of comfort, it's a matter of accountability," I said. "We're not talking comfort here."

White had not bothered to call Linda Densmore to tell her the good news. So we delivered it. Linda shot me a skeptical glance and said, "I won't believe it until I see it on paper." That was November 3, 1997. In true government drag-your-ass fashion, that paper announcing the change was not faxed to Linda until February 18, 1998. At the end of the letter, White wrote, "If I can be of further assistance, please do not hesitate to contact me." Right.

I don't know what it is, but some bureaucrats just love denial. They love to say no, that's against the rules. No, you don't qualify. No, you're too young. No, you're too old. No, you're too poor (you're never too rich). No, you don't understand. No, it's not a priority.

Not many Canadians would find themselves more punished by the rules than Maureen Sklapsky, a teacher in Castlegar, British Columbia. Maureen and her husband, Dwayne, suffered the ultimate tragedy, the loss of a child.

On January 18, 2000, Maureen was teaching at Stanley Humphries Secondary School, where her own seventeen-year-old son, Shawn, was a student. Suddenly, Maureen was called on the public address system to go to the activity room. There she found a group of students crowded around her unconscious son, who was lying on the floor. Maureen administered CPR to her athletic, healthy, 6'3" son.

"I wasn't panicking. I didn't know he was dying. I didn't know what was wrong. I just couldn't wake him up. It didn't matter what I did. I couldn't wake him up," said Maureen.

Shawn died of a rare heart defect. Maureen suffered post traumatic shock. She was emotionally injured and unable to work. Her family needed the money, so she applied for workers' compensation. Unbelievably, the WCB denied the claim. It said that she was acting, in this tragedy, as a mother, not as an employee.

Teachers and supervisors at the school and at the Board of Education could not believe the cold-hearted assessment. It was their strong belief that Maureen had been injured on the job, end of story. How dare the WCB make assumptions about how Maureen was feeling or in what capacity she was acting as she struggled to save her son's life.

When we called the WCB, it was clear they were highly uncomfortable with their decision. "Give us a reason to change our mind," the WCB seemed to be saying. The board wanted more "proof" that Maureen was acting as an employee.

We got supervisors and a superintendent of education to rewrite their earlier reports to the WCB. It was essentially the same message, but with different words. It gave the WCB enough wiggle-room to slide off the pointed stick upon which it had been skewered since the unpopular decision had been made. Said Allan LaPierre, from the WCB: "The issue was gut-wrenching, to say the least. In fact, quite frankly, I was happy when I found some reason to say, you know, it was an acceptable claim."

Sixty-eight-year-old Jack Ives of Tisdale, Saskatchewan, got himself into a lot of trouble with bureaucrats after he honestly checked off a little box on his driver's licence renewal form.

He had ticked off the box that asked him if he had high blood pressure. It was a minor medical problem, easily treated by drugs. It had no impact on his active life. But ticking off the box had a real impact.

He was sent a demand letter for an extensive medical examination. If he didn't have this examination, he could lose his licence. The exam called for, among other things, these parts of his body to be checked and certified healthy: teeth, gums, prostate, rectum, genitalia. What that had to do with Jack's driving was a mystery to Jack.

So we asked a few probing questions of Allan Cockman (I'm not making this up), a vice-president of Saskatchewan General Insurance, the agency that handles driver licensing. Read his answer carefully. Note the slippage.

"What rectal condition could prevent you from driving a car?" I asked with a decidedly straight face.

"I think you say, 'Now, what are the conditions that individuals have?' And sometimes the combination you have can make a difference. Now, the number of times people will do with anything from the rectal side ... prostate cancer, maybe things like that. But otherwise it's very, very, minor. And once this was brought to our attention, we said 'Hmmm. Let's take a look at it. Let's remove it because it's so minor. And it may cause more stress and irritation to people.'"

So SGI printed a revised list of requirements from the medical examinations it orders for about fifteen thousand drivers in Saskatchewan each year. Missing from the earlier list are such items as teeth, gums, rectum, prostate, and genitalia.

Said Allan Cockman, as he mused out loud at the end of our interview, "Maybe we're too close to this. We've been doing this for well over twenty years, and this is the first time someone really complained to us."

Jack Ives, a retired newspaperman, wrote us this thank you letter: "While I realize it was your platform that made the whole thing possible, it seems I have become a bit of a local hero for taking on SGI and bringing about the change. I have talked to so many people who were annoyed by that medical questionnaire but had no idea what to do about it."

Our story also prompted this letter to the editor of the *Saskatoon Star Phoenix*:

> On the February 13 edition of *Canada* AM, Goldhawk, inquiring into a Tisdale resident's complaint about a medical needed to renew his driver's licence, was told by the SGI that this was the only such complaint. Not so. On June 1, 1994, I was notified that my licence renewal was conditional to submitting medical information to SGI. I protested by telephone, to no avail. On July 12, 1994, I wrote to the supervisor that I was a long way from convinced that the condition of my rectum, prostate, and genitalia impaired my ability to drive. And after her 80th birthday, my wife had the same questions — regarding a pelvic examination, a breast examination, and a trip to Saskatoon for a mammogram. As I told my doctor, I can understand the SGI seeking help from the medical profession. But it doesn't excuse doctors from making a meal out of it.

All I know is that we eliminated fifteen thousand government-mandated rectal examinations a year in Saskatchewan.

3.

Bad Guys Dancing

Bad guys are all out to get the same thing — something for nothing. Bad guys will work their asses off seven days a week, twelve hours a day to get something for nothing. Bad guys will live the life of a jackrabbit, bolting when smelling danger, living on pizza and beer, with no fixed address to get something for nothing. Bad guys will take in millions with some elaborate scam and then risk it all by getting caught shoplifting golf balls.

I know bad guys who take pride in never paying for anything. With a million cooling in the trunk of his Cadillac, the true bad guy will still pull a midnight checkout to stiff the motel on a cheap room. A bad guy in a thousand-dollar suit and slippery Italian shoes will still stroll away from a bar tab in a five-star hotel. It's what they do. It's their gig. Their profession. Not that there is any honour among thieves. There isn't. Any bad guy worth his suit would suck a client dry, right down to his last buck, and would sell out a business partner at the drop of a hat. He would, however, never sell out his mother. Bad guys still have standards.

Bad guys almost never tell the truth. The truth is what they make up. The truth changes from day to day. I remember a conversation producer Marlene McArdle had one day with a notorious mover, a take-the-money-and-lose-the-furniture specialist:

"So your name is Peter," Marlene said to the mover on the phone.

"Yeah," came the reply.

Then later in the conversation, Marlene said, "What did you say your name was again?"

"John."

"I thought you said your name was Peter."

"It is. It's... John Peter."

The bad guys I meet, in the main, do not live what they believe is a life of crime. The bad guys are marketers, counsellors, consultants, topnotch executives out to make the big deal. It's not crime. It's business. Hold up a bank and steal $5,000, that's a crime. Sell an ointment guaranteed to grow hair on doorknobs, that's business — high profit, low overhead. Most of those bad guys never get caught, anyway. The secret is not to be greedy — piggishly greedy.

Say you are a bad guy. You can scam $5 million or $10 million, keep a low profile, know when to leave town, just before the vexatious questions start being asked, and you'll prosper. Scam $100 million or more, build a mansion, buy a yacht, let your screwees witness the screwer having a good time, forget to leave town when investors start to wake up, and your little empire might fold.

Of course, you will still have plenty of time, if you have any brains at all, to get out of town with a huge wad of cash, to live abroad in luxury for the rest of your natural, rotten little life. What's the downside to all of this? You will probably never get the Order of Canada. And running for school board trustee might be out of the question.

We had been on the trail of Robert Lawrence Brown for a long time. Brown, as with many of the characters we had met in our nine-year journey at *Goldhawk Fights Back*, was an odd man. He was short and rotund with lightly-tinted orange eyeglasses and a clipped white goatee of a style sometimes favoured by piano players in houses of ill-repute. Brown had a background in selling vending machine candy, but had more recently fallen into show business.

Brown worked for First Professional Video Inc., traveling the country selling video equipment to aspiring videographers. It was sold as a franchise for anywhere from $14,000 to $16,000. Videographers were promised they would make big money — as much as $75,000 a year — shooting, as a company brochure suggested, weddings; bar mitzvahs; graduations; and club, office, and private parties, to name a few. The brochures, supplied by FPV, for the use of the franchisees should have been a tip-off:

In the average family, one or more of the group is involved with an animal. Not just to the degree of having a house pet, but to the extent of raising and showing top class animals in competition. Attending the animal shows is fun in itself, but many people would like a videotape of the Blue Ribbon being awarded to their special animal. Taking the situation very seriously, why not tape the entire extravaganza for a later review of the competition... it just might enhance your chances for top honours in the event next show. (sic)

The camera gear supplied to new recruits was cheap. The budding videographers were outfitted with low-quality VHS video equipment — old-model cameras, several years out of date. Nobody we could find ever made more than a few hundred bucks. For some, the equipment, paid for up-front, never came.

We were always interested in exactly what kind of pitch Brown used on his customers. Once, Laurie posed as a prospective buyer as we listened to all the glowing promises on a hidden microphone. Brown liked to use the arty approach in selling — a gruff but benign producer-type who has been everywhere and done everything — trying to give the kids and the amateurs a grab at the old brass ring. The day Laurie met him, he was dressed all in black, with chicken soup stains down the front of his turtleneck. That became his code name whenever we were on his trail. Chicken Soup was working on what would eventually become a long list of complaints about these video franchises.

First Professional Video Inc., was owned and operated by David Nancoff of Toronto, a man you will meet up close in Chapter 4. Brown and Nancoff seemed corporately close. On January 11, 1991, Nancoff registered an Ontario corporation under the name "The Original Candy Man Inc." On April 22 of than same year, Brown registered almost exactly the same name as a British Columbia Corporation: "The Original

Candyman Inc." In another symbol of close business ties, Brown certified to the Ontario Ministry of Transportation that his home address on his driver's licence was "1881 Yonge Street, Apartment 706, Toronto." But 1881 Yonge is an office building. And Suite 706 is the office of First Professional Video Inc. But then again, having no home address can be a handy business tool.

We caught up with Chicken Soup at a posh hotel in Regina, Saskatchewan. Brown was making a cross-country sales tour, signing up young shooters and shipping the contracts and cheques back to Nancoff at corporate headquarters in Toronto. We decided it was time to put Brown on television so any additional young videographers might get the real picture when dealing with FPV. And we wanted to demand from Brown that some refunds, or at least partial refunds, of those franchise fees needed to be made.

The *CTV News* crew and I sauntered into the hotel, our video toys carried loosely at our sides as if it were mere baggage. We wanted to look like we were heading for the convention floor to shoot a wedding. We knew from sad, past mishaps that hotels frown heavily on marauding news crews busting up hotel rooms.

We had a deep-throat client make an appointment with Brown. He called from the house phone in the lobby to say he was on the way up. But we kept the appointment. Brown had the door of his suite open, ready for the throngs of eager investors.

Coming up in the elevator, we had time to fire up the camera and check sound. We were rolling as the elevators opened on Brown's floor. In just a few steps we were into his room. Brown had set up a little desk in front of the television. He was sitting behind it like a receptionist, a blank contract on the desk. The two beds were lined with dozens of brochures, pamphlets, and other gimcracks that spoke well of the wonderful world of video.

Brown had been about to light a cigarette, the lighter cupped in his hands. He dropped the lighter and grabbed the TV remote, trying to turn off the TV, but I was in the way. I was demanding answers, and there was Brown, struggling to command the TV with his remote, the unlit cigarette dangling precariously from the middle of his upper lip.

As Brown vainly punched buttons on the remote and trotted out the usual dumb excuses and explanations for misrepresentation, I wondered if he had seen Peter Sellers try to kill the bad guys with a remote in *Being There.*

I eventually extracted a promise from Brown that he would intercede with Nancoff when he got back to Toronto, to try to shake loose some refunds for unhappy customers, most of whom borrowed money to pay the franchise fees up-front.

Brown got ambushed again on the road across Canada — this time by the Royal Canadian Mounted Police, the Victoria, BC, Commercial Crime Section. We weren't the only ones on Brown's trail. Brown was arrested in Halifax, Nova Scotia, in the process of selling even more FPV franchises. It was just a few days after we had popped in on him in Regina.

Brown was charged with six counts of fraud in Victoria, relating to his company, The Original Candyman Inc. Brown faced an additional four charges of fraud in Edmonton, Alberta, relating to contracts he sold for Nancoff's First Professional Video Inc. The RCMP put him in a Halifax jail cell for the night, taking Brown to the airport the next day for a flight back to Victoria, where he was due to make a court appearance.

We were waiting, as an RCMP Suburban pulled up in front of the airport, to walk Brown into the terminal building. Brown looked deflated. And scared. He kept his head low as our camera followed him into the building — and into the legal system. We were done. There would be no refunds for victims, but there would also be no new videographers sucked into the exciting and way-too-challenging world of showbiz by Brown.

Machines that dispensed candy were always coming back to haunt us. Hardly a day went by that we didn't hear of some heart-vending story. The machines were everywhere. They beckoned with golden promises of big profits with no real work. "Buy fifty machines and then sit back and watch the money roll in." "Be your own boss."

The problem was, after working your butt off driving around to all your machines, shopping for good locations, trying to fix machines that were broken, dumping in some new candy, and emptying out the change, those eager new vending machine operators were usually left with nickels and dimes. The smooth talkers who sold the machines sold a dream that almost never came true. Instead of cleaning up in the candy machine business, the operators were all too often just cleaned out.

Phyllisteen Gibson bought fifty-four machines that dispensed chocolate mints from the North American Vending Company. Gibson dealt with the registered owner himself, Terry Swetlicoe. To clinch the sale, Swetlicoe toured Gibson around to a few established machines. They were all full of quarters, loonies, toonies and five-dollar bills. It sure looked good to Gibson. She signed up for the machines, already placed in retail locations, paying Swetlicoe $7,500. She never saw Swetlicoe again. She never saw much in the way of profits, either. Gibson said Swetlicoe told her she would clear $1,000 a month. Of course, that was Terry Swetlicoe math.

The real math went like this: It cost Gibson $800 a month to keep her fifty-four machines full of candy; she spent about $60 in gas to get to her machines; she paid another $100 a month to a charity. The name of the charity was stamped on the candy machine. The charity label was supposed to convince a storekeeper to donate space and tolerate the existence of the machine near the cash register. So Gibson's total monthly expenses were $960. Monthly sales, roughly $1200. Gibson's profit, her salary, was about $240 a month, or $60 a week. And Gibson had high volume. She was selling a lot of candy. Or a lot of people were stealing it.

In any event, the business didn't pay. Gibson started to believe that Swetlicoe had salted the boxes with cash before he took her on tour to show her the big money. Gibson never found anything beefier than quarters in her collection rounds.

And then there was the charity connection. All of Gibson's boxes were stamped with "The Lost Children Recovery Program" labels. The reason to give, the pitch to buy candy and pay as much for it as you can, was right there in black and white. After all, it went to a good cause — some of it, anyway. Gibson's contract with Swetlicoe read, in part: "It shall be the purchaser's responsibility to pay to the affiliated charity, The Lost Children Recovery Program, the sum of $2 a month for each candy dispenser in the route."

Nowhere on the candy dispensers did it say only $2 a month would go to the charity. Then again, it wasn't a charity. The Lost Children Recovery Program was just registered as a non-profit corporation. Tony Turco, a private eye, was one of the directors. Turco said he and other private investigators donate their time to locate missing kids. The money that went to LCRP paid for office space and a telephone. Turco told us that in the last three years, he had located three kids. Turco also insisted that he had severed ties with Swetlicoe because there were so many complaints about the candy dispensers from storekeepers.

Jo-Anne Brown, of Parents Against Drugs, seconded that motion. She said that her registered charity was once the recipient of little donations from North American Vending Company but she cancelled the arrangement because it was too much of a hassle. Hapless vending operators who could never find Terry Swetlicoe would call her to complain about lousy sales. And storekeepers would call, demanding that the charity pick up the candy dispensers because they were just dumped off at the store and left there with no permission.

And what about the customers who bought the candy? Shouldn't they have been told that only a portion, maybe a small portion, of the money they dropped into that charity box in a store actually went to the charity?

Yes, they should have been told, said Eric Moore, Director and legal counsel in the Charitable Property Division of the Ontario Ministry of the Attorney General. He told us, "If money is being collected in a charity's name and the charity isn't getting all the money collected, that ought to be disclosed to the donor without any request being made by the donor. The disclosure may be in any form — for example, a leaflet that accompanies the dispenser."

The next time you see a candy dispenser in a store, proceeds to charity, see if it tells you how much of the money collected is actually going to charity. If not, tell the charity about it.

We wanted to tell North American Vending Company about all the complaints we had, but the company was nowhere to be found. The directors of the company were Terry Swetlicoe and his wife Marina.

We finally traced them to a rented house north of Toronto. I knocked on the door. No answer. So we waited on the road in front of the house. Don and Kevin in the van, Laurie and I in the Beater. We were parked about fifty metres apart. Suddenly, the front door banged open and out strode a woman, obviously madder than a hornet. She headed for the crew van.

Don and Kevin watched her approach, their gear as out of sight as possible. Don had his camera lying across his lap, waiting for a signal from us. Laurie and I were out of the Beater and on the same heading as Marina Swetlicoe, heading for the crew van. She got there first, trailing a cloud of profanity.

Before Don could get out of the crew van and get his camera up on his shoulder and ready to shoot, she was at his door. Quick as a flash, Marina yanked up her sweater, screaming, "You want a picture?"

I shouted at Marina, "Yell at me, I'm the guy."

"You're the jerk," said Marina, yanking her sweater down to where it belonged in public.

"Yeah. Where's Terry?" I asked.

"I'm not talking to you with the camera. You think I was born yesterday?"

"I don't know when you were born. Where is he? All we want to do is talk to Terry." By now, Don and Kevin were out of the crew van and recording every word.

"Can you please take this out of my face? You take it out of my face or I'm going to smash it, I swear to God, okay?"

Nothing got smashed. Marina stomped off and we didn't find Terry Swetlicoe. And Don kicked himself all the way back to the city. He had missed a shot. It was not a shot we would have put on television, but that didn't matter to Don.

One of the best dancers we ever met was Josephus Lewis, sole director of at least three corporations we knew about: Business Referrals Associated Ltd., Search Group of Companies Inc., and Search International Marketing Group Inc. All of the companies were trolling for substantial investments by eager investors hoping to make 20 percent on their money.

That was always the clarion call of Lewis. Big money could be made. But it didn't take long for some of the investors to realize there would be no profit on investments. And there would be no investments. All the money disappeared.

In many, many conversations we had with Joe Lewis, he promised the moon. The money would be returned. Lewis even called my office number at midnight, reasonably sure I would not be there, to once again go on and on about how all the money was safe. It just wasn't in the hands of the investors, that's all.

Lewis took careful pains to explain that he was, in all these investment deals, "merely the conduit" through which the money flowed, apparently only one way. So Lewis was a money pipe, and the end of the pipe, to hear him tell it, was never stuck into his own pocket. We sparred with Lewis for weeks. No money came back. We thought it might be time to pay him a visit.

Lewis had no regular office, no known business address. Although he was still advertising for investors, the address was only a telephone number. So we set him up. Laurie became an eager investor, with $20,000 to invest. The plan was that Laurie would keep an appointment with Lewis, and at some point I would arrive with the camera crew. It was time that Lewis had a little publicity; time to issue a warning to other investors tempted to make a quick buck with The Conduit.

Lewis took the bait in less than a day. A nighttime meeting was set up at a huge office building that apparently had nothing to do with Lewis and his companies. We could find no connection. Did Lewis have a day job with a real company? Maybe he had a friend who loaned him a desk.

Laurie was wearing a wire; she would guide us to the meeting place by giving us clues in her idle chatter to Lewis. "Oh, we're getting off at the fourth floor... so here we go, here we turn right and then we turn left. Boy, I hope we can find our way out," Laurie joked expositionally. Lewis laughed obligingly. After awhile, the voices of Laurie and Lewis faded. They were deep in the building where Lewis was explaining the merits of investing in a movie project called *More Than A Brother: The Story of Billy, Stanley, and Elvis Presley.*

Outside, we saddled up, gear at the ready, and headed for the front door of the office building. Up the elevator, following directions, we crept through what seemed like miles of darkened office building. Finally, we heard Laurie talking, using her outside voice, to guide us in.

The three of us hustled into the office where Lewis was deep into his pitch. Without missing a beat or stopping for breath, he immediately stood up, smiling, to shake our hands and welcome us to his happy little hole of an office. Even Billy, Stanley, and Elvis would not have received a warmer welcome. Lewis did suggest, in the gentlest of terms, that we were interrupting his meeting with Laurie. "Oh, she won't mind," I said, flashing a glance at Laurie, who said, "Nope, I don't think I want to invest any money today," and left.

Lewis danced us around for the next half hour and then guided us out of the building, waving good-bye at the front entrance. He kept glancing around the parking lot, as if hoping to spot Laurie and her $20,000. Clearly, he had not made the connection. And despite his promises that night, nothing happened. There were a few more midnight telephone messages of assurance. Then nothing.

Whenever I think of Jory Lord, a young sailor from Vancouver, I think of bad guys dancing on the deck of a Chilean submarine, swilling Canadian beer.

On a foggy September night in 1994, in Juan de Fuca Strait, in Canadian waters on the West coast, a Chilean submarine, traveling at about eleven knots, rammed Jory Lord's fifteen-metre sailboat, *Moonglow*. The submarine came out of the fog about nine metres away from *Moonglow*, giving Jory no time to react before impact.

Moonglow sank in sixty seconds. The submarine, the *Thomson*, kept on going. Jory was left floating in the ocean, among pieces of his sailboat, wondering if this was the end of his young life. He shouted at the submarine as it disappeared into the fog. Twenty minutes later, the *Thomson* returned and rescued Jory.

What was a Chilean submarine doing in Canadian waters in the first place? War games. Submarines from the United States and Chile were chasing each other in the waters off Nanoose Bay on Vancouver Island. The games were being hosted by Canada, out of the Armed Forces Base at Nanoose, where giant wharves had been built years earlier to dock submarines. The *Thomson* crew had finished its assignment and was beginning a long journey to San Diego, California.

The Canadian Transportation Safety Board report on the accident would note later that "The submarine's crew denied having been in a collision (in radio transmissions) and did not acknowledge a collision until almost two hours after the accident."

Jory Lord said crew members had told him they heard cries for help and stopped to investigate. Apparently nobody inside the sub heard, felt, or detected that big bump that sent *Moonglow* to the bottom.

The TSB reports wondered out loud how this accident could have happened, as well. In its summary, the board wrote: "It is unknown why the *Thomson* did not observe the *Moonglow* on any of her three operational and manned radar systems." Putting it in language regular people can understand, how could a $600 million war machine, whose main claim to fame was its ability to pinpoint targets, manage to accidentally ram and sink a sailboat the size of a school bus?

The *Moonglow* was under sail, displaying its running lights at the time of the accident, and had its radar deflector hoisted up the mast. The radar deflector is supposed to make a boat easier to detect on radar, unless, apparently, you happen to be driving a Chilean submarine.

And what about the sonar on board the *Thomson*? That class of submarine, built in Germany, has an active sonar detector that should have been bouncing electronic "pings" off the hull of the *Moonglow* as the two vessels closed on each other. So what really happened?

Beer might have been the answer. Too much of it, just before departure. Sixteen members of the *Thomson* crew, out of a total crew complement of twenty-six, had been running up a big bar bill at the Spinnaker pub in Nanaimo on the day of departure.

The tab came to more than $400, which meant that, checking bar prices, the average crew member had five pints of beer in the afternoon, before heading off to a private party near the Nanoose base, where it is possible, even likely, that more than lemonade and tea was served to the already over-refreshed crew. Then off to the sub and out to sea, just in time to run down Jory Lord's sailboat.

And what a beautiful sailboat it was — a two-masted ketch built in 1939 for silent film star and glamour queen Gloria Swanson. It was mahogany and oak construction, lovingly restored by Jory, who hoped someday to turn his home on the water into a charter business.

Jory was a boat builder and sailor of considerable knowledge and experience for his twenty-seven years. But nothing would have prepared him for a showdown with a speeding submarine in a fog bank.

And nothing would have prepared Jory for the diplomatic, political, and legal mumbo-jumbo that boiled up in the wake of the accident. Jory wanted to talk to somebody about compensation for his lost $200,000 sailboat and home. But nobody wanted to talk to Jory. The Chilean Consulate in Vancouver declared diplomatic immunity; The United States Navy refused comment, citing national security; the Canadian Government said nothing.

From September of 1994 to March of 1996, we worked the telephones trying to get somebody to pay attention to Jory's plight and the gross unfairness of his situation. We compiled our own information packages, including summaries of what had happened, along with video interviews from Jory on precise details of the collision. We sent out the packages to back up our repeated telephone conversations and messages. But we were getting nowhere fast.

Foreign Affairs in Ottawa just didn't want to talk to us at all. So we ambushed Foreign Affairs Minister Lloyd Axworthy as he beat a hasty path out a back door in the House of Commons on the way to his office. I put the package directly into his hands. "We'll take a look at it and get back to you," said Axworthy. That's the last we heard.

We even dropped in on the Chilean Embassy in Ottawa with our camera crew. We got past some of the locked doors, and then I was summoned into the private office of Fernando Urrutia, a Chilean diplomat. He listened sympathetically to the story, as if he had never heard it before in his life, and smiled sadly.

The camera crew was still recording the conversation from the outer office. I was wearing a wireless microphone. Urrutia did concede at one point that "Perhaps from a humanitarian point of view, perhaps it's possible to reopen the case." We put that audio into our story, hoping it signalled a positive step. But it didn't. We were getting nowhere.

In November of 1996, Jory's lawyers managed to get a default judgment against the Republic of Chile. And later, he did get a settlement, although it was far less than the value of his beloved *Moonglow*. Jory has been traveling the world in the last few years. He captained a schooner in the South Pacific and spent a lot of time in Japan, Malaysia, and New Zealand. He has yet to replace *Moonglow* with another sailboat.

Of all the bad guys we invited to dance, nobody danced longer in a single performance than Glasford Alexander.

His advertisements ran in newspaper classified sections all across Canada: "Financial Consulting and loans for debt consolidation, business, personal, etc. Also first time loans. Good or bad credit, bankruptcy welcome." Wow. Who couldn't get a loan under those conditions?

As it turned out, almost nobody got a loan; almost everybody got the business. Alexander was director and administrator of both AAA Financial Consulting Inc. and SSKB Financial Corporation. The companies promised desperate customers instant loans, after they paid an up-front fee of about $400. But the loans never appeared, and the poor and penniless clients fell deeper into financial trouble after being ground up and spit out by Alexander's busy, profitable companies.

We caught up with Alexander, after one of his many brushes with the law, as he was leaving the courthouse at Old City Hall in Toronto. Alexander was carrying a heavy banker's box, filled with evidence filed against him in court by the Ontario Consumer Ministry and made available to Alexander as a matter of process in his trial.

We quickly surrounded him at a stoplight as he was about to cross the street into Nathan Phillips Square. The cameraman poked his lens right into Alexander's face as I tried to engage him in conversation. Alexander used the banker's box as a shield. He thought he was hiding his face from the camera as he crossed the street with us in tow.

Once in the pedestrian square, Alexander seemed unsure where to go. He patently ignored us but kept shifting the box to keep the camera lens from drawing a bead on his face, although the lens had done just that several times. Alexander then headed down the stairs into the parking garage.

Over the next several minutes, we followed him from floor to floor, as if he had forgotten where he parked or was worried about showing us his car, with licence plate attached. The dance settled into a routine. We tracked his every footstep, offering advice: "Sorry, I think that garage door is locked." "Nope, can't use your cellphone down here, it won't work."

Alexander remained silent, preferring to let his heavy banker's box speak for him as he jerked it around to protect his now well-shot facial features. Twenty minutes later, we were back at street level in the Square. Alexander either couldn't find his car, or thought better of showing it to us.

Alexander was clearly getting fatigued by the weight of the box. Carrying his alleged sins around with him, as it were, was tiring work. Suddenly, he put the box down on the sidewalk and ripped off the cardboard lid.

Leaving he box behind, he used the lid as a lighter, more workable shield. Out where he could now use his cellphone, he called an associate who came to his rescue. After he performed a few more dips and dives, a sports car screeched to a stop at the curb and Alexander finally made good his escape. The box of evidence, valuable court documents, sat forlornly on the sidewalk.

Years later, Alexander finally went to jail for promising loans that never materialized. He was sentenced to six months in jail and his companies were fined $10,000. Justice of the Peace Ian McNish called Glasford's scam a "sophisticated plan to take money from the weakest, poorest, and most vulnerable people in our society."

The Crown Attorney, Jim Girling, said it was a victory for Alexander's victims: "These people believe that after they have been ripped off one more time, that they are simply victims in society. This should empower them. This type of decision should let them know they are worth something."

Alexander's wife, Debbie Luhowy, was fined $3,000 for her role as director of Alexander's companies. We caught a glimpse of her that day as she was rushing away from the couple's new nine thousand square-foot mansion just north of Toronto.

Some bad guys don't like to leave their victims empty-handed. Not that bad guys have a heart. Most of them don't. It's a safety measure. Bad guys know that if they take all your money and give back absolutely nothing of value, it might be easier for police to prove fraud.

But if bad guys give you something when they gleefully suck up your money, that's a business transaction. The victim might not be getting a good deal, but since when is that against the law? Winning — the art of cajoling opponents to get the better deal — is pretty well what drives the economy.

Robert and Aurelienne Jolin of Toronto figured they were closing in on the big deal. They were close to the brass ring. They actually thought they were lucky to be targeted by a Montreal mail order company. Picked out of the blue. The Jolins had won, they were told, some big prizes — a car and $52,000 cash. All that would be theirs if they just bought some valuable merchandise offered for sale.

The Jolins bought, while waiting for their prize to arrive, a Norman Rockwell reproduction for $1950, a Steamboat Willie (an early Mickey Mouse cartoon drawing), a British silver crown for $6,280, one King Tut's Cartouche (an ornamental picture frame) for $1605, and a four-piece Roman coin set for $3110. That's a total of almost $13,000 spent while waiting for the big prize. There were other bonus prizes sent along the way, just to keep the Jolins excited about the big win.

The guy on the telephone said he was shipping out a hot tub for Robert and Aurelienne, and a boat, probably too big for the Jolins' driveway, said the guy. The hot tub arrived first. It was a kids' wading pool with an electric heater attached. The boat too big for the driveway arrived next. It was a rubber dinghy, almost too big for the Jolins' kitchen table. That guy on the phone from Montreal sure loved his work, selling dreams and happy times to hapless customers in Toronto.

When we came barging in the front door of a seedy walkup in Montreal, looking for executives from S.D. Prestige Enterprises, the people who had given the Jolins and hundreds of others lessons on sharp marketing, we found only an angry, growling dog. The hair on the back of his neck told us he was not having a good day and we were not welcome. The office was drab and messy, with boxes of what looked like cheap junk piled in one corner. On the wall hung a simple sign: "Never Give Up." A woman stuck her head around the corner to tell us nobody was there.

Later, we got a company executive on the line and he immediately went into his tap-dance act. The Jolins had received valuable merchandise for their money. How could there be a problem with that? Over several conversations that day, the executive, known to us only as "Jamie" promised a $5,000 refund.

But "Jamie" insisted that the $5,000 would be paid only on the understanding that all that valuable merchandise was returned. The company said it would send out a truck to pick up the spurned treasures right away. The Jolins got their $5,000 in the mail. The truck never came.

Some of our clients came to us with problems that money could never repair. Gary Allen from Victoria had carried a terrible hurt deep inside his soul for his whole adult life. Gary had always remembered clearly that he had been taken on a two-week road trip by his Big Brother, a volunteer for the Big Brothers and Sisters of Victoria Capital Region. The Big Brother had told Gary's mother he was going on a business and pleasure road trip to the United States and he wanted Gary to come along. Gary's mother was a bit hesitant at first, but the Big Brothers Organization said it would be okay. And Gary kept bugging his mother to let him go.

Gary was eight years old. Every night in motel rooms across Oregon and California, he was sexually assaulted. The pattern was always the same. The Big Brother would leave Gary in the room while he went out to buy beer. Gary told me later, "And then he would come back with the beer, drink it, and then more or less order me onto the bed and then perform sexual acts on me." Even in the retelling, Gary shuddered at the terror he felt. "I seriously thought that when he went out to get that beer, I should pack up my little bag and get out on the highway and hitchhike home. And I was just ready to do it when he walked in."

The Big Brother allowed Gary to send a few postcards back home to his mother — after he read the message first. One card says, in typical eight-year-old scrawl, "I am having a good time in a heated pool." The truth of it was, the motel pools were Gary's only safe refuge. "You know how motels have pools, so I used to stay out at the pool as long as I could because there were people there. But then, sooner or later, he would come and drag me out, back up to the room and the same performance again."

"How did you feel?" I asked Gary.

"I felt like I had a dirty secret to keep. That I couldn't tell anybody. And I felt that, somehow, I deserved it," he said with his head bowed and his eyes closed.

When Gary came to us, he was thirty-four. He had finally decided he wanted people to know what had happened. He wanted that Big Brother exposed. And he needed some psychiatric therapy to help him carry on in life. Gary identified his attacker as William Albert Elder. After several days of poring through Vancouver Island telephone books, we found him working as a janitor at a Victoria elementary school.

We shadowed that school for two days. We couldn't believe it, but nobody reported the presence of two large vehicles, with four adults carrying strange-looking gear, lurking around the school yard. On the second day, we caught him coming out the back door of the school and heading toward his compact SUV. We were shooting him tightly, camera in the face, to eliminate any possibility we would catch school children in our lens. He drove off as we trotted alongside his SUV. He would answer no questions beyond denying he knew Gary Allen. It was a bizarre scene — Elder driving his SUV down a school laneway crowded with baby strollers and mothers, a cloud of TV people swarming around his open window. Finally, Elder accelerated and was soon gone from the neighbourhood.

We put the story on television, with befuddled and panicked Big Brothers officials insisting that screening procedures had improved vastly from the time of Gary Allen's allegations about what happened to him in 1972. Big Brothers also told us they had turned the matter over to their insurance company for possible settlement of any damage claims. Gary got a lawyer and sued William Albert Elder and the Big Brothers and Sisters of Victoria Capital Region for damages. Finally, Gary settled out of court for a small, undisclosed amount of money that allowed him to get his needed therapy. Gary had also won a far larger battle. He had told the world. He had no reason to feel more shame. He was a victim. He was innocent.

In an unrelated incident, on January 16, 2003, William Albert Elder was convicted in the sexual assault of an eight-year-old boy he had been babysitting in Victoria. The judge sent him to jail for nine months. Gary Allen was there to witness Elder's day in court.

Gary heard how the eight-year-old had wanted to take a gun and kill himself over what had happened in Elder's house. Elder is banned for life from being around children under fourteen. He cannot go to parks, swimming pools, or any public place where children congregate. He is also prohibited for life from using a computer to communicate with children. He is not allowed to possess pornography or firearms.

Testimony showed that the eight-year-old boy's father had met Elder when he worked as a janitor in the very school where we chased him. The boy's father and mother trusted Elder and used him as a babysitter while they took an overnight trip out of town.

Gary told me after that trial that he had forgiven Elder. He had moved on. It was now in his past. But it would always be in his past.

When I open the *Goldhawk Fights Back* File labeled "Gold Digger," the first things that hit me are the photographs of Adele Darlene Andre, a veteran escort-service operator in Saskatoon. There she is, in full facial *flagrante delicto*. She was the bold, brassy, platinum-blonde with the big lips and voracious appetite for big money. She went after a widower — a lonely, confused, retired school teacher. Adele cleaned him out and put him in debt up to his neck. She was thirty-five, he was seventy. Edwin Born was exhibiting the early signs of Alzheimer's disease.

After he had met Adele, from September to December of 1996, Born went from a debt-free status to $116,000 in the hole. This was all discovered after the fact by an incredulous daughter, Karen, who had been worried something like this had been happening. She was given power of attorney for her father after he suffered a major stroke in February of 1997. That's when the whole sad story really came out.

In just a few months, Born had, for his new friend Adele and himself, run up a $25,000 line of credit at the Bank of Nova Scotia, charged his Visa up to $5,000, and got another loan from BNS for $12,000. On top of all that, the bank had approved a $57,000 mortgage on a house, signed by both Edwin and Adele, where Adele could live with her two young daughters. There were other incidental charges, as well — $7,000 owing to Sears and $3,000 owing to his credit union, just to name a couple. As Karen told me later, of her father's feelings for Adele, "I think he loved her. I think he did."

Adele apparently had extended use of Edwin's credit cards. Once, while he was on a brief holiday in Hawaii, Adele ran ads in the *Star Phoenix*. One read: "Naughty and Nice. Ultra Sexy XXX EXXXplicit, True Blondes Tammy, Barbi, Janice, and Michelle. 10 a.m. to 3 a.m." The number to call listed in the ad was Edwin's home number. Edwin's friends and family were horrified. So was Edwin when he got home.

Karen Born came to us because she was desperate. The family was being saddled with the $116,000 debt, now that Born was in a nursing home in poor heath. Karen told us she had been given every excuse in the book why the Bank of Nova Scotia could not help. Why hadn't somebody warned Karen about the debt her father was accumulating? One local bank representative told Karen that bankers are not allowed to share private banking information, even with other members of the same family.

We went to Bank of Nova Scotia headquarters in Toronto looking for a better answer. We found one. The bank closely examined the circumstances and decided it was time to demonstrate that banks can have hearts, too. The Bank of Nova Scotia took Edwin Born's name off the $57,000 mortgage and forgave an extra $20,000 of his loan debt. Said Diane Flanagan, a senior consultant in public affairs at BNS, "I think we want to take that extra care. And we're doing some important things like a sponsorship of a seniors' education program to help seniors become more aware of situations out there, become better consumers, better customers."

Back in Saskatoon, we tried to find Adele Andre. We thought it was time to put her on television. After several trips to the house that Edwin bought for Adele, it appeared nobody was home. I called her home several times on my cellphone. No answer. I left a message. Back came the call like a thunderbolt as I stood on the street just a few doors away from her house. Adele was sweet and lovely to me on the telephone until she realized I was the pest who had been banging on her door all day. I asked about her relationship with Edwin Born:

"He hired me as an escort. He's really a client," she said sweetly.

"Well, he's a lot more than a client, isn't he?" I said in a level tone. "I mean he's loaned you lots of money. And he co-signed the mortgage on the house that you're in." I could feel the mood change right on the line. Her breath seemed to be coming in short pants. She started to growl. I could hear that she was sneering.

"You're an asshole. Leave me the fuck alone. I'm calling the cops on you right fucking now and I'm telling the police that you're harassing me. And I'll have you charged with harassment right now. I'm calling the cops right fucking now."

"Okay," I said, trying to be cordial, "all right, you do that. I'll wait." The line went dead. That was March 19, 1998.

On April 26, 1998, in a matter totally unrelated to the Edwin Born case, Adele Andre was charged with conspiracy to commit murder. Police said she tried to hire three youths to kill a man. On December 16 that year, she was found guilty and sentenced to two years in prison.

Just about the same time that Adele Andre was trying to eke out a living in Saskatoon, financial advisor Patrick Kinlin was hitting the big time, living high off the hog in Hogtown. Kinlin was a high-school dropout with the gift of gab. He was a charmer with lots of high-end suits and slippery shoes. He started out as an insurance salesman, but soon moved to the more glamorous, if not more mysterious, world of financial advisers.

Kinlin opened a posh office right on Bay Street, in Toronto. His Kinlin Financial Services specialized in older clients with sizable savings. He invested their money for them and paid above-average returns. Naturally, his clients loved him. And he loved them right back.

He attended their parties, offered little gifts, and sent thoughtful birthday cards. His client list grew and grew, just as his appetite for fast cars, expensive wine, big houses, and even more expensive suits did. Then, just like that loose piece of yarn you carelessly yanked on that old sweater you once loved, it all started to come apart.

Suddenly, the investments were not paying dividends. Patrick Kinlin, once Mr. Ubiquitous to his friends, became scarce. At this point, Kinlin was managing more than $12 million for seventy-eight clients. Actually, managing was an odd word — he pumped all $12 million into his own account at a small Toronto Dominion Bank branch in West-end Toronto. Then it was withdrawn by Kinlin, and it left for parts unknown. As Kinlin fled to the United States, just before his investors went to police, only $44.61 remained in that TD account.

Kinlin surfaced at a mental hospital in Philadelphia, where hospital officials said he was being treated for trying to commit suicide. Police returned him to Toronto where he was convicted on twenty-seven counts of fraud and sentenced to five years in prison. Five years for all the lives he had ruined — for all the retirements he had destroyed. The Crown Attorney in the case, Bev Richards, told me after the trial, "Some of these people were wiped out. We're talking about people in their sixties and seventies, whose complete life's savings had been taken from them."

In her closing argument at trial, she had told Mr. Justice Hugh Porter:

> Like a parasitic insect that bores into the heart of its chosen host and proceeds to feed its every excessive need, Patrick Joseph Kinlin fed his lavish lifestyle by stealing from widows, aging retirees, trusting friends, relatives, and particularly any decent person he came across who had worked hard the last twenty or thirty years.

After the dust of the trial had settled, I got a call from one of Patrick Kinlin's clients, David Thut. He had lost $2 million to Kinlin, but the damage still had not run its course. Near the end, Kinlin was still managing to pay Thut his dividend cheques on the "invested" money. Or so David Thut had thought.

Actually, Kinlin took out an $11,000 loan at that TD bank branch, in David Thut's name. He forged Thut's signature on the application and then used the loan proceeds to pay Thut his phony interest. Kinlin was buying himself a little time, as usual, with somebody else's money.

Of course, the loan was never repaid by Kinlin. Thut found out about it after Kinlin had gone to prison and the TD bank sent Thut a letter demanding its money. Thut objected and sent off a letter to TD Bank President Charles Baillie.

Thut got back a letter from Colin C. Taylor, Director, Litigation, for TD Bank Financial Group. Lawyers might have called the letter fittingly aggressive. Mere mortals would have called it snotty. It said, in part:

> In the circumstances, you have had the full benefit of these funds and the Bank is entitled to look to you for the repayment of these funds under principles of restitution and unjust enrichment.
>
> In my view, the forgery, if any, by Mr. Kinlin of your signature is wholly irrelevant to your obligation to repay the funds received by you. I suggest you are also liable to pay reasonable interest from the dates of the withdrawals.

We argued with lesser officials who would listen to us that Thut was the innocent victim of crime and should not be further victimized. And how had the bank managed to approve a fraudulent loan application in the first place?

The TD Bank forgave the loan and said, in a terse, five-line letter to Thut, "The Bank will forgive your loan. We will ensure that our collections department is made aware of our decision and that your credit rating has not been affected by this incident. We trust you will find this satisfactory." David Thut did.

But just as that Kinlin mess was being cleaned up, Kinlin himself was busy with a new enterprise from inside prison. Corrections officials alleged that Kinlin and two fellow inmates were applying for old-age pensions on the Internet, using phony ID. The government cheques were sent to Kingston mailboxes and the inmates picked them up and deposited them in their own bank accounts while they were out of the prison on day passes.

The investigation into that scam was abruptly halted when Kinlin became ill with a heart ailment. He died in Kingston Penitentiary Hospital on March 4, 2001. He was fifty-five. Kinlin died poor, sharing that status with his ruined clients.

Promising big profits is a time-honoured way to get OPM — Other People's Money. But some bad guys sweeten the pot by adding a little glamour, some showbiz, and a touch of sex. Such was the combination of delights awaiting rapturous stars of tomorrow at the ritzy offices of Canadian Media Group International. The hot pink brochure said it all:

> When the time comes to embark on a career in the entertainment industry, there is always a need for guidance and refinement... Models are one of the most important parts of the fashion industry. Without models, the fashion industry would not survive... The Talent Division of Canadian Media Group brings together a number of gifted individuals who represent the widest possible range of acting styles... We believe in the three-dimensional actor, one who brings character and emotion to their (sic) craft.

Clearly, CMG did not represent writers. But then again, it really didn't represent anybody. We could not find a single client who got a job or a gig as a result of going to CMG and plunking down anywhere from $600 to $6,000 for publicity photos, videos, and agent representation.

Said the brochure, "Our support staff is knowledgeable, not to mention tenacious, capable of casting, booking, and meeting the demands of our clients." But when clients demanded their money back, support staff members were hard to find, not to mention unavailable.

The Toronto Better Business Bureau, the Ontario Consumer Ministry, the Toronto Police, and *Goldhawk Fights Back* got hundreds of complaints about CMG. We decided to pay a visit to their offices. We formed a delegation — a disgruntled mother and her hoped-for child star; Peter Lalonde, the President of the Toronto Better Business Bureau; and us. The mother wanted her money back. Lalonde wanted his little BBB sign back — he was revoking CMG's membership. We wanted to find somebody, anybody, who got their money's worth from CMG.

At the reception desk, with camera rolling, the staff went into a tizzy and disappeared behind a huge, fancy facade that surrounded the desk. Finally, a man we identified as Claude Wiseman came out.

"I'm here to inform you that we have to revoke your membership in the Better Business Bureau," Lalonde announced to Wiseman.

"And you need a camera crew for that?" asked Wiseman.

"We want to talk to you about some problems," I chimed in, helpfully.

Wiseman disappeared and returned to announce he had called security and we would be thrown out. He did give back Lalonde's little "Member of the BBB" sign. He would answer no questions about anybody who ever found happiness and work through the efforts of CMG.

Wiseman disappeared again. We were left alone. A huge portion of the facade in the reception area contained floor-to-ceiling, colour-coordinated filing cabinets. They were labelled with the great cities of the world: London, Rome, Paris, New York, Sydney, Tokyo. There was even one for Toronto. I eased open the Toronto file cabinet. It was empty. I tried them all. They were all empty. The facade was really a facade.

Then security arrived. A pleasant young woman announced she was head of security, and we would have to leave. I asked for identification. Without a word she left, returning ten minutes later with a business card.

I thanked her, but said we preferred to wait, hoping somebody inside CMG, beyond the facade, would talk to us. The head of security said she would have to call the police. I told her that was a wonderful idea, that I believed the police should be involved, and that I would eagerly await their arrival. She left again.

In the meantime, many of the staff members were escaping out a back door. We were not sure anybody was left. After another half-hour had passed, we left, too. When we got off the elevator on the ground floor, we were met by three large men in white coveralls and paint splatters. They were waiting to get on the elevator, but looked at each other sheepishly as we got out. I looked at them expectantly.

"We're supposed to throw you out," said one.

"Can't," I said. "We're leaving. Are you guys security?"

"No," said the one guy. "We're painters. Building management told us to pitch in and help."

"You're telling us to leave, and we're leaving," I said, trying to make this odious task as easy as possible for the poor painters.

"Great," said the painter, waving good-bye. The story was aired on *CTV National News* that night, October 6, 1998. On December 3, we ran a second story. Canadian Media Group had closed its fancy doors and disappeared without a trace, ending its seven-month performance.

A lot of bad guy performers never stop. Always on the move with some new scheme/scam, they leave behind a long trail of misery, financial hardship, marital breakup, and suicide. The best dancers almost never tell the truth, never look back, and never regret. They sell shoddy products, offer lousy customer service, promise impossible dreams, take money from anybody, and say absolutely anything to close a deal. That pretty well sums up a bunch of characters we came to call "The Universal Gang." Our file on the Gang grows to this day. It is now two banker's boxes big, even too heavy for Glasford Alexander to heft, to hide his guilty face.

The Universal Gang first came to our attention in June, 1996. We were curious about a company called World Venture Distributing (II) Inc. The president of WVD(II) was Paul Guy Beaupre. The company was located in Aurora, Ontario. And based on the theory you can always tell the wild ones by their ads in the classified section, this was WVD(II)'s little doozer in the *Vancouver Sun*: "Hot, new concept. Money back guarantee. No selling. No product. No inventory. First distributors of unique game, never offered in BC. Get best locations and quickest profits."

The scheme worked like this: Operators bought these little games that looked like mini pinball machines, WVD(II) placed them in busy, profitable locations, such as bars. And if customers won at the game, after pumping in a few quarters, the bar owner would hand out a prize. Maybe a drink. If a customer won in a coffee shop, she might get a doughnut. The commercial outlet got to keep 50 percent of the quarters.

Based on that formula, Wendy Tracy of Vancouver paid $11,000 for twenty-five machines, was promised she would make $900 a month for herself, and actually wound up making, on average, $22 a month. WVD(II) ignored her complaints, just like it ignored all complaints, and then went out of business.

By August 27, 1998, we were chasing another vending company that had just gone out of business, International Vendcorp Incorporated, with offices in California, Florida, and Mississauga, Ontario. The man behind the company was, once again, Paul Guy Beaupre, sometimes identified as Guy Beaupre or Guy Paul Beaupre. IVI had left behind scores of unhappy customers in five provinces, and about eighty or ninety hopping-mad investors in Florida. Police and government officials knew all about IVI (we had told them, countless times) but they essentially slumbered on, taking no action, just noting with a disapproving sniff that something didn't look quite right.

In the beginning, IVI was a member in good standing of the National Business Opportunity Bureau, operating out of Atlanta, Georgia. A member in good standing meant that IVI would operate, as its certificate said, to "protect the interest of the consumer and conduct business activities in an ethical manner." But a few months after registration, NBOB kicked out IVI after getting too many complaints from unprotected consumers.

Shortly after that, IVI proudly proclaimed it had become a member of NABOB, the North American Business Opportunity Bureau. The wording on the official certificate was identical to NBOB's wording. But NABOB (having nothing to do with coffee) operated out of a semi-detached house in Brampton. The president was the husband of an employee who worked at the Universal Gang's offices.

Meanwhile, in Florida, the Department of Agriculture and Consumer Services, after listening to complaints about the quality of the vending machines and misrepresentation, issued a cease and desist order against IVI. The company ignored it — at its peril, it turned out. The State of Florida filed a lawsuit against IVI and Paul Beaupre. It got a default judgment against the company. No default judgment was ever obtained against Beaupre because Florida couldn't find him to serve him the papers. He was in Canada, in Toronto, where Ontario government consumer guardians took copious notes, compiled files that were deemed protected under Canada's and Ontario's privacy laws, and then went back to sleep.

At *Goldhawk Fights Back*, we had been bugging Beaupre's office on an almost daily basis, but getting nowhere. Finally, a self-announced paralegal was assigned by IVI to deal with us, and gruffly proclaimed that Beaupre had no time for complainers. An inside source in the company was telling us at that same time that the paralegal, Frank Marshall, was really Beaupre's bodyguard, and would let no one near his boss, alleged by his employees to be a millionaire.

IVI was in the candy business, although it was never a sweet deal for any of the disillusioned investors who came to us for help. All the problems were, by now, standard fare for the Universal Gang. One woman from Prince Edward Island was a typical victim. She paid $11,000 for eighteen vending machines that dispensed Hershey Nuggets. She was promised exclusive sales territory on the Island but quickly found other victims who had also been sold exclusive territory by Beaupre's company.

After several arguments with IVI and its new watchdog, Frank Marshall, the woman got a $6,000 refund. She was one of the very few who got anything out of IVI. She remains just a she, anonymous at her own request. The woman was beginning a new career as a financial advisor and didn't think her past misjudgments would look very good out in the open.

Meanwhile, at Hershey Canada, President Rick Meyers was complaining that there was never a link between IVI and Hershey. IVI used the Hershey name and made it seem as if it were affiliated with Hershey Canada, to help boost sales. Myers said to me, "We have never given them permission to use any of our marks or to use our name in conjunction with the sale of their machines. They are trading on the goodwill that we have developed with our consumers and the trust that they have in our franchise. That's what deeply concerns us."

Investors had their own concerns. One was a "Guaranteed Agreement on Investment," a shining document of blind faith given to all victims. It said, in part, "If the purchaser has not earned through the Company's products at least 100 percent of purchase price after a full twelve consecutive months after initial location of all units, the Company will reimburse to the Purchaser the difference between initial purchase price and Purchaser's earnings." Fat Chance. It never happened for almost anybody we tried to help recover from investing in IVI.

Four months later, in January of 1999, we were off and running again. This time the Universal Gang's marketing geniuses focussed their creative guns on personal hygiene.

The new product was paper toilet-seat covers that would be dispensed, for a price, before seating occurred in any public washroom. The scheme, as usual, was fraught with peril, even to the consumer.

We market-tested the idea in the men's washroom at CTV. The tissue-paper seat covers had to be unfolded carefully, a little like a road map, and then placed gingerly on the toilet seat. A long, protruding piece of tissue dangled into the bowl, so that once the deed was done and the toilet flushed, that wet part of the tissue would cause the entire paper contrivance to be sucked neatly down the bowl.

Well, that *could* happen, with a lot of practice. There were drawbacks. While unfolding the tissue, it was far too easy to rip off the protuberance that was supposed to dangle into the bowl, thereby disabling the automatic feature. Placing the tissue was tough, especially in heavily ventilated washrooms. It didn't take much of a breeze to blow the paper cover onto the floor or into the bowl, before the butt could be placed into position. And finally, although we couldn't be sure, we had our suspicions that the paper cover might stick easily to bare skin. Under normal conditions, those difficulties might be enough to sink any new product.

But it didn't end there. The little vending machines were incredibly cheap. Some were plastic so that all a customer had to do was yank hard on the cover to remove a handful of little tissues and then grab the quarters in the change box, as well. And then there was the coin mechanism. Often, the quarter would be inserted and turned, and nothing would come out — not good if a vendor wanted to have any repeat customers.

But it didn't end even there. The vending machines were sold under the Cottonelle brand name, lending a great deal of credibility to the enterprise. But Kimberly Clark, the owner of Cottonelle, told us their name had been taken in vain. They had nothing to do with the venture. Does this sound at all familiar?

Distributorships for "Cottonelle Heath Guard Paper Toilet Seat Cover Dispensers" were being sold by Universal Vending Inc., George Katsoulakis, President. Universal Vending's offices were in the same ugly little office on Britannia Road in Mississauga where we had been looking for the defunct International Vendcorp.

Same address. Fancy that. And when we had gone looking for International Vendcorp at its last known address, who told us International Vendcorp wasn't there? George Katsoulakis himself. There was no Paul Guy Beaupre in the corporate documents for Universal. But there was a Leo Beaupre, Paul's father.

Jim Roe of Kindcardine, Ontario, had been one of many unhappy investors in toilet-seat covers. Roe bought twenty-one vending machines from Universal for $12,000. He dealt with George Katsoulakis himself.

Roe had watched a promotional video that said, proudly, that Universal was the company that invented paper toilet-seat covers and then test-marketed the idea across North America for three years. Maybe. Jim Roe sure couldn't sell many toilet seat covers in the Bruce Peninsula region of Ontario. He wanted his money back. We got him a partial refund, $5,430, just before the toilet seat cover business went down the drain. However, going down the drain in the case of the Universal Gang didn't always mean going out of business. Sometimes it just meant the company was shifting gears and would be back in the limelight with a great new product.

Sure enough, by May of 1999, just three months after the toilet seat cover brouhaha had settled down, we started to get complaints about a company selling pay telephones. A brand new video sang the praises of Universal Pay Phone Systems, Inc.

"Live the life you've always wanted. Welcome to the wonderful world of cash, with Universal Pay Phone Systems." The President, once again, was George Katsoulakis, who by then had lost part of his name and referred to himself and signed letters as George Kats.

In Canada, the CRTC deregulated the pay phone business in June, 1998, following a similar decision in the United States. So in this new world, it was possible for mom and pop operators to set up their own pay phones and make money.

The technical hurdles that needed to be overcome — the installation of special lines, the locating of a good spot for the pay phone, and the quality of the phone itself, created massive headaches for what turned out to be hundreds of investors.

Also, for many who spent money on pay phones, the phones were never delivered. Many customers came close to bankruptcy after their brush with Universal Pay Phones. Meanwhile, we had been sent company accounting documents by a Deep Phone inside Universal that showed Universal Pay Phone Systems, Inc. had registered gross sales of $25 million.

Jim St. Louis of Windsor, Ontario, was lucky in a way. He only lost $13,000 when he ordered three pay phones from Universal. He signed up for the phones, paid the money, and then started to get cold feet waiting for the phones to arrive. So he called the Canadian Business Bureau, an agency that lists Universal Pay Phone Systems, Inc. as one of its happy members. The wording on the Certificate of Registration, included in Jim's sales package, was the same as the wording in the NABOB certificate, a few corporate generations ago.

Jim St. Louis called the number for CBB. The phone was answered by a familiar voice. It was Ira Newman, the salesman from Universal who had sold St. Louis the phones. Ira said to Jim that he supposed this didn't look very good and Jim readily agreed. The official office for CBB was a post office box on Yonge Street.

We went back to Universal, to the same crappy little office out behind the shabby strip bar with a sign that said "Girls, Girls, Girls," only to have a Universal staff member slam the door in our faces.

In a last-ditch attempt to get through to somebody at Universal, we set up one of their salespeople to meet our shill, Brian Woodcock, on a busy outdoor patio at a Church Street restaurant.

At a signal, Brian cut short his meeting, suddenly deciding he did not want to invest thousands in pay phones, got up from the table, and started to leave. A cheesed-off salesperson, Tony Ferrari, followed him to the sidewalk. She had been expecting a cheque, not a brush-off.

As Brian kept her occupied on the busy sidewalk, we worked our way closer. I was carrying the sales packages for Hershey Nuggets, Cottonelle toilet-seat covers and, now, pay phones. I thought it was possible that Tony would not have known about the Universal Gang's long history.

Finally, I was standing quietly at her side. There was poor Tony — busy talking to Brian on her left, while I, the cameraman, and a sound man with a boom pole mike only a few feet away from her head, waited unseen at her side.

I said, "Excuse me," and Tony turned to look my way, instantly irritated she had been interrupted. Her eyes widened. She flashed a glance at Brian, who had already melted into the crowd and then instantly formed her strategy: flight. She started to move — fast.

"Is this what you're selling?" I asked, showing her the sales packs.

"Oh my God," said Tony, hustling across the street as we followed.

"Were you also selling these?" Then Tony added denial to her escape dance.

"I don't even know what you're talking about," she said.

"You know the company you're working for? Universal Vending?"

"I don't know what you're talking about," she said again, emphatically and slowly, as if I were too stupid to get what she meant. Then she was gone, ducking into a busy restaurant. We stopped at the door. No sense ruining everybody's lunch. Tony didn't seem in the mood to really talk to us, anyway. A few weeks later, Universal Pay Phone Systems Inc. closed its doors and disappeared.

We didn't hear from the Universal Gang again until early in 2001. This time they relocated, put on a fresh coat of paint, and returned to their core business: candy. The Blue Corporation was located in Kingston, Ontario. The President was Donna Peden, the wife of Leo Beaupre, and Paul Beaupre's stepmother. There was, of course, the usual fancy corporate video and a well-known brand name to grease the wheels of investor participation.

This time it was M&M candies. And the vending machine had a little Mr. Blue, who waved his arms whenever anybody got close to the machine, and pitched M&M candies in a recorded message. The motion-activated Mr. Blue looked like the M&M characters seen in television commercials. It was a great selling gimmick. Too bad the

Blue Corporation had no permission and no licence to use the patented trademark.

In the beginning, the little Mr. Blue vending machines, stuffed with M&M's, sold quickly to eager distributors. It was a brand new product for the Blue Corporation, but the same old problems soon started to surface.

The first thing was the little plastic mechanical Mr. Blue in the vending machine. He was tough on batteries. Every time anybody even walked by the machine, Mr. Blue would wave his arms and go into his little act. Distributors complained they could have gone broke just replacing the batteries in the overactive Mr. Blue.

Then storekeepers where the machines were located started to complain that the Mr. Blue mini-commercial was driving them crazy. The recording featured some white guy doing his imitation of Louis Armstrong. It was annoyingly amateurish. The voice sounded like one of the Universal Gang's better-known salesmen.

Janice Quick, who lived near Grande Prairie, Alberta, bought forty candy machines from Blue Corporation for $40,000. A few weeks later, she discovered that two other investors had also bought the same "exclusive" sales territory in Grande Prairie. There just wasn't enough territory to go around. There was hardly a building in Grande Prairie that didn't have a Mr. Blue Machine waving his arms until his little battery died.

Besides that, the Mr. Blue vending machines were designed and built in the United States, and some staff at the Blue Corporation doubted that the machines would take Canadian quarters.

The Blue Corporation told us that Janice Quick would probably get a refund. She didn't. Then the Blue Corporation closed its doors. This time, however, the company announced it was closing after it had been sued by Effem, Inc., the owners of the Mr. Blue trademark.

The court judgment ordered the Blue Corporation to remove the Mr. Blues from all its vending machines and pay $5,000 in fines. The Blue Corporation was told it could carry on selling M&Ms without the Mr. Blue figure. Instead, the company chose to cease operations.

Just a few weeks later, another vending machine company opened its doors just down the street in Kingston, selling distributorships for cheap silver jewelry. It closed down, too, after eleven complaint-filled months in operation.

During all this time, there was one business bureau that was intensely interested in the Universal Gang. It was the Better Business Bureau of Mainland British Columbia. Valerie MacLean is the Vice-President of Consumer Affairs. She makes bad guys shake in their boots. She is probably the only BBB official in North America who still answers her own phone. The rest have all succumbed, as have most of us, to the comfort of voicemail. Bad guys did breathe a temporary sigh of relief when MacLean ran for Mayor of Vancouver. Thankfully, she lost.

MacLean was usually one step ahead of the Universal Gang, getting newspapers to yank their sleazy advertisements whenever she could. Also interested, as the Universal trail got longer, was Corporal Phil Bailey and his team at the Royal Canadian Mounted Police Commercial Crime section in Kingston, Ontario.

Our files on the Universal Gang never stop growing. We are now into our third banker's box, with these late-breaking news items, written on deadline as *Getting What You Deserve* goes to press:

On January 16, 2003, Royal Canadian Mounted Police in Kingston charged three people with several counts of fraud and conspiracy to commit fraud. The charges relate, said the RCMP, to a $5 million international marketing scam operated out of Kingston and Toronto. One of the three charged is Guy Paul Beaupre, thirty-nine, of Godfrey, a small community near Kingston. A warrant was issued for Beaupre, who was believed to be in Mexico.

On March 14, 2003, Mexican police arrested Beaupre at his home outside Mexico City. Beaupre was kept in a holding cell near the Mexico–United States border for about a week, and then shipped to *Reclusorio Norte*, a notorious prison in the northern section of Mexico City.

Frank Armstrong, an enterprising business reporter for the *Kingston Whig-Standard* has also been following the movements of the Universal Gang. On April 22, 2003, Armstrong wrote that Beaupre had complained to his mother and sister back in Kingston that he had been beaten, raped, and made to sleep on a urine-covered concrete floor at *Reclusorio Norte*. The RCMP brought Beaupre back to Canada in early June, 2003, to face charges in a Kingston courtroom.

4.

Cut to the Chase

We were in convoy. Cruising streets in lower Mississauga, Ontario, working our way into Oakville. It was a two-vehicle convoy — the Beater up front and the crew van behind. We were checking a few addresses where we had reason to believe we would find our quarry. We were on the trail of a company called First Dominion Financial Corporation. A mortgage broker. The company arranged a $70,000 mortgage for our client, Kostas Giancoulas. He needed the money to finance his comic book business. Kostas' aunt and uncle put up their home as collateral. The mortgage went through. The cheque was picked up by First Dominion. It never got to Kostas. Not much of a con job. Just a smash-and-grab. The cheque went to First Dominion, and then it got cashed. Kostas got nothing. By the time he realized he'd been had, the company had disappeared. We were looking for the two characters behind First Dominion. Alan Clarke was the owner. Teddy Herbert Dent was his mule. He was the guy who picked up the cheque and took it to Clarke. We had collected all the vital statistics. We had a physical description of both, home addresses, and a list of vehicles and plate numbers. Clarke tended to the flashy. He had a red Porsche, a black BMW, and two Harley-Davidsons. Dent had a previously-enjoyed white Pontiac.

We banged on Clarke's door many times. No signs of life. No activity at Dent's dump of an apartment, either. We had left dozens of phone messages at home phone numbers and cellphone numbers. No reply. So it was time to raise the temperature of pursuit. We decided to give ourselves a couple of hours to cruise Clark's neighbourhood. He was the main guy, not Dent. And we had reason to believe that Clarke was in his house and might decide to go out, if he thought the coast was clear. We did what we could to remain hidden in plain view in Clarke's neighbourhood. We had our best chase crew locked and loaded.

Producer Laurie Few was in the shotgun seat in the Beater, juggling her cellphone, answering mine, and chattering with the boys in the crew van on the walkie-talkie. In the van sat cameraman Don and sound man Kevin. They were the best, the biggest, and the toughest we had. Laurie called them the ugly crew. They loved it. We made a good team. We almost always got our man. And this day, we had a civilian on board. You know, we just loved that military mumbo-jumbo — locked and loaded, riding shotgun, civilian on board. Very early in the chase game, after too many hours cooped up in surveillance vehicles, we adopted the soldier lingo. We thought it was uproariously funny. Some people thought we were serious. We thought that was funny, too. The civilian was Russell Smith, a freelance writer doing a profile on *Goldhawk Fights Back* for *Toronto Life* magazine. He was just a kid, sort of swallowed up by the too-soft, plush velour seats in the back of the Beater. Smith was along for some action. He had pleaded with us to let him join us in a chase. We told him we couldn't just conjure up a chase. It took time. It was real. We couldn't make it happen just for him.

He didn't look like he was having much fun in the Beater, so we tried our best to entertain him. We regaled him with past adventures. We engaged in all kinds of profane insults and jibes with the crew. He still didn't look happy. After only two hours he said he had to go. We drove a few blocks out of our patrol area and called him a cab. Two small hours. A mere moment in the waiting game. In the nine years of *Goldhawk Fights Back* at CTV, we estimated we clocked six months of pure waiting time.

Not two minutes after Smith had left us, Don started squawking on the radio. "Hawk, we got a car in the driveway," he shouted.

"Take it easy," I said. "Stay low. Don't move. What kind of car?" Laurie and I were racing back to the neighborhood, just two minutes away.

"Old Pontiac."

"Geez, that's the mule. Teddy Dent. A tall guy, big nose, grey hair?"

"Yup. Like Ichabod Crane's dad. He's banging on the door. I'm pulling out onto the road, about five houses west of him," said Don.

"Okay, we're almost at the street on the east side," I said.

"He's coming back to the car," barked Kevin. Don had handed off the radio and put both hands on the wheel as he crept eastward toward the Pontiac, which was backing out the driveway.

"Roger, we see you," shouted Laurie from our end. We were closing on the Pontiac, moving slowly westward. As both of us converged on Teddy, he backed onto the street and turned west.

"Our side," shouted Laurie, slouched down in her seat so the hapless Teddy wouldn't see her on the radio in his rear-view mirror. I had slowed a bit to let Teddy out into traffic and then stuck casually but securely to his tail.

"Go down a block and head back to Islington," shouted Laurie, checking her street map. "You'll be parallel to us. Get ahead and wait at Islington. If he goes that way, you'll see him. Then tuck in behind us."

Sure enough, just as if Teddy had been listening for instructions, he turned at Islington and drove right past Don, two blocks down. As we passed the street, my rear-view filled with a charging white van.

"I'm here, Hawk," said Don. "You want me to drive lead?"

"Tell him to wait. I haven't worn out my welcome yet," I said to Laurie.

"Wait, Don," said Laurie. "Geez, this guy is all over the road." True enough. Teddy was a lousy driver. He liked weaving from lane to lane and blasting through yellow lights. I was starting to get worried that Teddy would notice, if he ever checked his rear-view mirror, that an Oldsmobile Delta 88 Brougham Royale was hot on his tail.

"Tell Don to go. I'm backing off to the right lane."

"Go, Don, go, " said Laurie. "Come by on our left."

"Roger," shouted Kevin. "We're on him." The Dodge Caravan screamed past us, bouncing low on the shocks with all the video gear in the back. You could almost see the nuts and bolts spewing out the tailpipe. Teddy sped up. The Dodge remained stuck to his bumper like Velcro. Don was not a subtle driver. And he was damn sure he was not going to lose Teddy in the traffic.

"Back off, Don," said Laurie, "or you'll spook him."

"Roger. No spooking." Teddy, indeed, did not seem spooked. He wheeled into a large shopping plaza. Don and I came charging in and immediately spread wide in opposite directions, giving Teddy as much room as possible, but still keeping him in sight. Teddy was heading for a coffee joint. Obviously, he hadn't made us at all. His mind was probably on other things, such as the whereabouts of his partner in crime, Alan Clarke. He probably wanted to find Clarke just as much as we did.

"Okay, Don. We'll take him outside. I'll keep him busy. You guys saddle up and charge when you're ready." I didn't get a reply on the radio. I didn't need one. Teddy had pulled into a parking spot in back of the coffee shop and I pulled in on his left. Teddy and I got out of our cars about the same time. Laurie, meantime had slipped behind the wheel and was backing out as soon as I approached Ted. I noticed the doors of Don's van opening, quietly, about thirty feet behind Teddy.

"Teddy. Teddy Dent," I said smiling and all friendly-like. I stuck out my hand. Teddy just stared at me and said nothing.

"Teddy, we've got to talk," I said. Teddy just stared, then turned to look over his shoulder as he heard the ugly team crunching through the hard snow, decked out in full video regalia, and wearing parkas that made them look as big as polar bears. Naturally, they were recording his every move. Teddy's eyes shifted to his back bumper, where Laurie sat inches away, idling in the Beater, blocking his retreat. Teddy bolted for the coffee joint door. We followed and stopped when he went inside.

We gathered around the idling Beater. Laurie was behind the wheel on the cellphone, talking to The Desk. Funny how our news managers suffered from such a definite lack of personification. The Desk Editor was pondering over the last script I had sent him. It needed his approval before we could edit the story. Laurie handed me the cellphone and rolled up the window to keep warm, giving me a "You're on your own, pal" look. I had to downshift fast. Forget for a moment about Teddy, trapped like a rat inside the coffee shop, and focus on the case we were putting the finishing touches on back at the shop. Oh, yeah. It was called "Phone Bug" — all about how a nice family got stuck with a strange, unjustifiable $73,000 phone bill. We made the phone bill disappear, but the Desk was apparently having problems with the math of the case. I used to joke to Laurie and the boys that my mistake was habitually writing scripts at the grade eight level of comprehension. It should have been grade seven. So here I was, stomping my feet by the Beater, the -30° wind chill making it harder and harder for me to talk as my jaw was stiffening up in the cold, arguing some boneheaded point with a bonehead back in a nice warm office. Finally, he seemed to get it. I conceded to a word change or two and he reluctantly approved the story.

Back to the present. I turned to the boys — frozen, snowy, video-sasquatches standing silently in the bitter wind. Kevin's bushy red moustache was frozen white. It was as if you could reach way up and snap off one of the ends. A careless thought, to be sure. Laurie remained inside the warm Beater, a case file open on her lap, talking on the phone. She'd make a face at us once in a while to acknowledge our frozen discomfort.

"Okay, boys," I said. "You wait here and I'll go read him his rights."

"Great, Hawk," said Don, his camera on his shoulder, ready for action. Kevin just grunted, sticking the long boom pole on his shotgun mike into the snow. I walked into the coffee shop only to be greeted with open arms by the Chinese proprietor.

"Missa Gohawk, you wan coffee?"

"Gee, that would be great, but first I want to talk to my friend over there at the counter," I replied, pointing to Teddy Dent, heavy wool coat still on, collar up, hunched over a coffee and a *Toronto Sun*, doing his best to ignore me.

"Okey-dokey," said the coffee man, already pouring a coffee.

I sat down at the stool next to Teddy. "So, Ted," I said, "this is the deal. You come outside, talk to us about what you know. Tell us what happened to all that money. We have an open and frank conversation lasting, at the most, ten minutes, and we pack up the camera and leave. Or you can say no, and we'll just wait outside the coffee shop for the rest of our natural lives. I'll give you five minutes to decide." Ted said nothing. He stared at his *Sun*. I walked outside and joined the boys in the cold. We shivered silently for a minute or two.

Then I reminded Don and Kevin why we were on Dent's tail. Dent had picked up a $70,000 cheque from the mortgage lender that had been intended for Kostas Giancoulas. Dent took the cheque to Clarke.

Clarke deposited it in the First Dominion bank account. Prior to that deposit, the First Dominion Financial Corporation account boasted a $62 balance. Clarke then turned around and withdrew most of the money. Dent got $25,000. Kostas got nothing. His aunt and uncle were worried they would lose their home because the lender was now threatening to foreclose on the mortgage.

"That's who we're dealing with," I said.

"Has it been five minutes yet?" asked Don. My ultimatum to Teddy had been picked up by my in-parka microphone and transmitted to Don and Kevin outside.

"Damn right," I said, heading for the door. We, of course, were exercising the third option: We come inside and get you anyway.

"Rock and roll," said Don. All three of us barged through the door and headed for Teddy at the far end of the long counter. The coffee proprietor smiled, counting new heads, and pouring more coffee.

"Teddy Herbert Dent," I proclaimed. I liked the court-like sound of full names. "Will you tell us about your role at First Dominion Financial Corporation? What happened to a $70,000 cheque you picked up and delivered to Alan Clarke — a cheque that really belonged to Kostas Giancoulas?"

Teddy stood up slowly, looking around for options. He turned to me, as if trying to comprehend my questions and then quickly ducked down, out of camera range. His hand went quickly to an inside pocket. Don began pulling back, trying to locate Teddy, when suddenly, he popped back up intro frame, wearing wraparound gangster sunglasses. Now travelling incognito, Teddy started walking quickly along the counter, his TV picture framed by a rapidly changing panorama of doughnut trays.

"Talk to us, Teddy," I said.

"Missa Gohawk. You wan cream an suga?" asked the proprietor.

"Yes, thank you," I shouted, as we kept pace with Teddy, who was now clearly headed for the men's room. He opened the door and then tried to slam it in our faces, but the door became jammed. He banged away at it until he looked down and saw Don's size twelve army boot wedged in the door. Teddy retreated to one of the stalls, went in, and slammed and locked the door. Don zoomed-in to a crack in the door, and there stood Teddy, staring blankly at the wall straight ahead, doing nothing. So much for the high-flying, trustworthy personnel at First Dominion Financial Corporation.

With Teddy in seclusion, we sat down for coffee with the coffee man. Thanked him for his kindness. We tried to explain to him and his customers what the hell we were doing there, and why Teddy would not come out of his stall. We didn't see Teddy again until he made several appearances in court, facing charges related to First Dominion Financial Corporation.

It had been bitterly cold that first day we met Teddy, but at least the pursuit was reasonably short. Nothing at all like the fourteen-hour vigil we endured outside a dental office in Brampton, Ontario. We were living the final chapter of a case we called "Dental Duplicity." It was the story of Dr. Terry Papneja, a hard-working, hard-drilling dentist with a passion for finding cavities. He even found cavities that were invisible to other dentists. We first heard about it when Monique Gillan, a flight attendant who had gone to Papneja for the first time, was told she had five cavities. Papneja drilled the five cavities and gave her fillings. Monique's regular dentist had been unavailable at that time. Monique eventually saw him, the man who knew her dental history, and he told her she had no cavities and that the fillings were probably unnecessary. We helped Monique take her complaint to the Ontario College of Dental Surgeons. A complaints committee found the work was "consistent with the standards of the profession."

We didn't leave it there. First, we needed a mouth with no cavities. No problem there. Producer Laurie Few had never had a filling in her life. We compiled a dental history: Checkup by Dentist A on October 26, 1993 — no cavities, no dental work required. Checkup by Dentist B on March 17, 1994 — no cavities, no work required. Then Laurie booked an appointment with Papneja for April 8, 1994. He told her she had five cavities and two teeth which "required sealing." We had this from Papneja himself, with help from a hidden microphone. Laurie left the office and said she would book an appointment for the work later. During the next five months, Papneja's staff called her five times to remind her she had seven cavities to be filled and a wisdom tooth that needed pulling. It would take four appointments to do that work, she was told.

To complete our case, on October 21, 1994, Laurie's teeth were examined a fourth time by a leading expert in the field, a man who teaches dentistry at the University of Toronto. We nicknamed him the King of All Dentists. His opinion, Laurie had what he called "nearly perfect teeth." They were "teeth so healthy," he said, "that she only needs a checkup once a year and X-rays every eighteen months."

I got on the phone to Dr. Papneja to share our research results with him. He remained silent as I laid out the facts. I told him we planned to take our information to the College of Dental Surgeons and that we would like to interview him about what we had discovered. He politely declined and gently hung up the phone. It took us a few days to get together all the Papneja coordinates we needed — where he lived, what vehicles he drove — and we did a detailed survey of the Brampton shopping plaza where Papneja operated his ten thousand square-foot clinic. We checked for the usual bits of crucial information. What were the escape routes from the office? How many back doors were there? Where did he park his car? Was there any plaza security? Could we remain unnoticed in the parking lot for long periods of time? We made repeated dental appointments we would later cancel to figure out Papneja's working hours.

The dental office looked like a tough nut to crack. Hard to get past the front counter. And Papneja's office was like the factory ship of dental clinics. A huge stream of people in and out, all day long, made busting up the place with a video crew out of the question. We always worried about video collateral damage — scaring innocent bystanders as we tried to grab pictures of our target.

So we decided to try the house. Some house. It was a huge mansion on Mississauga Road South. We chose to drop by, camera rolling, early one evening when our detective work had told us he was home. We rounded the circular driveway and climbed the several sets of stairs to the magnificent front door, surrounded by huge panes of intricately designed glass that gave just a hint of a giant main hallway beyond. A huge chandelier blazed high above. The nanny answered the door, apparently amused as our camera lights fired up, ready to record every move and every word of Dr. Papneja.

"Not here." She chimed pleasantly, in answer to my equally pleasant question. "Still at work," she added. Well, we had blown our cover at the mansion. No more looking for Papneja here. Our so-called element of surprise had vanished. There was nothing left but the office. So we planned a vigil. We would wait for the doctor at his office. Get him on the way in or the way out.

We got to the shopping plaza at six a.m. It was almost deserted. We were in two vehicles: a rented Dodge Neon and an unmarked crew van with Paul and Marek inside. The Neon was a mistake for long-term occupancy. It was cramped, uncomfortable, and it had less than a quarter-tank of gas. The Beater had been seen in Papneja's home neighbourhood, so we didn't want to take any chances spooking the dentist at his office.

"A Neon?" I said to Laurie, who was behind the wheel.

"It's all they had left at the car rental joint."

"Why no gas?"

"I don't know. Maybe the gauge is broken."

"Maybe" I said. "Or maybe we'll run out of gas."

"Maybe. But I bet we freeze to death before that."

"Probably."

We always tried to look on the bright side. We took up positions in the parking lot to give us two views of the dental clinic. I was wearing a wireless microphone, so that anything I said was heard in the crew van and could be recorded instantly when the camera was turned on. Each of the four of us had a cellphone, as well. And the vehicles had two-way radios. We brought new meaning to the phrase "staying in touch." By six-thirty, we realized Dr. Papneja had beaten us to work. We were plate-checking vehicles and found a van registered to him. We hadn't really paid much attention to it before, but we knew it had been there when we first arrived. I guess we expected he would be driving one of the flashier vehicles he owned. The van was parked about a hundred yards from the front door of the clinic. Both good and bad. We would have a hundred yards to engage Dr. Papneja in conversation as he left work, but we might have to wait until seven or eight that night for the clinic to close. We had all had small coffees before we got to the plaza. Marek had a muffin, as well. But that was it. Based on the relatively safe principle of nothing in, nothing out, we settled down for the long fast. We had no idea when Papneja might pop out of his office and head to the van, so we remained at the ready for the next fourteen hours. Limbs became numb. The damn Neon was cold because we could only start it up, briefly, once an hour, afraid we might run out of gas. And the Neon had running lights that could not be shut off by depressing the parking brake, a feature found only on more expensive cars, trucks, and vans. We were worried the running lights would also signal to the observant that something was up in the parking lot.

We saw people arrive for work, step outside for cigarette breaks, go to lunch, and shop at other stores in the plaza. We figured out the plaza-people patterns of friendship. We observed the incidents of flirting, and discerned by reading body language the people who couldn't stand each other. By the end of the day, as they all headed for home, we knew all the players by sight. We had given them names so we could keep track of them. It was a soap opera unfolding without the TV set. We joked back and forth on the radio. I performed little skits, based on the people we saw moving about the plaza. We all laughed and then fell silent for long periods of time, knowing that at a moment's notice we could be out of our vehicles and chasing a dentist to his van. The Neon's windows started steaming up. We tried to wipe them clear. That just made it worse. As it began to get dark, at about the twelfth hour, I started to get worried.

"Laurie," I said. "When was the last time you ..."

"What?" said Laurie.

"When was the last time," I started again, "that you ..." And then I started to laugh. I couldn't stop. The more I tried to stifle it, the more it hurt.

"The last time I what?" said Laurie, trying not to laugh, but snorting mightily.

"When was the last time you stood up?" We both started to laugh. They were frozen, brittle guffaws. Paul tried to say something on the radio, but it was lost in their laughter. Slowly, it died down. Silence once again. It was almost eight o'clock. Didn't this guy ever go home?

The north wind whipped around the almost-empty plaza. We shivered and fidgeted and crossed our legs.

Suddenly, a muffled radio transmission. Paul, closest to the van, had shouted a few words of warning. We figured out he was trying to tell us Papneja's van had started up, all by itself. We could see the exhaust. Turning to the front door of the clinic, we saw a man coming out the door. He must have started the van with one of those remote starters. He was dressed in a dark overcoat, wearing one of those tea-cozy hats, the kind the guy was wearing who was choked by Prime Minister Jean Chrétien. The flaps were pulled down over his ears; the bottom portion of the flaps were sticking out at right angles to his head. Papneja? Yes. Was this a disguise or was he just cold? I poked Laurie, who was already shouting something and trying to get out her side of the Neon.

"Hey boys," I shouted into my open microphone. "It's Papneja. In the hat! In the hat! Go! Go! Go!" My feet hit the cold ground and I took a few tentative, Frankenstein-like steps.

"Laurie, block the van," I shouted. Laurie fired up the Neon and went blasting past me as I loped toward Papneja.

"Dr. Papneja," I said in my most pleasant tones. "I need to talk to you. It's Dale Goldhawk. At first, Papneja turned toward me, big smile on his face. When he heard my name, he stopped dead in his tracks. Just then, from behind, Paul and Marek arrived and lit up Papneja like a Christmas tree. Papneja climbed into the van, not saying a word, only to find a Dodge Neon pulled up to his rear bumper, blocking his way. I tried several times to get Papneja to talk to me. He said nothing.

"Let him go," I finally said to Laurie, who moved her Neon block-ade. Papneja backed out of his parking spot and sped off into the night. We were already at full gallop toward a fish-and-chips shop in the plaza. Blasting in the front with all our gear, I shouted at the cashier.

"Washrooms?" I said, way too loud. He just pointed. We ran. I shout-ed over my shoulder, "Fish and chips all round, please. And beer."

We saw Papneja many times after that. We sat in the same hearing room for days, as Papneja appeared before a Discipline Panel at the Ontario College of Dental Surgeons. He pleaded guilty to an act of pro-fessional misconduct relating to the Laurie Few diagnosis. He was fined $10,000. His certificate of registration from the College was suspended for six months. He was prohibited from practicing dentistry for that time. He was also ordered to pay the $5,000 cost of the hearing. Meanwhile, flight attendant Monique Gillan was left to wonder how many other patients might have suffered her fate. Monique has a mouthful of new fillings that will have to be maintained for the rest of her life. We had opened the file on the Papneja case in May of 1994. We closed it in May of 1996.

Some people we chased more than once. Vic Harris was a mover who specialized in countrywide moves where the move would cost customers twice as much as the estimate he gave them. In some cases, he just "lost" several loads of furniture. Harris was a broker. He would sell you a move and then go to a real mover to book trucks and men. He was never very fussy about the trucks or the men.

We had dealt with Harris many times on the phone. Usually, he would refund money when we demanded it for some of his unhappy customers. When the stream of complaints continued, month after month, we went looking for Harris to find out if he was the world's most incompetent mover or just a cheap crook. Harris had no office. He worked out of his car. He would flit from household to household, giving estimates to customers unlucky enough to have responded to his enticing newspaper ads. Once you gave Vic a sizeable deposit, there was at least an even chance you would never see him again.

Bagging Harris was embarrassingly easy. How do you get a mover? Call and ask for an estimate. He comes to you. And we were waiting. As soon as he came out of our contrived moving job in a sting-bungalow in west end Toronto, we were there. We caught up to him on the street and walked along as he fended off our questions by complaining about his cash flow problem and how hard it was to find good movers. We agreed with him on that part. We let Harris go on the promise things would get better. There would be no more complaints about him, he said. If only it had been true.

In the next few months, we had dozens more complaints. And the police had become interested in Harris, as well. It was time to say hello to Vic again. We wanted to remind him about a whole pile of new complaints. He never replied to our numerous messages, so with the help of one of our young operatives, Brian Woodcock, we set him up again. This time we had him trapped on the twenty-second floor of an apartment building. The apartment was bugged so the crew and I could hear what was going on from the hallway. We were ready when he bid goodbye to what he thought was a customer and stepped out into the hallway. He was hit with an instant blast of camera lights and me yelling "Vic Harris!" He must have jumped a foot. Then he rolled his eyes and shouted at me, "Does this mean I have to look over my shoulder every time I go out on a call?"

"Yeah, Vic," I said. "You got it."

It was a tight fit in the hallway as we all walked toward the elevator. I had brought my file of names and was trying to ask him about the status of dozens of moving complaints. Don and Kevin stuck to Vic like glue. He punched the elevator button and we all climbed into the car — four big guys and all the gear, boom pole banging against the ceiling, a little shoving from Vic. Then Vic decided to pop out of the elevator. He ran down the hall to the stairs — twenty-two floors down. We chased him down all twenty-two flights. At about the tenth floor, Kevin, the sound man, stumbled and fell, twisting his ankle. We unhooked him from the camera and told him we'd come back for him. He grunted. We continued. By the time we ran through the lobby, with tenants all yelling, "He went that way," we got outside just in time to see him flip us the bird as he drove off down the street. Such eloquence. The justice system flipped him the bird later that year when he was convicted of fraud and sent to jail.

One of only a few other guys we ever chased for a second time was David Nancoff — a man of many talents and trades. He was, among other things, a self-made paralegal, a legend in his own mind as a movie producer, and a seller of franchises for both video cameras and home doughnut-making machines. Nancoff told his women clients he looked like Al Pacino. Not many agreed once they saw him. If the women were even remotely friendly, he'd ask them out on a date. We first met, or at least started chasing, David Nancoff in 1996. In the beginning, Nancoff made a bit of an effort to keep his investors and customers happy. He would refund a little money here and there. But he always stayed out of sight. He refused to be interviewed and, despite our best detective work, we could never find where he lived, until in later years we discovered that he usually lived in the offices he rented for his various enterprises. He left several locations where the back rooms were filled with pizza boxes and pop cans. A few landlords complained to Nancoff that his lifestyle was attracting mice and rats to the building. If he left in a hurry, you might find a sleeping bag, maybe a sock or a shirt.

David Nancoff peddled dreams that almost nobody could make come true. Housewives were told they could make a fortune frying doughnuts at home and then delivering them for sale at offices, car dealerships, and other places of work. All that happened there was that people stole the doughnuts instead of putting money in the honour box. The artistically-inclined could buy a Nancoff video kit and make big money shooting wedding videos. Besides, Nancoff would hire them to work on movie sets, since he was in with all the big movers and shakers. Most of the video guys went broke. Some didn't even get the equipment they had already paid for. Nancoff would also teach you how to be a paralegal — for $1500. The classes would be conducted in doughnut shops or sometimes hotel rooms. Hardly anybody ever graduated or got a job as a paralegal. Over the years, we collected about fifty solid complaints about Nancoff, from fifty angry people who had invested more than half a million dollars in his schemes.

We tried to corner Nancoff several times at his office/home in midtown Toronto. But when Nancoff smelled trouble, he would stay in his car and circle the block for hours until his henchman back at the office would signal that the coast was clear. Nancoff knew we were on his trail and always managed to stay one step ahead.

One day, while our two vehicles were parked on side streets near his office, three police cruisers came screaming down the street and, with their guns drawn, officers surrounded both the Beater and Don's crew van. The sergeant stuck his head in my car window and then did a double take. "Oh, shit, Goldhawk. It's you." Nancoff had phoned in a tip about suspicious vehicles around a ground-floor bank. Nancoff told the cops he feared a robbery was being planned. When we told the officers why we were there, they wished us luck and, with friendly waves and smiles, they drove off. This was never going to work.

So we set him up with a phony customer in Kitchener, Ontario. When Nancoff stepped out onto the dark porch, leaving behind what he thought was a promising client, we zapped him with our lights. "Why don't you satisfy your old customers before you sign up new ones?" I said. Nancoff tried to get back into the house. I heard the deadbolt slide closed just before he turned the doorknob.

"What about all those complaints?" I persisted.

"But I am fixing up the complaints," he said.

"No, you're not."

"Yes, I am." This went on for twenty minutes. We finally let him drive off in his sleek black Lexus after we extracted one more promise he would resolve the fifty complaints we had. Well, that never happened. Then Nancoff seemed to drop out of sight. We heard nothing for years. But in 2000 he was back, selling paralegal training courses again, under his old company name, the Paralegal Association of Ontario. We were getting complaints.

So we set him up one more time. We wanted to challenge him about the fifty unresolved customer issues and warn new people to stay away from his schemes. Laurie Few answered one of his ads and played him for a sucker. She was very eager to become a paralegal and Nancoff, on the telephone, could clearly smell the money. He agreed to meet her at a doughnut shop in Kitchener.

From our hidden position, we watched him arrive in his Lexus. It looked not-so-sleek then, and had a huge dent in the driver's-side door. Maybe an unhappy customer had finally caught up to him. Through the shop window, we watched Nancoff set up his little display at a table. He carried a legal case — a square, black leather briefcase favoured by lawyers. Out came the "training manuals" and contract forms. Nancoff could almost feel that money in his own back pocket.

Laurie blocked the Lexus while we marched on the doughnut shop. Nancoff was at the counter buying a coffee. I slid up beside him, camera rolling, and guided him to the table where he had laid out his wares. He sat down slowly, his hand shaking as he sipped his coffee. I sat down opposite him and the argument began.

"So, tell me a little about the Paralegal Association of Ontario and who you represent."

"Well, it's a group of paralegals throughout Ontario."

"Give me the names, sir, of two paralegals that you work with. Just two. Forget the hundreds. Give me the names of two people. Could you do that?"

"Yes, I could, but I'm not going to do it without their permission."

"What, is it a secret that they're paralegals? Sir, you operate in the public, you're trying to sell this course to people, to members of the public, and now everything is private? Give me the name of a single paralegal you've taught who is out there practicing."

"Well, I could ..."

"Could you?"

"Yup."

"Well, write it down," I said, pushing paper and a pencil to his side of the table.

"Well, I'm going to get their approval," said Nancoff, returning to his old theme. Nancoff promised to send me all that information later but, as usual with a Nancoff promise, nothing happened. Unfortunately, he is currently not facing any charges.

Then there was the King of the Runners. Reverend Narvin Wray Clarence Edwardson. He was the fastest, the biggest, the slipperiest, and the oldest sleazy marketer we ever chased. For many years, Edwardson, a cunning cockalorum who called himself the Moderator of the Baptist Church of Southeast Asia, preyed on pensioners and churchgoers in much of Western Canada. Following his paper trail, we estimated he had been able to get investors to give him close to $7 million for his various schemes — everything from used cars, to rice programs at orphanages in Manila, to complicated projects involving giant industrial machines that were supposed to fight pollution. We never met anybody satisfied with the "investment" they had made with Edwardson.

We got onto his trail trying to help retired business executive Tom Johnson, who lived in Kelowna. Johnson gave Edwardson, in total,

$300,000 as an investment in the used car business. It didn't work out. Johnson lost almost all the money.

How did it happen? Edwardson steeped himself in the righteous bombast of religion. Once he had his victims believing he was a special man of the cloth, the rest was easy. Who better to invest with than your friend, the Reverend. He would often cry and get down on his knees to pray with you, said Johnson. He spoke with loving tenderness of the orphanage he said he supported back in Manila.

The Reverend, at 6'4", made very large footprints. He and his wife drove white Cadillacs. They lived in various mansions and upscale houses in and around Kelowna and Vancouver. But when it came to pinning the Reverend down, he was extremely fleet of foot. Some of his victims compared him to a large, high-strung jackrabbit. He was always on the move. He couldn't sit down for long. Couldn't stay in one place. He was always glancing around warily, as if looking for pursuers. Edwardson had spent so many years staying ahead of his unhappy investors, no wonder he was jumpy.

We needed to get him out in the open where we could get a good picture of him. Make him famous. Try to warn new investors to steer clear of the Reverend. Just running up to the Cadillac or banging on his door wouldn't do. All we would get then would be screeching tires and a slammed door. We needed him out in public, at least a few yards away from any refuge where he might hide, thus avoiding getting his picture on television.

In the weeks we trailed him, we often saw him at a distance. There he was driving his Cadillac, disappearing into his house, ducking into a restaurant. We stayed low, knowing how easily he could be spooked. We gave up on the idea of trying to tail the Cadillac. He was too smart and too careful to be followed. One day all of us were brainstorming over the problem.

"It's too bad we can't track him electronically," I said.

"Well, we could, you know," said our chief gadget guy and sound man, Jim Ursulak. "They use these little transmitters in TV sports shows, to keep track of skiers in the mountains. They have a range of seven miles."

"Geez, can we get one?" asked Laurie.

"Sure. Give me a day," said the man who knew more about electronic neat stuff than anybody I ever met. The bug was just a little thing. I didn't have much faith it would work. We planted it and waited. Jim was in the crew van, in radio contact with us in our truck. The beeps were stationary. Then they started to move. We were in a neighbourhood in Surrey, and for the next two hours we followed this signal all the way to West Vancouver. It became stationary again. After another half-hour, we had tracked it to the posh Salmon House Restaurant, up in the hills overlooking Vancouver. The Reverend was inside.

Laurie and Jim made like a couple and slipped into the restaurant. They got a table right next to Edwardson and two other men. The cameraman and I stayed outside in the shadows, while Jim and Laurie had at least part of a wonderful meal. Without warning, Edwardson was on his feet, calling for his bill. Jim slipped out the back door and joined us, strapping on his sound gear. Laurie was talking into my earphone, giving me a play by play of Edwardson's movements. Suddenly, he came striding out the front door all by himself — his table companions were still behind in the restaurant. With the camera lights off, I walked up to him in my best jovial manner and said, "Reverend?" I stuck out my hand.

"Reverend, we need to talk about money," I said. As soon as the magic word was out of my mouth, his big smile vanished; he jerked free of the handshake and began trotting away.

"Light him up," I shouted and off we all went on a jog. I shouted after him to stop several times but the Reverend, usually never at a loss for words, said nothing. I thought he would jog to his Cadillac and drive off. No way. He jogged to the end of the parking lot and then out onto the roadway, heading for the nearby highway.

As soon as he reached the highway, he kicked up into a sprint. Man, could this guy run. He was a very young sixty-eight. We clattered after him, gear and all, trying to keep up. At one point, halfway down a huge hill, he ducked off into the bush. We caught up and began shining the light up into the trees, trying to figure out where he had gone. There he was, lying on his side in the grass, on a steep slope, talking on his cellphone. He slid down toward us, trying to get up. We had no choice but to bounce the light off his huge ass as he scrabbled to his feet and ran past us.

The cameraman lost his footing and hit the dirt. We picked him up and continued the chase, across the busy highway. A big black car screeched to a halt. Edwardson jumped in. It was gone. The Reverend may have been praying for help but he had also called for reinforcements on his cellphone. Within hours, he called my cellphone.

"Are you going to put those pictures of me on television?" he asked.

"Absolutely," I said.

"But you'll ruin all the business deals I have going in Canada."

"Sorry about that."

After the story ran and Edwardson had attained new fame in the country, he vanished. I got a fax from him, sent from the Business Lounge of the Singapore Airport. The Running Reverend condemned Tom Johnson and then me. He wrote, "The difference is I am truly a Christian and under God's promise. No weapons forged against me can prosper. I put my full trust in Him." *Sure, pal,* I remember thinking at the time. *Just make sure you get it in writing.*

We were always aggressive with the camera and with the tough or embarrassing questions, but never aggressive ourselves. For us, going in rolling was a bold but benign move. I fancied myself as an edgy Good Humor Man or a delegate from the neighbourhood Welcome Wagon — without the ice cream and goody basket. I would never bang on doors or slam my fist on a counter just because some cowering crook was hiding in a back room beyond our grasp. I would never shout or scream or get angry.

To us, going in rolling was something like a spur-of-the-moment public forum. All were invited to hear the guy responsible explain his actions. The questions may have been tough, but they were also fair. Sure, we had ambushed the guy, but once the target was there in full view of the camera, I just did my thing as an interviewer — with the added responsibility of looking for a solution.

Part of the ambush was pure performance. If we were asked to leave — if we were on private property — we would leave, although I would dawdle as long as possible to let the crew get as many pictures as they could. I would leave behind my business card, but first I would have to rummage through my pockets looking for one. Then I would explain which numbers were best for calling me back. As an after-thought, I would suddenly remember to write my cellphone number down on the back of the card, once I had found that pesky pen. I had one somewhere. Sometimes I felt like Peter Falk in his cheap, wrinkled *Columbo* trench coat.

The ambushees were never amused. Since we were so darn good-natured, it was easy for the ambushee to get angry. A lot of them did just that. I would always try to douse the anger, knowing we were gaining the upper hand with our camera rolling. The ambushee could say or do anything he wanted, as long as he didn't mind doing it in full public view, from coast to coast.

I remember the day we stepped into the busy offices of Brooks International in Toronto. They were loan brokers. People desperate for money would give Brooks $500 up front to arrange a loan. The loan never came. The desperate people just wound up $500 poorer.

We went in rolling and asked to see the boss. It was pandemonium. Customers scurried out the door. About a half-dozen clerks behind the counter started running around screaming. Some held sheets of paper up to their faces and shouted at us from behind their flimsy shields. One guy picked up some heavy paperweight or doorstop and started waving it wildly.

"Excuse me," said the man at the counter.

"Good Morning," I said

"Turn it off."

"Are you the man in charge?"

"I'll talk to you if you turn it off."

"I just want to talk to the man in charge. I am not trying to make your life difficult."

"Turn it off," said the man, grabbing at the camera.

"What's your name, please?" I asked.

"Turn it off."

"If you roll that shit, I will definitely sue your ass," chimed in a new guy.

"We want to talk to you."

"No. Get out. Get out!"

The office closed down a few months later.

When I knocked on the door of County Sheriff Walter Thompson's home in Campbellton, New Brunswick, in the fall of 1993, with cameraman Graham Alexander rolling at my side, I had no idea what kind of reception we would get.

We wanted to talk to Thompson about a gravel pit he owned, and an expansion he planned for the pit, with the addition of a noisy rock crusher. Nearby residents had put up with the gravel pit for years, but they drew the line at a rock crusher.

Thompson, surrounded by three or four grown sons, answered the door. He glared, and said I could come in if the camera stayed out. It seemed like a good deal. I needed to talk to Thompson about the facts of the case. I walked up the steps and into the house; Graham stayed behind, shooting me through a pane of glass in the door as I disappeared into the house.

If you review the video from then on, you see the door open quickly and a burly hand grab the camera lens. With one huge upward motion, the camera is wrenched from Alexander's shoulder and flipped high into the air.

Still rolling, the camera falls back to the driveway, but before it does, it takes a perfect picture of the camera tosser, one of the sheriff's sons. Damage to the camera: $25,000.

We convinced the town council to prohibit the use of a rock crusher at Thompson's gravel pit. But the Sheriff had that council decision struck down in court.

Damian Duchene, a man who called himself a lawyer to his clients but was, in reality, a paralegal (maybe), was seething when we came upon him sitting in his brand-new Corvette.

"You want me to smash that fucking camera?" he asked. I guessed it was a rhetorical question. Then he began looking in the glove box and then under the seat, as if to find something he could use as a smasher.

I wanted to know what Duchene had done with a $25,000 retainer a client had given him. He started swearing at the camera (as if it cared), and so I handed him my card. He used the card to try and shield his face from the camera. I knew it would look pretty funny on television.

Gradually, conversation became a bit more civil. But then, as he drove out of the parking lot, with the camera rolling, he gave us the not-very-eloquent middle finger.

5.

Bring to a Boil

Most movers and shakers know about the glare of publicity. They have had extensive media training. They know how to handle the annoying questions posed by TV reporters in cheap suits; they know not to look angry when the radio reporters stick a dozen or so little tape machines in their faces; they are adept at ignoring or pretending not to hear the really embarrassing questions posed by newspaper reporters — the ink-stained scribes who can't write down what you don't say.

Then there are those who love the limelight. They bask in it the way lizards soak up sun. In this group you will find politicians, top bureaucrats, captains of industry and commerce, and flamboyant entrepreneurs. To them, publicity is a natural resource to be used freely to further one's own career and deepen one's pockets.

Publicity is not hard to get. It's amazing what kind of crap can wind up as news just because somebody called a press conference. But sooner or later bad news happens. The limelight lovers just take it in stride. With their superior knowledge and performance skills, they will be able to handle any situation and answer any dumb questions from reporters, who in many cases haven't two hot clues about what is really going on. At least, that's what big guys and bad guys are tempted to believe.

Kofi Hadjor was a chartered accountant who specialized in helping people in show business. In his heyday he had about four hundred clients and, in some way or other, he screwed them all. Kofi Hadjor should have hung up the phone when I called to find out what was going on.

He should have slammed the door when I came calling with a camera crew. And he should have kept his mouth shut. But he didn't.

Kofi Hadjor, the son of a cab driver, came to Canada from Ghana with just a few dollars in his pocket. He went to school all day and washed dishes at night. Three degrees later, Kofi Hadjor was a chartered accountant. But he was never an ordinary CA. For one thing, he took jazz dance classes. And once he had fallen in with the arty crowd, he got the idea that he should specialize in clients from show business.

Dancers, producers, directors, makeup artists, cinematographers, set designers — all came to him for a kind of total-package financial service designed for people who were too busy to pay much attention to their personal finances.

Hadjor created CATS (Creative Arts Tax Service). He marketed his services by telling clients he could answer "Yes" to these leading financial questions:

"Can I sit down with you guys four or five times a year to make sure everything is on track?"

"I think I'm paying too much tax. Can you help me reduce my tax bill?"

"Can you come up with a plan that will help me retire in ten years?"

Hadjor served his clients with a flourish that would have impressed Cecil B. DeMille. He took a few friends and flew them to the North Pole for his fortieth birthday. They sipped champagne in parkas during that $40,000 trip.

He bought a huge, seventy-five hundred square-foot mansion, had it lavishly renovated, and then filled it with what he called a half a million dollars worth of art. The front yard, overgrown with vines and enough wooden trellises to build another house, he called the Garden of Eden. Over the front door hung a sign that read *"Palacio de Cristo"* (House of Christ).

He called himself the father of his flock. He was the goose, laying golden eggs for his clients. He bought a Lincoln Navigator and hired a driver so he could visit them all to attend their parties, weddings, and funerals. He wore long, flowing African robes and once gave a ceremonial African scarf to grinning Ontario Lieutenant-Governor Hilary Weston. The photo was in the *Toronto Sun*.

A fawning feature article in *camagazine* in March, 1995, called him "The Dream Maker." Writer Marie Wiese wrote: "Hadjor offers clients in the Toronto arts community more than filed tax returns — he's there for deep soul-searching and hand holding. Servicing 400 creative types, including musicians, designers and film producers, he not only aids them in charting their financial course, but helps them fulfill their dreams."

Hadjor liked the Dream Maker handle so much that he borrowed it as a title for some supercharged propaganda he included with every information package handed out to a new or prospective client. The words were so Hadjor-like, he could have written them himself:

> It's Thursday morning and Kofi is still wearing his cape, bright orange neck scarf and army combat hat that he wore to his weekly bible study class as he enters the lobby of his office…he shows me into his simple, chaotic little office sporting an ominously large calculator in the middle of the desk. Soothing tones of Mozart play in the background…Kofi is his own personal tornado, crammed full of ideas unleashing energy and creativity at every opportunity he encounters. Cosmic art throughout his offices reflect both his spirituality and the infinite nature of his dreams.

Hadjor's clients were willing to tolerate the quirky, self-oriented behaviour as long as he delivered on his promises. He promised to do their taxes. Any tax owing would be sent by cheque to Hadjor, who would then send it on to Revenue Canada. Clients never had to lift a finger, except to write a few cheques, payable to Kofi Hadjor. He took care of everything.

Soon Hadjor was offering to give his clients a 20 percent return on their money. They went for it. The process was as unusual as he was. The clients would loan money to Hadjor, then he would pay it back later, plus 20 percent. The clients never knew where the money was being invested. One client told me she thought she was investing in the fashion business. For a while, the big dividends paid off and everybody was happy.

But then Hadjor's merry little money train ran off the track. His clients' cash disappeared. Hadjor became scarce as his "dividend" cheques to his clients started bouncing all over town.

Hadjor blamed the bank. He blamed his employees. It was never his fault. There were never any apologies. The money would come back someday, maybe. Makeup artist Janice Shantz remembers once when she corralled Hadjor on the telephone. He told her he had to go, *The Young and the Restless* was on.

About a dozen clients, representing a larger group of showbiz types who had lost about $670,000, went to the Fraud Squad at Toronto Police Services. The cops said they were too busy. Besides, the alleged fraud was less than a million and the Fraud Squad, they were told, didn't really handle that kind of small stuff. The cops suggested they hire a private investigator to get the goods on Hadjor.

Enter Brian J. Patterson, a Certified Fraud Examiner. He got the goods. One of the first things Patterson discovered was that many of Hadjor's clients were in trouble with Revenue Canada. Hadjor hadn't filed income tax returns for some clients. Other clients had sent income tax payments to Hadjor, made out to Hadjor, on the understanding Hadjor would forward the money to Ottawa. It never happened. Other clients had income tax refunds coming, but since Hadjor had managed to reroute all Revenue Canada mail to the *Palacio de Cristo*, the cheques were deposited in Hadjor's bank account.

The personal losses for Hadjor's clients were devastating. They had worked hard to set aside savings in a cruel business, where one day you're hot and the next you're not, and given it to Hadjor for safekeeping and wealth accumulation. Many of the clients had their life's savings wiped out; others took major hits.

Movie set decorator John Rose lost $150,000. To add injury to injury, Hadjor had not filed an income tax return for Rose, so he was in trouble with the Feds on top of everything else. An unnamed producer, who had not yet told her mother what happened, lost $120,000. Cinematographer Simon Mestel lost $40,000. Set designer Ian Brock said goodbye to $35,000. Janice Shantz initially lost $20,000. She managed to get half that money back — one of the very few who got anything back from Hadjor — but she spent the

$10,000 hiring her own forensic accountant and then later putting money into the pot to hire Patterson.

Patterson attacked his assignment with great zeal, working day and night in a paper chase for documents and hard facts. At *Goldhawk Fights Back*, we were conducting our own investigation: interviewing victims, gathering evidence, and preparing to confront Hadjor once we were convinced he had permanently borrowed his clients' money. Our approach in this kind of case was pretty simple — follow the money and try to get some of it back, while the rest of the country watched.

The first telephone conversation I had with Hadjor was on the high side of cordial, with a lot of lame excuses about temporary banking problems that would soon be fixed. Hadjor chuckled and guffawed. It seemed to help him paper-over his flimsy stories about where the money really was. Hadjor said he did not want to be interviewed on camera, and would write out a statement and fax it to me.

"Great," I said, "then I can stand in front of your house, read your words out loud and tell everybody in TV Land that you won't talk to me."

Over the next few hours, Hadjor and I had maybe six or eight telephone conversations. Clearly, he had been advised by a lawyer to keep his mouth shut, but here was a challenge Hadjor could not resist.

We were invited over, crew and all, to tour the *Palacio de Cristo* and the Garden of Eden and then sit down to a nice interview.

On the way over in the crew van, I was going through my menu choices. Would this be a brief sear? A quick fricassee? Or would there be time for a longer barbecue? Would some early tenderizing be necessary? By the time he met us at the door, gushing over our presence, intent on showing us every nook and cranny in his huge pile, I had deciding that coddling was the answer — the old slow-boil.

The *Palacio* was magnificent with beautiful little offices everywhere, all equipped with the latest in computer equipment. The floors and woodwork had been lovingly restored to their original gleaming beauty. Art hung everywhere. Then we toured the yard. The Garden of Eden was all vines and flowers and wood and stairs and pathways, looking a bit like it had been designed by Rube Goldberg. We even got to see the huge three-vehicle garage. The back wall was covered in shelves containing two or three hundred banker's boxes. His clients' files.

We picked a beautiful upstairs conference room for the interview. Hadjor chose his own background — a huge stained glass etching of Christ. Throughout the thirty-minute interview that was to follow, Christ loomed large over Hadjor's shoulder.

In the beginning, he was in his glory. Bathed in television lights, the camera rolling, four of us hanging on his every word, how could it get any better than this? I let him ramble. A lot of it was Biblical. I thought he was going to paraphrase all of Genesis before we could get down to the point. I started to focus in on the money. Hadjor smiled and gestured around him at the paintings, the room, the *Palacio*. I kept asking the same question: "Where did the money go?"

"Look around you," said Hadjor. The answer was staring me in the face. Hadjor told me he had used his clients' investment money to renovate and expand his huge home office. So this was the intricate investment plan that would offer a 20 percent divided to investors.

Give me all your money and I'll fix up my house.

I stopped dead, staring at Hadjor over his frank admission. His smile shone on, but as the silence grew I was dreaming of a huge frog, luxuriating in hot water, then suddenly realizing he was being boiled. Kofi Hadjor was an instant television celebrity from coast to coast on CTV. Later, the entire interview would be played for the jury at his trial.

Brian Patterson initiated an unusual private prosecution of Hadjor. The evidence supported six charges of fraud, involving the disappearance of $400,000. Patterson managed to convince a Justice of the Peace that Hadjor was a flight risk, so the JP issued an arrest warrant. Patterson had the warrant executed by Toronto Police, early on a Saturday morning.

We were there as officers brought out the Dream Maker, walking him through the Garden of Eden to a waiting cruiser. Hadjor was dressed for the occasion in a sweatshirt and sweat pants. The smile was pasted on his face. Later, Hadjor would break-down on the witness stand as he recalled the police strip search he endured and the night he spent in jail.

After a three-week trial, the jury convicted Hadjor on March 14, 2000. He remained out on bail, awaiting sentencing by Ontario Justice David McCombs. On May 27, Hadjor was back to hear his fate. As he walked toward the courthouse on University Avenue in Toronto, I caught up to him. We shook hands, our normal habit, always initiated by him. His hand was wet.

"Well," I said, "I guess we won't be seeing you for a while."

"Why?" he replied. "Where am I going?" He genuinely seemed to want to know.

"I think you're going to jail, aren't you?"

"I guess you know, eh?"

"Well, I don't know yet. I'm just asking if you have any last words."

My question, for the first time since I had met Hadjor, was answered with silence. A few minutes later, Judge McCombs sentenced Hadjor to two years less a day. Hadjor was immediately slapped into handcuffs by the court constable and taken into custody, to begin his journey through the system.

Hadjor served eighteen months behind bars. He was released in November, 2001. A restitution order had originally been issued against Hadjor. It sits on a shelf in a court office somewhere, gathering no more than dust.

Finally, Janice Shantz is able to laugh, a little, at her ordeal. She still remembers bitterly how she handed over that $20,000 cheque to Hadjor. It was two days before Hadjor bought the *Palacio de Cristo*. Janice's money had no doubt helped with the down payment. Janice herself still lives in an apartment. Her hope had been that Hadjor would have turned her savings into enough money for her to afford her own house.

Looking back on the case over a beer and a steak sandwich, Patterson had to laugh about his larger-than-life opponent. "If there was one thing that Hadjor believed," he said, "it was that there was no such thing as bad press. He sure was flamboyant — the most flamboyant I ever met. But when you look at the financial damage he did to his clients, he seems like just another bandit with a funny story."

During his trial, Hadjor had referred to Patterson as the "Pit Bull" who pursued him. Patterson scoffs, but wears the description like a medal. Both Patterson and Shantz, plus a whole gang of former clients, are wondering where Kofi Hadjor is today, and if he will ever step onto a public stage again.

Checking those old files now, I note with some interest that during the summer of 1998 when Kofi Hadjor and Hilary Weston had their picture taken together, after Hadjor had been committed to stand trail on fraud charges, another bizarre public spectacle was taking place in Salt Lake City, Utah. There, Lorena Riffo, as Division Director of Corporations for the State of Utah, was issuing a certificate of good standing for Renaissance Capital Group, Inc., a Utah-incorporated company since 1983.

That was one of many documents given to investor Claude Henry by Merv Bodnarchuk, the founder, chairman, and director of renaissance. The company seemed to be everywhere. It had offices in Salt Lake City; Orange, California; Blaine, Washington; and Vancouver, BC.

As busy as he was, Bodnarchuk found the time to travel all the way to Sudbury, Ontario, where he convinced Henry and another investor, Keith Rogerson, to climb onto his bandwagon. Henry borrowed $20,000 and gave it to Bodnarchuk. Rogerson invested $55,000. In all, we found about fifty investors from across the country who had invested with Bodnarchuk in a scheme called Majik Rent-a-Car.

A chain of outlets would open from coast to coast. Henry says he was told it was going to be "Big. Really big. He told us the shares would go to $18 and then to $50." And at $50 a share, Henry, a retired Inco worker, would be a millionaire. But only in his dreams. His stock dropped to three cents a share.

It was being traded on the highly-unregulated OTCBB, the Over-The-Counter Bulletin Board, penny-ante trading system in the United States. As RCMP commercial crime investigator Constable Richard Bergman told me, "The OTCBB is a dangerous place. People should be aware of that. People would probably have greater luck on a slot machine in Vegas."

We talked to Bodnarchuk at his Vancouver office. He said investors should just hang on. The stock will go up. As for Rogerson, who never even got his share certificates after investing his $55,000, Bodnarchuk said he would go to Utah and look for them.

We went looking for Bodnarchuk. There was a long trail to follow — clear across Canada. Mervin Michael Bodnarchuk had been convicted of more than fifty offences under provincial securities legislation and fined more than $140,000. He had been banned from trading in Manitoba, Saskatchewan, Alberta, and British Columbia. Under the bans, Bodnarchuk was not allowed to solicit investments. In other words, he can't approach potential investors to buy securities. Maybe that's why he was in Ontario, visiting Sudbury.

We could never find Bodnarchuk in when we called at his office. We had cased the joint earlier and knew exactly where it was in a high-rise building near the Vancouver Airport — not exactly the financial district. We even knew that Bodnarchuk's desk was in a corner of his office and, with the door open, he could see clear down the hallway.

So we tracked him down at his home. We called him from our cellphones, parked on the street outside his house. He was aghast. He didn't believe we would track him down to his home. I told him to look out the window. Bodnarchuk made an appointment to see us the next morning at his office. We took him at his word and left the neighbourhood.

In the morning, Bodnarchuk met us in the lobby of his office building. We would do the interview right there, he said. So we set up our lights and Bodnarchuk and I talked high finance while we sat on a kind of park bench, right inside the front door to the lobby.

Bodnarchuk, a big man with a big moustache and big eyes, just stared at me as I laid out our case. He was clearly cheesed-off, and surprised that we seemed to know what we were talking about.

After an initial ten minutes where Bodnarchuk droned on about the hugeness of his investment opportunities and the bigness of his company, we got down to small brass tacks. The interview turned an abrupt corner with this question:

"Manitoba, Saskatchewan, Alberta, British Columbia — you are prohibited from doing any trade in those provinces at all, aren't you?" I asked. There was a pause. Bodnarchuk seemed to be thinking.

"Ah, that's true," was his answer. It went downhill from there.

"Mr. Bodnarchuk, you're running out of provinces."

"My answer to that is my company is an American company. I am doing business in the States. I'm not selling in Ontario."

"But you did sell in Ontario."

"I didn't do these transactions, initially."

"The money came to you. The money was wired directly to you. Doesn't that involve you in the transaction?"

"These people received stock for their investment."

"That was wired to you, personally. I saw the bank drafts."

"These people purchased stock in a company. They received stock in a company."

You know the interview is just about over when the interviewee starts repeating lame excuses, as if it were some kind of protective litany. Bodnarchuk abruptly got up from the bench and walked away, probably wondering what had possessed him to show up in the first place.

We told the country about Merv Bodnarchuk on April 28, 1999, the same month that *Saturday Night* magazine ran a feature story on Bodnarchuk entitled, "Drinking, Fighting and Curling with the Anaheim Earthquake."

It was Bodnarchuk's other life. He was a curling aficionado who sponsored a team called the Anaheim Earthquake. Bodnarchuk had plans to make curling big in the United States. He paid players big money to play with him. He boasted to *Saturday Night* writer Guy Lawson that he had spent more than $500,000 US on curling in the last four years.

One of the photos shows Bodnarchuk grinning, with a $1,000 bill pasted to his forehead. The story is punctuated with incidents where angry investors show up at curling rinks looking for the big spender, yelling at him from the stands. No kidding.

Putting one over on the media isn't much of an accomplishment. Anybody can do it. Quite a few try. The most common method used is a bit of a blunt instrument, but it works better than it should: Lie. Maybe the reporter will take the lie at face value. Better yet, lie about something that's tough to check out, involves a lot of research, or requires more than normal intelligence to verify.

My friend and colleague Andrew Mitrovica wrote about systemic lying in his best-selling book about CSIS, the Canadian Security and Intelligence Service. In *Covert Entry: Spies, Lies and Crimes Inside Canada's Secret Service*, Mitrovica described the standard machinery of falsehood delivery inside CSIS like this: Lie, deny, and act surprised. It works. Test it yourself. Imagine you are a lying politician.

"No, I did not place a whoopee cushion on the mayor's chair and I cannot believe you would accuse me, the councillor from Ward 45, of doing such a thing."

Debbie Ervine of Brampton, Ontario, felt betrayed and belittled when she became the target of lies. In the summer of 1994, Debbie was desperate to find work. She found a fetching half-page ad in *The Employment News*: "$27.10 an hour plus benefits. Pay guaranteed in writing. Customer Relations Personnel needed to liason (sic) with existing Bell Canada customers. Full time or part time, no experience, comprehensive training. Students welcome."

Debbie went for it, and so did a lot of other students hungry to make some money before going back to school. It was a cruel con. Debbie sat through a training course with hundreds of other victims. They all heard the $27 promise. Then, as they hit the road, they discovered the cold hard truth. They were selling long distance telephone service door-to-door. No $27 an hour unless you signed up three customers every hour, at $9 a crack. No benefits, either. They were signed up as "independent dealers." These young kids were being used as marketing cannon fodder.

"How much money did you make working there?" I asked Debbie. "Try to summarize that for us."

"Well, it's easy to summarize because I made $10, although I haven't been paid yet," said Debbie. "I worked eight hours, so that's $1.33 an hour."

We paid a visit to the offices of the Home Phone Club, the company that made the promises to Debbie and signed her up, even though Debbie at first thought she was working for Cam-Net Telecommunications, a Vancouver-based long distance service provider, one of Bell's early competitors. It was another little lie told to Debbie.

We took it all up with Home Phone Club Vice-President Vern Ralphs. Before that, we had done our homework. We took hidden cameras into an employment seminar and recorded all the tall tales. I had a small tape player with me to play back the lies when the time was right. Once the big camera was rolling for Ralphs' interview, I asked him about complaints from the young people who thought they were working for Cam-Net.

"For what it's worth," said Ralphs, "we do have the whole seminar on tape and, quite clearly, as the independent dealer agreement says, you are seeking to be an independent dealer with the Home Phone Club, not with Cam-Net."

"Well, Vern," I said, reaching for the tape machine, "we have it on tape, too. We have it on tape and it runs quite counter to what you're telling me."

"I would love to hear it," said Ralphs, looking like he wouldn't love it at all. I punched the "Play" button, and on the little screen, company representative Gloria Gomez appeared, saying, "I think it's important for you to know who you're applying with in terms of Cam-Net's credibility, Cam-Net's financial status." I stopped the tape and turned to Ralphs once again.

"Doesn't that sound to you like Gloria Gomez is talking as an employee or an officer of Cam-Net, welcoming new people to the company when, in fact, that's not the case at all?" I asked.

"I think there's a mixture of Cam-Net and Home Phone Club in there," said Ralphs, hopefully. "I think what she's doing is trying to give credibility to Home Phone Club."

"She never mentions Home Phone Club," I countered.

"Yes she does."

"She can't give any credibility to a company she's not mentioning."

Eager to move on, I cued the tape to the part where Gloria Gomez talks about the pay: "The pay is $27 an hour," chirps Gloria on the tape, speaking to the crowd at the seminar. "So for one week of work, you are looking at $810 a week." I clicked the tape off and looked at Ralphs once again.

"So you have people saying, 'Oh boy, I'm going to make $27 an hour. It's guaranteed in writing,' when that's not true."

"It is true, if..."

"If, if, if — there's no guarantee. You can't put a qualifier on a guarantee of $27 an hour. Either you're guaranteed $27 an hour or you're not."

"If, as I mentioned, once we review that tape, if we have to change our approach, we certainly will," said Ralphs, with nothing left to deny.

Sometimes, no matter how long the interviewee sits on the barbecue, the goose just cannot be cooked. The goose is too cooperative, too willing to concede a point, too willing to blame himself. Even though the goose richly deserves to find himself on the grill, he's just too damn pleasant.

If Ed Rayment had a goose, it was cooked in 1991, when his printing company went bankrupt. It put seven people out of work and drained Rayment's personal savings. Rayment blamed it all on one huge overdue account with a company called Canada Opportunities Investment Network. Rayment signed a contract with COIN to supply $99,663.60 worth of brochures advertising COIN's services.

COIN was the brainchild of Jim Carnegie. He was COIN's president and chief operating officer. He was also the executive director of the Ontario Chamber of Commerce. The two organizations, while incorporated separately, were one and the same to Rayment.

COIN was run from the Chamber offices. Carnegie ran both organizations from the same desk, the same telephone. The literature Rayment printed for COIN said clearly at the bottom, "A project of the Ontario Chamber of Commerce."

Rayment felt comfortable dealing with Carnegie, even though COIN was a new project, knowing that COIN was backed up by the resources and stability of the Ontario Chamber of Commerce.

As well, Carnegie was the Commanding Officer of the Toronto Auxiliary Police. It was yet one more reason for Rayment to feel comfortable in his dealings with Carnegie on such a huge printing job for such a relatively small company.

COIN was a service of the Chamber that promised to pair up investors with entrepreneurs. They were matched up by computer, a little like computer dating. That's all there was to it. The whole project was self-supporting, said the literature. COIN employed one clerk to key in all the information from subscribers, who paid a small fee to be listed. When names were matched, it was up to the investors and entrepreneurs to take it from there. COIN offered no further assistance.

COIN was blessed with government largesse. From 1988 to 1991, the Mulroney government gave COIN $600,000. The Peterson government in Ontario handed over an additional $150,000, for a total of $750,000. Imagine Ed Rayment's surprise when he was told, after printing $100,000 worth of COIN brochures, that COIN was broke, out of money.

"So COIN, the Canada Opportunities Investment Network, and the Ontario Chamber of Commerce, were, as far as you were concerned, the same thing," I said to Rayment.

"It was the promotional program, 'the premier promotional program,' as we had printed in all the Chamber brochures. They all list COIN as their most important project," said Rayment as we stood in the vacant shop that had once been his printing business.

"But then COIN tells you it doesn't have any money, and you say, 'Wait a minute, it's the Chamber.'"

"That's it."

"What did they say?"

"They said, 'Tough luck. That's the way it is, Ed. COIN is in no way connected to the Chamber at all.'"

Rayment did get a partial payment — $23,000 — but it wasn't enough to keep his company, admittedly tight on cash, afloat.

Naturally, Carnegie and Rayment had different stories about what had happened. Carnegie says that he told Rayment to print the order a little at a time, since all government funding was not in place. But Rayment, Carnegie told me, decided to print the whole order all at once.

Rayment said horsefeathers to that. He produced for me a letter from Carnegie, on COIN letterhead, with "A Project of the Provincial Chambers of Commerce in Canada" printed at the bottom. The letter said:

> Dear Ed: This letter will serve as a purchase order for your firm, Litho-Offset, to proceed with the printing of the materials for COIN as outlined in your invoice dated March 28, 1991, a copy of which is attached.
>
> We understand that the project will cost $86,664.00, plus taxes, for a total of $99,663.60. Thank you for quoting on this project, and we look forward to receiving the material. In the meantime, please do not hesitate to contact us should you have any questions.

Rayment also managed to get his hands on a copy of an application COIN had made for provincial financial assistance. On the application, COIN was required to give details of any other government financing already granted. Jim Carnegie listed a federal grant of $100,000 for "the printing of promotional kits and brochures."

It might have looked good on the application form, and the money apparently had been sent to COIN, but only $23,000 actually trickled down to the printer. Rayment had argued that since COIN and the Ontario Chamber of Commerce were part of the same organization, the Chamber should pay up if COIN couldn't.

In a letter to the Ontario Chamber of Commerce Executive Council, triggered by our investigation, Carnegie insisted "there is no legal or moral connection between COIN and the Ontario Chamber of Commerce." Carnegie apparently felt so strongly about that point that he repeated in for a second time at the end of his letter.

Carnegie readily agreed to an on-camera interview. First we talked about what Carnegie considered a solid financial firewall between COIN and the OCC. He did concede a person might be confused about the relationship.

"You've got the same man running both organizations, using staff that works at the Chamber here; the address is the Chamber — maybe he (Ed Rayment) can be forgiven for thinking it's all the same thing," I said to Carnegie.

"Maybe he can," responded Carnegie, who was a man of few, well-chosen words that day about COIN, an operation that apparently had become "dormant" due to a lack of funds. But COIN had been given $750,000 worth of public money.

"Where did all the money go, if this thing is self-supporting?" I asked.

"Where that money went, in the very simplest of terms," replied Carnegie, "was to do advertising, to do design, to do a first-run of printing, to do distribution." I showed Carnegie a copy of the application form where Carnegie had said that a $100,000 federal grant had been earmarked for printing.

"So this document is not to be believed?"

"That document is to be believed."

"If it's to be believed, there should be $100,000 for printing. Isn't that what it says?"

"That's what you're telling me it says."

"Mr. Carnegie, please. It says printing of promotional brochures and registration kits."

"That was one cost of the entire program."

"It doesn't say that. It says the purpose was '$100,000 for printing of brochures and registration kits.' It doesn't say 'And other stuff.'"

Carnegie shrugged sadly, as if to say I didn't understand. I handed Carnegie the purchase order he had sent to Rayment — the purchase order that had made no mention of delivering the project in stages, as money became available.

"It doesn't say anything there about it being delivered in dribs and drabs and I'll pay you when I get some money," I said.

"No, it doesn't," said Carnegie.

"Well, that isn't a very good way for either of you to do business, is it.?"

"No, it isn't."

So that was it. Minor concessions from Carnegie, but no consideration for Rayment. COIN was broke and the Ontario Chamber of Commerce had nothing to do with it, and no legal or moral responsibility to pay a bill that would have saved Ed Rayment and his company. Carnegie smiled, thanked us for coming, and said goodbye.

Later that year, at Christmas time, Jill and I had our young kids lined up on the sidewalk on Yonge Street, waiting for the Santa Claus parade to begin. Police were everywhere — regular force and the auxiliary officers. One of those big, black, unmarked police cars rolled by. In the back seat was the Commanding Officer of the Auxiliary Police, decked out in full dress regalia. He was waving at the kids.

"Where's Santa?" I mumbled under my breath.

Sometimes it's the attitude that really makes our blood boil. It's one thing to be wronged, to be treated unfairly, to be victimized. It's quite another to be ignored, flicked off like a bug when we try to complain.

Ray Deardall, a wheat farmer near Outlook, Saskatchewan, had a simple enough problem. He figured he would find a simple solution. A fuse on a power line that runs across his field blew one day, the hot fragments set the wheat field on fire, and in just a few minutes, with a big Saskatchewan wind to fuel it, the fire had destroyed twenty-five acres of wheat, and maybe forty tonnes of alfalfa and hay bales. The fire also damaged a hay baler and melted the tire on a tractor.

Total damage, according to Ray, was $14,588.77. Deardall did what he thought was the obvious thing: he invoiced Saskpower, the government suppliers of electricity in Saskatchewan. Saskpower sent it back, without explanation, and said no, it would not pay.

This went on for a while. Deardall would demand payment. It was Saskpower's pole and Saskpower's equipment that set fire to his field. Saskpower would say no. The only thing that happened was that Saskpower's excuses for saying no got longer. Here's part of a letter from one of their lawyers:

> It is possible that the fire resulted from the failure of a lightning arrestor and fuse which comprise a portion of Saskpower's electrical distribution system. However, Saskpower is only liable if the fire was caused by some negligent act or omission on its part. The equipment that failed was purchased from reputable manufacturers. Additionally, there is no evidence of negligence on the part of Saskpower. I would therefore suggest that the occurrence can fairly be described as an unforeseeable accident.

If Ray Deardall had been barbecuing on his own property near a Saskpower pole and set it on fire by mistake, I wonder if Saskpower would have considered that an "unforeseeable accident."

The first few times we called Saskpower, they didn't bother to return the call. Finally, it happened. Saskpower told us they were reconsidering the Deardall case, although they had neglected to tell the Deardall family about it.

Saskpower also pulled out the privacy argument. It goes like this: Saskpower must protect the privacy of its customers, even though one of its customers, Ray Deardall, had given his written consent to us to negotiate with Saskpower and then tell everybody about the results across the country on television. Deardall was eager for Canadians to know what had happened to him and what, if anything, Saskpower was going to do.

The privacy card was a popular card to play for government agencies, departments, ministries, or even giant corporations in the private sector that offer services to customers. It had a nice, noble ring to it. We will protect the privacy of our customers and clients at all costs. We will wrap ourselves in the flag of privacy protection. It didn't seem to matter that the customers and clients did not want their privacy protected. They wanted other Canadians to see their stories.

When we made that argument, it was usually dismissed. Doesn't matter what the customers want, we're protecting them anyway (and conveniently covering our own asses in the process). The argument always reminded me of that old army joke: "We're here to protect democracy, not to practice it."

Saskpower finally settled with a satisfied Ray Deardall, after getting him to sign a nondisclosure agreement that would prevent him from telling anybody about it. More privacy protection.

Bad guys use the privacy protection line. It's a great catch-all and so much more modern than the old "No comment." When a bad guy invokes the privacy protection line, he's trying to tell you he cares about his client or customer — or just plain victim — when usually only the opposite is true. The bad guy might as well be saying "Have a nice day." We know what a patented insincerity that line has become.

Stephanie Nolan was heartbroken that she was not able to get to Montreal fast enough to see her dying father. As Stephanie and her mother mourned the loss together, her mother said, "You've got to help me. Mr. Duval has stolen all of your dad's money."

William and Cynthia Rosevear put all of their life's savings into mutual funds with The Mutual Group. That's when they met one of

Mutual's investment counsellors, Andre Duval. He was solicitous, friendly, and more and more in their lives as time went on.

Duval would drop by their home to chat, and gradually the conversation would turn to the Rosevear's investments — about $110,000. Duval told them he could do much better things with their money on his own, if they would just withdraw their cash from The Mutual Group and sign it over to him.

Duval started with small amounts — $10,000 here, $15,000 there. But in the end, Duval cleaned out the Rosevears. He got all $110,000. Duval dealt mainly with William Rosevear. He tried to come between William and Cynthia. William's behaviour, according to what Cynthia told her daughter, began to change. In the end, he trusted only Duval and listened to only Duval's advice. Soon, the thin veneer of investment counsellor wore off and Duval would come to the house demanding money.

Cynthia Rosevear explained how one time Duval wanted $15,000 to buy a car. William objected, but eventually wrote out a cheque to Duval that day for $12,000.

In the final few days before he died, William Rosevear realized that he was being victimized by Duval and broke down in front of his wife, lamenting that Duval had taken all of their money. "What am I going to do?" William said to Cynthia. "I'm finished and I'm ruined."

After the funeral, Stephanie went after Duval for the money:

"I asked him, I said, 'What have you done with my father's money?' And he said, 'It's none of your business. I'm looking after everything, and your mother wants me to look after everything, and you have nothing to do with it.'"

Naturally, it was all a lie. We tried several times to call Duval. He ignored our many messages. Other messages left for Duval's bosses in Montreal were also ignored. So we went to The Mutual Group head office in Waterloo, Ontario. Key officials there listened. We asked Mutual to investigate and to compensate Cynthia Rosevear if officials were able to verify for themselves that what we were saying was true.

Mutual issued a cheque to Cynthia Rosevear for $128,531. That represented the original amount that had been "borrowed," plus interest. Cynthia was happy and relieved, only wishing that William had lived to see this day. To its credit, The Mutual Group did not demand that Cynthia Rosevear sign a gag order. She was free to talk about the settlement. A Mutual Group vice-president (the company is now known as Clarica) agreed to be interviewed.

William Rosevear had died at age seventy-seven. His death certificate listed cirrhosis of the liver as a cause of death. Stephanie could not believe what she was reading. As far as she had known, her father had been an abstainer for his whole life. Cynthia, in a flood of tears, finally told Stephanie what had happened.

Cynthia admitted that William had been drinking, and drinking heavily, for the last two years of his life. Most of the alcohol was supplied by Duval, who brought it as a gift for William. When Stephanie was cleaning out her parents' home in preparation for moving her mother to a nursing home close to her, she found eleven unopened bottles of gin and a few bottles of bourbon.

Once the cheque was cashed and safely in a savings account, we went to Montreal. The Mutual Group office was near Dorval Airport. It was a single building with a massive parking lot out back. We cruised the parking lot several times, looking for Duval's car. We knew the model and plate number.

Finally, we spotted it and discovered he parked in the same place every day, up close to the building. The building had good security. We knew we would never get past the front lobby with our gear, and the back door was locked, with security-card access.

We would have to wait him out. Get him as he left the building, just as he approached his car, a long walk from the back door. Even if he decided to go back into the building, he would have us tagging along for a good hundred metres.

It was June, 1995. Hot. Real hot. Duval had come to the office. His car was in its usual spot. We waited. We had two cars and kept in touch with our two-way radios. Cellphones were too slow. By the time you dialled a number and waited to be connected, the bad guy could be long gone. Two-way radios were instant.

We moved the cars once in a while, hoping to look less conspicuous. We couldn't use the air conditioning. The cars were pointed toward the windows of the building and the running lights would have shouted, "Look over here!" Only the more expensive cars had that special feature where if you put the emergency on, the running lights went out, even with the engine and the air conditioning on.

We had the cheap wheels again that day, so we sweltered. We kept the tinted windows on the cars closed so nobody could spot the TV gear. We were buns in an oven. Meanwhile, Air Canada DC-9s approaching Dorval roared by only a few hundred feet in the air, some so close they shook the cars.

It may not have *been* Hell, but you could see it from there. When I mentioned the bun analogy to Dave the cameraman, he started laughing uncontrollably. Dave, a great cameraman, was not known for his sense of humour. He was delirious.

Our cover was slowly disappearing as people left to go home. The parking lot was emptying out. There was no place to hide. It didn't take long. Soon there were only three cars left — our two and Duval's luxury Toyota, tucked up close to the building.

We could see Duval in his office, staring at us. We had been made. Now it was just a standoff. Who could last the longest. We were tired, hot, hungry, and thirsty. Our water supply had run out. Obviously, Duval was likewise not having a good day. He had known for some time that we would, sooner or later, come looking for him. Now he was trapped.

At twilight, a pizza delivery car pulled up to the building. He buzzed, and a janitor opened the door and took the pizza. We saw the janitor deliver the pizza to Duval's office.

"That bastard," said Pierre, the sound man. "He's got pizza." Laurie kicked open the car door and stomped up to the pizza guy, still in his car, sorting out his orders.

"I'd like to order a large pizza and four drinks," she told a surprised pizza guy. "For delivery."

"Delivery to where?"

"To that car over there."

"Sorry, I have to have an address."

"We don't have an address, just a car. Two cars."

"Sorry, I can't deliver a pizza to a car."

"Well, geez, you delivered a pizza to the bad guy. Why can't you deliver one to us? We're the good guys."

"The bad guy? In the building?"

"Yeah."

"Well, sorry, I had no idea," said the pizza guy, who thirty minutes later delivered a pizza to a car for the first time in his career. We pulled the two cars right up to the building entrance. We slapped the pizza box onto the hood and stood there, eating and drinking, watching Duval watch us. We wanted him to get the idea that we were going to wait for him forever.

We knew Duval, close to running water and bathrooms, could outlast us, once nature had her way. So we decided to put on a little performance once it got dark. The cars were still lined up at the building entrance, one behind the other. All four of us got out and started making a big show of packing up to leave. We dragged boxes out onto the pavement, rearranged equipment, all the while chatting away about catching flights and calling it a day. Pierre got in his car first and drove off, as the three of us waved goodbye. Then we piled into the station wagon, Dave and I in the back seat, and Laurie driving.

We had to drive down a laneway, right by Duval's car, to get out of the parking lot. It was around the corner from the windows where Duval had been watching us. Laurie went just far enough past Duval's car to put the station wagon out of his line of sight. She stopped long enough for Dave and I to scramble out the back door and dive into a huge row of shrubbery on the other side of the lane. Laurie then roared around the block and found a hiding spot beyond the parking lot that gave her a bead on the door Duval would come out.

Dave and I, in the bushes, nursing our scratches, were soon joined by Pierre, who had ditched his car and walked back. It was full dark, but still hot. We could see, through the shrubbery, Duval's car. It was only thirty feet away. Then we heard thunder. Soon there was lightning. And then the downpour. It rained for twenty minutes. We did the best we could, protecting the camera and the sound gear with our shirts. Still no Duval. The next hour was agony. Dave had the heavy camera on his shoulder, ready to go. Pierre was struggling in the dense underbrush with his boom pole and shotgun microphone. We stayed in that position, as close to motionless as we could.

Then we heard footsteps. Around the corner of the building came Duval and the pizza janitor. We were ready. Laurie had spotted them first and had given us a signal. Duval was walking purposefully, carrying his briefcase. The janitor was edgy, looking around, as if suspecting something was going to happen. We didn't disappoint him.

We came blasting out of the shrubbery as I shouted, "Andre Duval. Goldhawk. *CTV News.* We need to talk to you about William and Cynthia Rosevear." Duval kept walking. The janitor crouched into a Kung Fu kind of stance, then instantly thought better of it as he watched us pursue Duval. As he reached the car, Duval looked down his nose at us and said, "I do not discuss the private matters of my clients."

"Little late for that, isn't it?" I replied. Duval got into his car and sped away. The janitor looked at us.

"I knew you guys were still here," he said.

Cynthia Rosevear died peacefully on April 16, 1996, her daughter at her side. Just before her death, Mutual had told Stephanie that Andre Duval had been fired. The case was closed.

Some organizations seem to have a natural talent for getting into trouble. If there is only one issue in the whole pasture, rest assured some people will step in it every time. School boards come to mind. The elected trustees are usually political neophytes, holding public office for the first time, getting a first whiff of power, maybe a future prime minister in their midst. They try to work together as a democratic group without becoming a gang that values compliance and loyalty to the team over public service. At least they try.

Sharon Villani was a veteran in a war she and many other parents were waging with the Simcoe County Separate School Board in the Barrie area, north of Toronto. In a move designed to save money, the board instituted all-day kindergarten. Sharon and the other mothers pleaded that all-day kindergarten was too much of a grind for kids that young. They campaigned for the retention of half-day kindergarten, and after a long, at times emotional battle waged during board meetings and in the local newspaper, the mothers lost.

Somewhere in the long war, the school board trustees lost their patience. Sharon had appeared in roughly twelve delegations before the board over the kindergarten issue. Now that the board had managed to hang on and not bow to the pressure, the board moved to deflate that pressure for future meetings. A board trustee proposed that delegations would not be allowed to bring up the same issue any more than once a year. Sharon, and a growing number of parents, were really getting angry. They called us to see if we could talk some sense into the SCSSB and win one for democracy.

We figured the best way to demonstrate democratic behaviour might be to attend the public meeting where the board would vote on the anti-democratic motion. Before the meeting started, we lit up the small board-room with four large, bright, and hot television lights. We didn't want any trustee to get the idea that this would be a quiet, slipped-through decision. If the board was going to move to drastically limit parental input, it would have to do it in the full glare of national publicity.

Sharon Villani and other mothers who accompanied her to the meeting, had expected that the gag order would pass. The mothers had heard no words of support for parents in all the discussions and telephone calls that had happened when word of the notice of motion had slipped out. It had come as a result of an in-camera session of the board.

But as the meeting got underway, the trustees — with damp foreheads — seemed to be pulling back from their earlier intransigence about democratic discourse from the unwashed public at the board table. When the topic of the gag order came up, Trustee Paul O'Leary spoke of the offending motion: "I had written out another one here but I'm not going to read it," said O'Leary, of an obvious amendment to the motion. "We should let sleeping dogs lie. It does not behoove us to put this motion on the books," he concluded.

The other trustees either stared blankly ahead or intensely studied their notes. For the next thirty minutes, as the canines dozed on, trustees pussyfooted around the issue. Then the chair called for a vote.

In the end, nobody voted for the motion — not the trustee who had seconded it, not even the trustee who had proposed the motion in the first place. The mothers were dumbfounded, but happy.

"Motions like this one tonight," said Sharon after the meeting, "are going to get passed if parents are not here to watchdog over what the trustees are doing." Later, as we packed up the gear, getting ready to head out of town, I told Villani that if she felt so strongly about these issues that maybe she should run for trustee herself.

The next year, in the November 14, 1994 election, Villani ran as school board trustee in Bradford West Gwillimbury and Innisfil. Among her campaign promises was this item: "As your trustee, I will make certain that the concerns of parents are heard by their school board." She won.

In April of 1997, we got involved in another school board issue in a different part of Ontario: Cobourg — home of the Northumberland–Clarington Board of Education, just east of Toronto. And this time, it was a trustee who needed our help. Marg Connor had been banned from all in-camera meetings of the board. It was a severe penalty.

Many school boards and municipalities, especially the smaller ones, love the in-camera mode. It's often where all the real business is conducted. Once in open session, a board or a town council just votes on motions. All of that bothersome debate on the issues has already happened behind closed doors, where it carried no risk of provoking a public fuss. I asked Connor how she could do her job and represent the people who voted for her if she couldn't attend those closed meetings. Her answer was, "Well, I can't. That's a real problem."

Connor had been kicked out of the inner circle by doing exactly what the inner circle is designed to prevent: triggering that public fuss. She revealed to a reporter from the *Port Hope Evening Guide* that the board, in-camera, had set up a special $83,000 fund to provide merit pay for non-union employees, and had set aside $334,000 to pay retirement gratuities to upper management.

That's where upper management gets rewarded for not calling in sick. Sick days not taken can mean extra pay at the end of a career. The board was ending this practice for non-union management, and the $334,000 was the estimated wrap-up money to pay-out the sick days accumulated up to that point.

It should have been no big deal. These payments are made. Unionized teachers still get this benefit. But when the information dribbled out of a closed meeting, it carried with it that whiff of scandal. The NCBE was embarrassed by the leak. Trustees accused Connor of breaking the rules, of not being a team player.

From Connor's side of the table, she was just doing her job. She thought those funds should be public information — after all, where did that money come from in the first place? The board insisted it had kicked out Connor because of other concerns as well, but those other concerns were never specified.

Board Chairperson Bob Willsher told me that before Connor could come back behind closed doors, the board needed assurance from Connor that she would "comply with the confidentiality of in-committee proceedings; in particular, the protection of individual privacy in accordance with the Municipal Freedom of Information and Protection of Privacy Act."

Connor said sure, she would continue to comply with that act and the Education Act, and another act that was tossed into the debate, the Municipal Conflict of Interest Act. She would comply, she said, as she believed she had complied in the past. She violated no confidentiality, revealed no facts about any individual who worked for the board, just mentioned overall figures that she thought were important information for taxpayers.

That produced a letter to Connor from the board's lawyers, Keel Cottrelle. Robert Keel wrote, in part: "you indicate you will 'continue to comply' with the legislation. This suggests you do not acknowledge any possible past non-compliance."

Connor felt she had no choice at this point. She had her lawyer send a letter to their lawyer. David Brown, of the Toronto law firm Stikeman, Elliott, wrote, "Your letter was unnecessary. Mrs. Connor's assurance more than meets the request of the chair." Then Brown attacked the board's earlier decision: "Either the Board misunderstands the public nature of board financial information as set out in s.207(4) of the Education Act and s.6(2) and 52(4) of the Municipal Freedom of Information Act, or the Board is attempting to treat as confidential that which it has no authority to treat as confidential and keep from its ratepayers."

A few days later, the board, in an in-camera session, accepted Connor's earlier assurances of compliance with all the rules and voted to let her return to the education inner sanctum, leaving long-suffering parents to wonder how much real work, on behalf of real students, had to be set aside to deal with all this procedural grunting and snorting.

6.

Striking Out

Along the way, we lost a lot of cases. It hurt each time. You could always tell when it happened. File drawers would be slammed a little harder than was necessary. There was unusual silence. Normally, the office was encased in bedlam — telephones ringing, people dropping in off the street looking for an appointment. We were involved in loud exchanges, arguing with each other over cases, using just enough profanity with each other to fuel honest conversation.

We broke a lot of phones. Well, no. *I* broke a lot of phones. I always felt the new ones did not slam down as efficiently as the old ones. The new ones were flimsy, and parts fell off constantly. The old black ones, made of granite-like plastic, were indestructible. Incidentally, we never slammed the telephone down on clients. Never. We saved that for meddlesome inquiries from our bosses about what we were doing, or in arguments over vetting a story. The desk tended to pussyfoot our items, soften them up, while we wanted them hard and raw. It was usually a compromise in the end, closer to what we wanted than what they wanted.

To save ears, I never really hung up when someone was talking. Well, I did. But not hard. The phone-slamming could be engaged in after the annoying party on the line had hung up. I would bang it in its cradle, rapidly, six or seven times, real hard, just to perform for the staff and signify my disapproval. The slamming usually brought laughter, but not from Producer Stacey Johnson. She would shoot me one of those "how childish" looks of hers. Then her admonishments would become part of the act, and in the end we would all laugh. Through that kind of manic behaviour, we managed to survive.

But when we lost a case, that silence hung in the air. It was as if something had died. It had. A little bit of fleeting hope. We were our clients' last chance at winning. After us, nothing happened — except for the stalwart few who took their grievances to court.

Cleo Barra, who lived in Vancouver, was poor. There could be no courtroom at the end of her long, painful trail. It was us or nothing. When I look in Cleo's file now, I see notes detailing what happened during 106 telephone calls, trying to get some life-saving action for Cleo, from November of 1993 to July 31, 1995. The file ends there.

Cleo had a mastectomy for breast cancer in 1977. She thought her nightmare was over, not beginning. The radiation treatment after her surgery eliminated all signs of cancer. She was given a saline breast implant in 1982. Only one year later, it had to be removed. She was developing serious health problems with the implant. Her breast was then re-constructed using part of her stomach muscle. A few months later, her stomach ruptured. The plastic surgeon repaired her stomach. It ruptured a second time, and the same plastic surgeon said he was not sure what he was doing with this kind of procedure and suggested she should find another doctor.

So Cleo went to another surgeon and had her stomach muscles repaired again. This time, the surgeon put in a plastic mesh, a patch, over the rupture.

That was 1983, the beginning of a long, gradual decline in her health. She developed chronic abdominal pain, joint pain, fatigue, chest pains, insomnia, poor memory, facial lesions, sore throat, and vision problems.

Cleo also became allergic to a wide variety of common substances: cigarette smoke, ethanol, formaldehyde, ladies' perfume, men's cologne, newspapers, fabric softeners, and unleaded diesel fuel. She started to lose her hair and her teeth. Cleo believed her body was reacting to the plastic mesh. She wanted it removed. But no doctor would perform the surgery. They were worried that it couldn't successfully be taken out. And quietly, they admitted they were nervous about legal problems that might crop up if the operation went wrong.

That's when Cleo came to us. We quickly established that her family doctor and a specialist both backed up Cleo's argument about the plastic mesh, but no surgeon would remove it. So we opened negotiations with the British Columbia Ministry of Health.

The battle was on, opened on two fronts: the health bureaucrats and the BC medical profession. Almost every day, there was a new hurdle to jump, a new panel of doctors to convince, or, yet again, another form to be filled out or another level of approval needed. The bureaucrats fought our involvement every step of the way. They made nothing easy. Every small step ahead felt like a major victory.

We even enlisted the aid of the Health Minister himself, David Ramsay. He told me he would do all he could to prod his bureaucracy into action. After a while, as Cleo's health continued to slide, it looked like approval was forming on the distant horizon. The approval meant that the operation, deemed not possible to perform in BC, could be performed in either Halifax or Dallas, Texas, where doctors had some experience in this kind of surgery.

But there were still bumps along the road. The Halifax operation became impossible when BC learned that Nova Scotia would not perform surgery on out-of-province patients, due to health funding shortfalls in Nova Scotia. So much for nationally accessible medicare.

The Dallas option was all that was left, but first BC Health wanted to send Cleo to Dallas for tests, bring her back to Vancouver, and then decide, based on test results, if the operation could be financed. Then she might be sent back.

Cleo made the gruelling trip to the internationally known Environmental Health Center in Dallas. She was examined by the head man, Dr. William Rea. Dr. Rea was listed as a thoracic and cardiovascular surgeon, an abdominal and general surgeon, and the first world professional chair in environmental medicine at the Robens Institute, University of Surrey, in England. This was his matter-of-fact assessment, tinged with an edge of urgency: "After history and physical exam, it is my opinion that the mesh is responsible for all of Ms. Barra's symptoms. We recommend that she have surgery to remove the mesh. It is imperative for the patient to have surgery in the Environmental

Unit with doctors who specialize in environmental medicine and surgery. Her condition is precarious."

The doctor added that without the operation in the special facilities of the Environmental Health Center, "it can be dangerous and potentially fatal to the patient."

We were elated when we read the letter. At last we had categorical proof from a world authority that Cleo needed to have this mesh removed from her body to save her life. What more could the Health Ministry in BC need?

Well, believe it or not, more proof. More detailed test results from Dallas. Then when that was all in-house and studied by the Health Ministry in Victoria, if it all looked okay they would first try to find a doctor in BC to do the operation, or in Halifax, but if nothing else worked, then in Dallas.

We reminded them we had been through this whole dance just a year ago, but that seemed to make no difference. The bureaucrats who spouted the bafflegab and paid slavish attention to some "process" that was never clear to us, always exhibited selective hearing when we tried to interject a note of reality. I wrote on the file, on the back cover, "Common sense is not necessarily applicable."

We tried to get back to the ministerial assistant/flak/fartcatcher who guarded the door of the minister. This time we could not get through. In fact, since we were becoming more annoying by the day as Cleo's condition worsened, the MAFF decided we should be punished for our impertinence. He proclaimed that we would never be able to interview the minister about Cleo or about this issue and that the MAFF himself would no longer return our telephone calls.

On July 31, 1995, Cleo Barra died at St. Paul's Hospital in Vancouver. She was fifty-five.

Contrary to most public opinion from Canadians who do no live there, all of Saskatchewan is not flat. Saskatchewan has beautiful rolling hills in the north, and way down in the south Saskatchewan has the Big Muddy Badlands. It's breathtakingly beautiful — rolling hills and wooded valleys where wildlife flourishes. Some parts of the land have been left undisturbed for five thousand years. No plow or spade has broken the ground. It is, as farmers like to say, "as God made it." Even Hollywood liked it. *Butch Cassidy and the Sundance Kid* was filmed there.

Much of the Big Muddy is Crown land — government-owned and leased out to farmers as pastureland. The Noble family has been looking after the same piece of land for seventy-five years. Cattle graze there. A biology professor from the University of Regina examined the site closely and called it "An outstanding example of undisturbed mixed-grass prairie.

"The land is remnant upland between two valleys. All other land in the immediate area with a similar topographic situation has been broken for crop production. There is very little of this native prairie left and every attempt should be made to conserve it for wildlife habitat and biodiversity."

Well, good luck to the land. The Saskatchewan government ignored its natural and historical value, even though the land had been protected from exploitation by the Wildlife Habitat Protection Act (WHPA); even though scientists noted the existence of seventeen teepee rings, circles of rocks that were used to hold down the edges of the teepees, marking traditional native encampments that had doubtless been used for countless centuries; even though many suspected ancient burial sites had been found.

Here's how it all came apart, and how expediency and big money ruled the day:

In 1996, Ron Noble got a letter from the Saskatchewan government, from the Crown lands biologist. It reported that department officials had recently visited the land and decided that it was not as critically important or significant as had once been thought. Therefore, the government was removing Noble's custodial lands from the WHPA.

While the Nobles wondered about the sudden change of attitude, and wondered if they might be able to now buy the land themselves to keep it untouched and use it as pastureland, the light bulb soon clicked on.

A later letter explained that Luscar Limited was being allowed to expand its nearby open-pit coal mining operation into the formerly-protected lands, to mine the coal used by Saskpower to generate electricity for the province. But never mind, officials said, the area will be re-seeded with those nice modern-day grasses once the coal has been dug out and all that untouched pastureland is ripped apart.

Ron Noble and many of his neighbours were angry at the heavy-handed tactics and sad to lose a critical section of unbroken land. In all of the Big Muddy, only 1 percent of it remained untouched. They came to us to see if we could help.

We couldn't. Coal mining and power generation form a giant juggernaut in Saskatchewan. The government readily consents to big project/big money enterprise and ordinary people do not count. They just get in the way, but they can be easily brushed aside.

We tried to get the premier himself, Roy Romanow, to intercede. To at least speak to us. Instead, Romanow tossed a couple of cabinet ministers our way, hoping that would do. It didn't. John Nilson, the minister responsible for Saskpower, said it was all okay by him. The Minister of Environment and Resource Management, Buckley Belanger, said it was okay by him, too. The environment had been weighed against the juggernaut, and the environment had lost.

The mining company was careful to tell us that its people found a few artifacts on the site. They were counted and classified and taken away, a quick nod to environmental and historical sensitivities. Belanger seemed pleased the company had done that.

"This information has all been taken out and documented and catalogued for our interest," said the environment minister.

"So the land can be dug up," I added.

"That is correct," was the brief reply.

"Have you seen it? Have you seen the land?"

"No, I haven't."

"Pity. I wish that you had. Maybe you'd feel differently about it."

"Okay," was all Belanger said in reply. I knew he wasn't saying, "Okay, I'll go out and have a look." It was more, "Okay, this interview is over."

On the way out of Coronach, we stopped for a last look. It was cold. A biting prairie wind blew over the summit of the doomed hill, much as it had done since about 3000 BC. I got down for a close look at the grasses. Almost every tiny plant was different, and many of the plants I had never seen before coming here. Some were in bloom — little yellow flowers the size of confetti. I took off my glove and patted the ground, knowing that if I ever made it back to the Big Muddy, this original patch of Canada would be gone.

It was the first time we had tried to preserve a piece of history. Usually, we tried to save people. We saved them from themselves, from their families, from an uncaring government, an unfriendly corporation — and for Rose Green of Calgary, from a too-friendly young man. That's not her real name. I promised the family I would do what I could to protect her reputation as a highly successful and well-known stockbroker and investment dealer. Rose was wealthy, and a widow. Her husband had also been wealthy.

One day in a supermarket, Rose, who was eighty-eight when we first met her, was struggling with lifting a bag of milk into her shopping cart. A nice young man, he was thirty-two, offered to help. Joel Mason even assisted her in carrying the groceries to her car. It was the beginning of, if not a beautiful, then certainly a profitable relationship for Mason.

As Rose and Mason were becoming friends, Rose's family across the country were becoming increasingly worried about Rose. She began to shut herself up in her huge home. She started to hear the voices of her dead relatives. She began to avoid all her friends and family, spending more and more time with Mason.

And who exactly was Mason? He worked for a Calgary company selling burial plots in cemeteries. To those who asked, he also called himself an investment consultant for widows — a somewhat narrowly focussed, if not suspicious, profession. Family members discovered that Rose had cashed in about $1.5 million in investments and just put the money in her savings account.

They also knew, and we confirmed, that Mason would frequently drive Rose to her bank in his old Lincoln Continental. Rose would make large cash withdrawals as Mason watched.

With a little well-meaning snooping, the family also found out that Mason apparently had ample access to credit cards belonging to Rose. In all, figured family members, Mason had been given close to $200,000.

He had also, according to documents that had been retrieved from the home, added himself to Rose's long list of beneficiaries in her will. The family was understandably worried that all of Rose's money would disappear. Rose was also executor for her husband's estate, worth an additional $5 million.

The family asked us if we could help, not even sure what we might be able to do. In similar circumstances, we had been able to shoo away or drive away suspicious young friends who had attached themselves to older people.

But there would be no shooing away of Mason, not as long as Rose had anything to do with it. She was told by Mason that we had been snooping around and trying to track him down on the telephone.

I got an angry call from Rose, telling me to mind my own business. It was her money, she told me, and she would do anything with it she wanted. Nothing I said could change Rose's mind about Mason. He was a good boy, she told me, and she wanted to help him.

Without revealing Rose's identity, we made Mason famous. We caught him on tape, using a hidden camera, and later put his picture on television, in March of 1994, just in case Mason had other "special clients" who might need to be warned.

Mason refused to talk to me on camera. We sat outside his house for an entire day trying to convince him, by telephone, to come out. He stayed inside, all the curtains in his little house drawn tightly closed.

All of the attention we were giving Mason soon attracted the attention of the Calgary Police Service. Constable Tim Potter, from the Fraud Detail, launched an investigation.

Joel Mason was charged with fraud, but the charges were stayed, with the agreement that he sign a Deed of Disclaimer, barring him from the estate of Rose Green.

Rose Green died in July of 1999. She was ninety-three. Mason hired a lawyer and argued he had signed the Deed of Disclaimer under duress and was now claiming his share of Rose's estate. The family, knowing that he could tie up the estate for years, gave Mason $100,000 to get rid of him.

We closed the file on Joel Mason after almost five years. Our oldest file remains open after nine years. It belongs to a former cop, a Royal Canadian Mounted Police undercover narcotics officer, convicted of throwing his wife from the balcony of their seventeenth-floor condominium on Toronto's waterfront.

Patrick Michael Kelly was convicted in the first-degree murder of Jeanette Kelly on May 31, 1984. He got the mandatory life imprisonment, with no chance of parole for twenty-five years.

The only eyewitness to the crime was a woman by the name of Dawn Bragg, a one-time love of Kelly's, who testified she was in the Kelly condo that day and saw Kelly throw Jeanette from the balcony. It was that smoking-gun testimony that helped convince the jury that Kelly was guilty of first-degree, or premeditated, murder.

Kelly appealed his conviction to the Ontario Court of Appeal and was turned down. The appeal court, in refusing to overturn the verdict, stressed how important it felt the Bragg testimony had been:

> When the evidence of Bragg is considered, there is an air of total unreality about the proposition that the appellant's acts were not planned and deliberate. She stated that after she heard what sounded like a blow, she left the room in which she was and saw the deceased lying on the floor, presumably unconscious, with the appellant standing over her. The appellant then picked up the deceased, carried her across the living room, across the balcony floor and dropped her over the balcony. He returned with a certain coolness, telling Bragg he loved her and arranged for her exit from the apartment building. The actions, as described by Bragg, are inconsistent with the dropping of the deceased over the balcony being an impulsive act, and, of course, totally inconsistent with the evidence given by the appellant.

Kelly then applied for leave to appeal to the Supreme Court of Canada, and was refused on February 28, 1986.

Through all of it, Kelly insisted that his wife had fallen acciden-
tally from the balcony. He said she had stood on a stool on the balcony,
trying to investigate a rattling sound the strong wind was making that
day as it blew past the metal flashing at the top of the balcony. She lost
her balance and fell. As she was teetering, she screamed for Kelly, who
rushed to the balcony and caught her briefly around the waist but was
unable to hang on, and she fell to her death. That had been Kelly's
story in court. He stuck to it relentlessly.

He also said that Dawn Bragg had not even been in the Kelly
condo that day. Kelly's story was dismissed as improbable and implau-
sible. The Crown called expert witnesses who testified it was highly
unlikely that Jeanette Kelly lost her balance, fell from the stool and
over the balcony, with Kelly arriving just in time to grab her around
the waist but unable to hang on.

In 1993, as Kelly was serving the ninth year of his twenty-five-year
term, Dawn Bragg (now remarried and known as Dawn Taber) changed
her mind about what she saw in Kelly's condo.

She said she had either been coerced by police or somehow talked
into believing, with the help of a police psychiatrist, that she had seen
Kelly drop his wife over the balcony. She said she had heard what
sounded like Kelly hitting his wife from the other room, but that's all
she saw. At this point, Taber was living in the United States, and was
worried about coming back to Canada to tell her new story — worried
she might be charged with perjury.

That's when Kelly wrote to us. He wanted us to help him get another kick at the justice can. Kelly was making a special appeal under
Section 690 of the Criminal Code, a section that allows the justice minister, in special circumstances, to order a new trial for someone convicted of a crime, or refer the case to an appeal court and have the court
decide if a new trial is warranted. Kelly had hired a big gun to handle the
appeal, celebrated defence lawyer Clayton Ruby. Kelly wanted to know
if we were interested in helping on the bureaucratic and political fronts.
Section 690 applications are famous for their snail-like pace. It can take
years to get an answer. The wheels of justice turn slowly enough as it is.
Ask any lawyer how glacial the process becomes when the system is
asked to throw itself into reverse and reconsider the already-considered.

I remember at the time we had no real opinion about the ultimate guilt or innocence of Kelly. The point was, the Section 690 application was a legal remedy open to Kelly and, now that Taber had said, in effect, that she lied at trial about being an eyewitness, Kelly deserved some consideration, and maybe another day in court.

The Taber testimony had been instrumental in his conviction for first-degree murder. As soon as Toronto Police had it in writing that Taber was an eyewitness to murder, Kelly was charged. The rest of the evidence was all circumstantial — damning in some respects, but circumstantial.

Kelly was involved in money laundering schemes; he was once charged and later acquitted on arson and fraud charges; he was living way beyond his means; he was an incorrigible womanizer; a few days after Jeanette Kelly's funeral, Kelly left for Europe with his girlfriend — although to balance that out, Jeanette was about to catch a plane the day she died, to visit her Italian boyfriend in Europe.

But the absolute icing on the cake was that Taber said she saw Kelly kill his wife, then she said she didn't.

Kelly was by now a famous ex-Mountie. A book was being written about him that would illustrate his bad boy ways but cast doubt on his conviction. Then a movie was made about his life and the death of his wife, starring actor Paul Gross. I think Kelly liked the casting and even said parts of the movie were accurate. I was with him when he watched the movie for the first time.

I had brought a tape to William Head Institution in British Columbia. The assistant warden let us watch it together in an unused classroom at the prison. Kelly remained mainly emotionless (his usual state) during the movie. He smiled or laughed a few times. He flinched and let out a moan when the movie portrayed Gross dropping his movie wife from the balcony.

I had been to see Kelly at William Head many times over the years, discussing the details of the case, the evidence, and the progress, or usually the lack of progress, with his Section 690 application.

Kelly remained lean and wiry during his prison years. Life at William Head, a medium-security prison, was a lot better for Kelly than his early years spent at Kingston Pen. Targeted as a former cop, facing some of the inmates he helped put in prison, Kelly said he fought for his life almost every day.

William Head was better. Fewer fights, less-dangerous fellow inmates. But the high fences, the razor wire, and the observation towers were a reminder that it was still prison. We would walk the fence line for a little exercise. I could leave. Kelly couldn't. Kelly once told me his stone-faced demeanour had been developed in prison as a defence mechanism.

He expected nothing. Life was a minimal existence. He could not allow himself to hope. He studied. He spoke of God, as many inmates do. And of course, he was obsessed with the details of his case, as many inmates are.

We were working hard, making ourselves unpopular with the Department of Justice in Ottawa. We were having success attitudinally but making no real progress otherwise. Justice officials clearly wanted nothing to do with us. They could never answer our questions about how long all of this 690 stuff was taking.

Dawn Taber had recanted her testimony in 1993. It would take until 1997 for that development to trigger a new hearing before the Ontario Court of Appeal.

In that four years, we annoyed Justice Minister Alan Rock several times, catching up to him in the House of Commons hallways to ask him when he would decide on what to do in the Patrick Kelly case. After that got us nowhere, we even ambushed Prime Minister Jean Chrétien, as he attended a function at the University of Toronto. When I reached out to shake his hand and ask him to look into the Kelly case, he grabbed it and pulled me along in the crowd as he headed toward his limo. He told me he had faith in his justice minister. But he was clearly annoyed. Whether that sped up Rock's decision to refer the Kelly case to an appeal court, we never knew.

We tracked down many of the former witnesses in the trial, looking for new details. We discovered that while Kelly's story of rushing to catch his wife as she teetered might sound like a tall tale, the expert called to disprove that possibility readily conceded to us that Kelly's version could be true. It was possible.

The police psychiatrist told us he had been concerned about the mental and emotional stability of Dawn Taber as he questioned her, with the police, when Taber first said she saw Kelly kill his wife.

We found Dawn Taber in the United States and spent many hours on the telephone with her. She was always emotionally fragile. We were gentle with her, but it was difficult to get hard information.

Then her story starting mutating. In her recantation, she said she was in the condo, but did not see the murder. Then she said she was not even in the condo that day. She had been there, possibly, the day before Jeanette Kelly died. That's what she told the Ontario Court of Appeal after the Justice Minister Rock finally decided that the court should decide Kelly's fate.

But the Court, in a rare 2–1 split decision, said Kelly's conviction should stand. Mr. Justice Coulter Osborne and Mr. Justice George Finlayson agreed that Taber was probably telling the truth during Kelly's trial but lying, or being delusional, with her recantation. Besides, they both said, there was enough circumstantial evidence to convict Kelly, anyway. Osborne and Finlayson wrote:

> We do not believe the testimony of Ms. Taber taken before this court and believe that she told the truth at the trial. In this regard, we are not satisfied that her most recent version of events is her own. It is apparent from this record that Ms. Taber's cerebral travels to these fresh insights into her mental state was a journey that she did not make alone. She was either pressured or at the very least felt pressured to change her trial testimony.

The judges detailed in their decision they felt that Taber's evidence had been tainted by Clayton Ruby, who cross-examined Taber at the hearing, on behalf of his client Patrick Kelly, and in preparation beforehand, had, as normal practice, talked to Taber on the telephone, preparing her for her testimony as lawyers do.

Her evidence was also tainted, said the judges, by Michael Harris, the author of the book about Patrick Kelly, and by us at *Goldhawk Fights Back*. We had talked to Taber frequently. We had spent most of our time just listening to Taber, making notes on what she said, trying to comfort her about her upcoming testimony and making sure we understood what she said she believed. We never told her what to say. We made a hard practice of not telling anybody what to say.

Mr. Justice Stephen Goudge disagreed with his colleagues. This is some of what he wrote. The parenthetical information is mine, added for clarity:

> Ms. Taber's evidence at (the original trial, in 1984,) evinced significant frailties in a number of respects. First, it emerges from the tortuous evolution (the police and psychiatrist's extended questioning of Taber) which I have described. Then there is the substantial degree of coincidence in Ms. Taber's arriving unannounced at the Kellys' apartment on the very day of Jeanette Kelly's death, not having seen the Kellys in more than four months.
>
> In addition, there is a degree of improbability in all the actions of Mr. Kelly which, on Ms. Taber's description of events, must have occurred in the two to five minutes that independent witnesses said elapsed between the body landing on the ground and Mr. Kelly's arriving on the scene. He had to help Ms. Taber up after she collapsed on the balcony, calm her down, take her to the elevators on the seventeenth floor, get the elevator and ride with her up to the twenty-fifth floor, change elevator banks, get the elevator for her (express) descent, and put her on it. Then, he had to go back down to the apartment on the seventeenth floor, and move the stool from which he said his wife fell from the kitchen to the balcony, where it was discovered by the police. Ms. Taber testified that she was sure there was no stool on the balcony when she was taken from the apartment. Mr. Kelly then had to get to the site of the body. For Ms. Taber to be right, all this had to happen within approximately five minutes.

Finally, there were a significant number of inconsistencies between Ms. Taber's trial evidence and objectively demonstrable facts. For example, she testified that Jeanette Kelly's suitcase was in the bedroom and her travel suit was on the bed, whereas the luggage was actually in the hall and there were no clothes on the bed. She also testified that she had no recollection of the Kelly's large and playful sheepdog being in the apartment that day, whereas the first police officers to enter the apartment found the dog there.

She said she exited the building through the garage door, but the security guard on duty said that no one exited on foot through the garage in the half hour within which this would have happened. She testified that she did not see either Mrs. Kelly's body or people rushing to it as she walked to her car, yet she would have passed within eight car lengths of the body and the growing commotion surrounding it.

Delmar Doucette, one of Clayton Ruby's law partners, went to the Supreme Court of Canada to get permission to launch an appeal. The Crown argued that Kelly had no right of appeal to the Supreme Court of Canada. The judges refused to grant leave to appeal on a 4–1 ruling. In this case, the situation is that Kelly has no right of appeal to the highest court in the land, but if Kelly had won his case before the Ontario appeal court, the Crown would have had the right to appeal. Doucette asked Justice Minister Martin Cauchon to fix what Doucette calls an unfair situation.

Meanwhile, Kelly is out on parole, still proclaiming his innocence. His lawyers applied for special consideration under Section 745 of the Criminal Code of Canada, the so-called "faint hope" clause that brings a bit of compassion to the law. Patrick Kelly is living in a halfway house now, trying to adjust to a world he left twenty years ago.

Barry Robinson was summarily thrown out of his world — a world that preached peace, love, and justice, but practiced harsh judgment, character assassination, and rule by bureaucracy.

Barry Robinson had been a United Church minister for twenty-eight years. It was a profession, a calling, he had always known was right for him. Both he and his loving wife and preaching partner, Susan, had watched over and cared for several congregations in their careers.

None would be as challenging as the congregation at Wilmar Heights United Church in Scarborough, on the eastern side of Toronto. In accepting this ministry, Robinson knew the congregation had problems — conflicts between a handful of influential members who were accustomed to getting their own way, and the rest of the members. He accepted the challenge.

He had been invited to bring a fresh, proactive, and participatory kind of Christianity to Wilmar Heights, far beyond the proverbial comfortable pew. And he did. Or at least he tried. The vast majority of the congregation loved it. A much smaller group, led by the Troublesome Handful, set out to get rid of the Robinsons.

They found fault in everything he did. He was observed to have odd habits. He occasionally didn't make eye contact in conversation. He once sat with his head down in church, as if listening to what was going on, or perhaps, dare I say it, even praying. There was an argument over where altar furniture was to be placed. And, oh yes, he couldn't get along with the organist, or the organist couldn't get along with him, and didn't like Robinson's choice of hymns, to boot.

It was a festival of trivialities. But after awhile it gained its own goofy momentum. It was disrupting the business of the congregation. It was getting out of hand. The stories grew wilder and wilder. They assumed a life of their own. Finally, to put an end to this whisper campaign, to deflate the hate-mongering, Robinson agreed to a church dispute-settling mechanism known as a Final Hearing Panel. If that sounds a bit like Judgment Day, the comparison is inaccurate. The Final Hearing Panel was much tougher. Everybody had a lawyer — the Panel, the Troublesome Handful, and Barry Robinson was advised to get one, too.

The FHP had three responsibilities: to consider the effectiveness of Reverend Barry Robinson as Minister of Wilmar Heights, to consider the state of the Wilmar Heights pastoral charge (the warring church members), and to consider the oversight of the Toronto–Scarborough presbytery in respect of Reverend Barry Robinson.

The FHP got right to its task. It fired Barry Robinson and ordered him to vacate the manse as soon as possible — or in the pseudo-pious language of the hearing, the panel proclaimed that "The pastoral relationship shall be dissolved effective immediately."

Then the panel "recommended" that Robinson take a career-counselling course in Princeton, New Jersey, to see, among other things, if Robinson was "fit for pastoral ministry, or second if the first answer be negative, whether he is fit for any kind of ministry, and if both answers be negative, where should he be advised to direct the remainder of his working life."

Attendance was outwardly voluntary, but if he didn't agree to go he would never get assigned to another congregation in the United Church.

The panel had a few choice words for Robinson, the Wilmar Heights congregation, and the Toronto–Scarborough presbytery. It accused Robinson of causing conflicts in his last two pastoral charges, without detailing the seriousness or accuracy of that accusation. Then it went on to place, in writing, this indictment on Robinson's reputation, without a stitch of proof to back it up:

"We do not know whether or not the Minister is the way he is because he has peculiar views out of which he might be educated or whether he is that way because of some neurosis or psychosis which needs treatment. Were are only certain that he must not be allowed to go on destroying congregations."

Of the Troublesome Handful, and even of the majority of members who loudly supported Robinson, the Panel said:

> Members of (the Troublesome Handful) were the leaders when this crisis arose and thus had the burden on their shoulders. If some of them lost their cool we are of the view they should be forgiven. We are certain that each member of that group and others in the congregation, including some of the minister's supporters,

has his or her own personal regrets to think about...
We propose that the individual members of the congregation who were criticized in the course of the proceedings be forgiven for excesses, be thanked for their
service to date, and be welcomed to render any new
service which from time to time the Lord or their
church may ask of them.

The presbytery was blamed for letting things get out of hand at
Wilmar Heights: "Here is a crisis and a mess. A congregation is in a
critical state; the minister will lose his position and may lose his liveli-
hood, and many individuals in the congregation are in deep grief."

But only Barry Robinson paid the price — unemployment. He said
to me, well after the hearing when some of the raw emotion had sub-
sided, "We just couldn't believe that this was happening. That people
would be that malicious."

Most of the congregation, about 130 members, including nearly all
of its leaders and elders, were on Robinson's side. Said Doug Milne,
who no longer worships at Wilmar Heights, "Nobody would treat their
dog the way he was treated. It's just dreadful."

Robinson's brush with church justice left him with a $90,000
legal bill. The panel decided it would pay half. Then the Wilmar
Heights Board voted, 21–5, to pay the rest out of Wilmar Heights'
surplus funds. Wilmar Heights had $800,000 in the bank, money
from land it leases for housing in the neighbourhood. The Wilmar
Heights Board did not want Barry and Susan both unemployed and
$45,000 in debt.

But the Toronto–Scarborough presbytery overruled the Wilmar
Heights Board, said Presbytery Chair Rev. Lorne Taylor-Walsh. "We
felt giving half was both generous and the most stewardship we
could exercise."

"Regardless of what the board said?"

"We listened to what the board said. We did not agree with them."

If there was any comfort for Barry Robinson in those dark days
it was in the fact that he was not alone. Casey McKibbon, a former
United Church minister himself, runs an organization called the

Clergy Support Network. He showed me rows of files at his Ottawa-area offices — two thousand case histories of what McKibbon calls "clergy abuse."

All the stories sound roughly the same. They sound like Barry Robinson's. McKibbon told me that once a handful of influential parishioners gets into a power struggle with the minister, the minister always loses. "Once you've defined the clergy as the bad guy, then anything goes to get rid of him," said McKibbon.

"Another common theme seems to be, 'Well, if you're having problems with your congregation then you must be crazy,'" I said to McKibbon.

"Exactly."

"There must be some psychological problem."

"You must be sent out to the psychiatric unit to be assessed."

We were playing church bureaucrat and morbidly enjoying every minute of it. It let out some of the frustration over our inability to do something for Barry Robinson. We had pursued dozens of top officials over several months, trying to point out the injustices. We were met with polite shakes of the head. Nobody could help. There was a church process that must be followed. No single church official would venture any kind of public opinion. We saw no bravery.

At one point, we asked officials repeatedly if we might interview the Moderator of the United Church, Bill Phipps. We were hoping he might be able to, well, moderate. We were told in no uncertain terms the moderator did not get involved in these disputes. Ever.

So we caught up with the moderator one day as he spoke to a church group in Toronto. Some of the staff made us as we waited for the moderator to emerge from the church. We were waiting quietly at the main door, as we might have waited for any official, at any time, to grab a comment or two.

The staff bundled him out a side door, all huddled under a large trench coat and hat and into the back seat of a waiting car. Producer Jennifer Sheriff, sometimes brave to a fault, stood her ground behind the car, her hands planted on the trunk as it began to back up, waiting for the camera to get into position for a shot. I yanked her out of the way when it became clear the driver was not intending to stop.

Once we had that embarrassing picture of the moderator in inexplicable full flight, it was easy to trade it for a sit down interview to be used on air instead of the great escape footage. But all the moderator said was that "It would not be appropriate for me to make any comment. I don't know a lot of the details, anyway." It looked hopeless for Barry Robinson.

The next stop in the church justice system was an appeal of the Final Hearing Panel, which apparently wasn't final at all. All the players were called to testify, including Barry, who arrived in his Roman collar, thinking it might be one of the very last times he would be wearing it. Many of his faithful congregation were there as well. There was no sign of the Troublesome Handful. Former United Church Minister John Oldham was there. He was kicked out of his church in Rama, Ontario, a year earlier.

"Psychiatrists, psychologists, other counsellors. They did all kinds of tests on me. And you know what they found?"

"No," I said, guessing I had a pretty good idea what they found.

"I had personality features. Everybody — hey, you have a personality feature, Goldhawk, maybe you should go away for an assessment. You're a bit of a troublemaker," said Oldham. "Organized religion does not seem to have a place for people who may be slightly different. Sad, eh?"

"Yeah, it's really sad," I agreed.

"Well, look what they did with Jesus, for Christ's sake."

When the appeal panel wrote its final report, there was a mild but meaningless victory for Barry Robinson. That panel said the charges against Robinson had been both "trivial and unfair." The panel also said there was "no basis, beyond pure conjecture," that Robinson had any mental or emotional problems. In fact, said this panel, the earlier panel had ignored testimony from a well-known psychiatrist and psychologist that Robinson was solidly, mentally sound. Robinson quoted some of the words he had waited a long time to hear: "Due to the 'inconsequential nature of the allegations' — those are their words — the panel refused to accept the presbytery's recommendation that I be put on the Discontinued Service List," he said, after reading the decision.

It was a hollow victory. No presbytery in Canada would hire a minister with a ruined reputation, no matter what was said in retraction a long time later. In 2003, for what it's worth, the United Church did finally put Robinson on the DSL. At least that helped close the book on a sad tale.

The Robinsons have moved, much earlier than they thought they would, to their retirement cottage on a remote beachfront property on the Bruce Peninsula in Ontario. There, amid winter storms that push snowdrifts higher than the cottage, amid the slow but welcome rebirth of spring, the glorious heat and sunshine of summer, and the vivid, bracing cool of autumn, Barry and Susan have returned to their own ministry.

They call it Fernstone. It offers "thought-provoking and inspiring writing, healing stories, personal growth workshops, communication skills training, behavioural management, and family counselling."

In an e-mail, Barry Robinson wrote:

> My counselling practice in Owen Sound has tripled since we last talked. I have contracts to provide clinical therapy for six clients of employment assistance programs, as well as some psycho-social/rehabilitation assessments, as well as work for correctional institutions. Two-thirds of the additional business has come from our own advertising, and referrals from other clients. Seventy-five percent of my work is with couples who come in all degrees of disarray. Tough work, but deeply satisfying when it takes. 'Keeping the Faith in Babylon,' my weekly publication through the Fernstone website, is still going around the world to places like Berlin, Argentina, and New Zealand.
>
> So, I'm doing what I was called to do and the church ordained me to do may years ago — just outside the walls — and receiving a much more appreciative response for my work.

Susan Robinson wrote, in another e-mail:

> I hear the Rainbow are biting these days. A neighbour said we had a medium-sized black bear on the road last

Thursday. I just hope the people on the road remember to be bear smart. We are also aware of a mother and cub roaming in the vicinity. I certainly would rather deal with them that some human beings I've met. Oh, how I love the wild. So good for the soul. It keeps us grounded.

What a loss for the United Church.

7.

Show Us the Money

It wasn't until our seventh year of operation, 1999, that we started to realize that we were vacuuming a lot of money out of the system and dumping it back into the wallets and bank accounts of our clients.

The only money we usually thought about was the money we were spending. The GFB team was not known for its economy, and had not been hired to wreak havoc with the system because it was cheap. It wasn't. Our annual budget was about $500,000.

For that, CTV got one item a week. An item that might have taken us months to resolve, but it was still only one item, as opposed to four or five items a week from hard-working sluggoes who covered press conferences and media scrums.

We were low on quantity but high on quality, at least in our own minds, where there was no disagreement or criticism. We took a certain defiant pride in the fact that we did not fit in all that well in the Network Atmosphere. We were too loud, we laughed too much, we seldom deferred to the superior wisdom of our superiors, and we were severely allergic to bullshit.

I remember the day I tromped into network headquarters with some of the real thing on my cowboy boots. I was fresh back from interviewing a cattle farmer and needed to take exception with a writer who had screwed up the introduction to one of our stories. There were more than the usual looks of disapproval that day.

So that's why, in 1999, I thought it was high time we gathered some evidence to show that we were worth all the money and trouble.

We were confident that we had already been given enough rope to hang ourselves but we still wanted to stave it off as long as possible.

Working on *Goldhawk Fights Back* was addictive. Despite all the setbacks, hardships, failures, and friendly-fire incidents from the newsroom, we were making a difference.

I couldn't believe it when we added up all the refunds, insurance settlements, compensation payments, pension entitlements, and compassionate disbursements — $3.2 million that year alone. I immediately dispatched a self-congratulatory note to Carpetland at CTV headquarters. They didn't seem all that impressed.

We were. Not so much for the money, but for what the money did. It repaired lives, saved homes, allowed people to live independently, restored dignity.

Gerard Comeau had been in mourning for several months over the loss of his job. But it was more than that. Gerard had lost the rest of his working life. He had worked in the bush as a tree cutter and was totally disabled when the trunk of a felled tree took a strange bounce and struck him in the back.

Gerard was done. He could walk, with great care, but there was no work he would ever find in the bush or in the small town of Petit Rocher, just north of Bathurst, New Brunswick, where he lived with his wife, Louiselle, in their tidy little home. It was now a home they both worried they would lose. Money had become so tight they sold the wood stove, and then their car, just to make the mortgage payments.

The New Brunswick government had recognized Gerard's disability and had begun sending out a small monthly pension. Gerard's life insurance company also recognized his disability and also sent a modest pension. But the Comeaus could get no action from the disability insurance they had on their mortgage. They had filled out all the necessary forms and send them along to L'Industrielle Alliance, their insurance company in Montreal. But the company seemed to be saying that Comeau still had the ability to find less-physically demanding work elsewhere.

We went to Montreal to argue the case. It was a short debate. As soon as the company discovered from us that Gerard Comeau was illiterate, they agreed to pay off the Comeaus' mortgage. As company Vice-President Marc Gagne told us, "From that situation, all we could do is conclude this person, because of his education, could not do anything other than what he had been doing. He is, in fact, disabled."

"So the rest of the story is simple," I said, trying to nail it down. "You send a cheque to his bank and pay off the mortgage."

"So now this person can stay in his house, which is why he took out the insurance in the first place."

The Comeaus were at first shocked at their good fortune, then vastly relieved. L'Industrielle Alliance paid out the mortgage within days — $76,625.44.

Vic and Annette Thiessen of Strathmore, Alberta, had pursued a big dream for many years, and if it hadn't been for the cattle rustler, they would have made it.

The Thiessens had worked day and night in their restaurant, salting away the money they would need to start up their cattle-ranching operation, a lifelong ambition. Finally, with a little money ahead, they went to the bank for a loan (an old farming tradition) and paid a licenced and bonded cattle dealer $80,000 to buy them seventy-four cows.

The dealer bought the cows with the Thiessens' money, then turned around and sold them, pocketed the money, and left town. The Thiessens were suddenly near financial ruin before their farm had even gotten off the ground.

The Alberta government had a Livestock Protection Act that protected farmers and compensated for losses through the Cattle Industry Fund, but the protection offered was way too narrow to help the Thiessens. The Act would only compensate if somebody had written a bad cheque.

The authors of the Act, even though they were in Alberta, never thought cattle rustling would be a problem. After a lot of long, spirited conversations with the Alberta government, an offer was made. The government would let an arbitrator decide. He did. He said the Act should cover the Thiessens, a decision that might help other farmers in the same mess. A cheque was delivered to the Thiessen farm for $74,000.

By the time Hans Terbeek came to us for help, all hope of saving his business, or his home, was dead and buried in a sea of red ink. The Bank of Montreal had demanded immediate payment on a $225,000 business loan, forcing his small steel construction company, Hans Steel, into bankruptcy. Fifty workers lost their jobs. Hans and his wife and family lost their home. They had signed, at one point, to personally guarantee the original company line of credit.

The bank first declared financial war against the Terbeeks in 1982. It had gone to court, and got a judgment against the Terbeeks for $274,000. But the Terbeeks came to us for help in 1995 after that debt, with the interest-meter ticking every day, had climbed to $332,000.

At any time, Hans Terbeek could have declared personal bankruptcy and ended the agony. But he wouldn't. Hans Terbeek was claiming that the bank's figures were all wrong. He said, in fact, the bank owed him money.

Back in 1982, Terbeek had gone to work one day to find a bankruptcy trustee sitting at his desk. Terbeek was out. The trustee would wrap up the business and liquidate to satisfy the court judgment obtained by the Bank of Montreal. But Terbeek's argument then was the same as his argument thirteen years later: The company had enough accounts receivable to pay off the bank debt. If the trustee had done a decent job of collecting on money owing to Hans Steel, the bank would have been paid off, along with all the expenses of bankruptcy, and there would still have been $145,000 left over for Terbeek.

The Bank of Montreal never really listened to that argument. It went ahead with its normal debt collection procedures, even though, at one point, Terbeek convinced an Ontario judge to order the bank to disclose all the accounts receivable information that had been compiled after Terbeek had been show the door. The information was just a bank computer printout that arrived after much delay, and told Terbeek and his lawyer nothing.

And so the argument went on, year after year. The file was passed through the hands of four senior bank officers. At one point, Terbeek got a former neighbour, a retired senior official with the

Office of the Superintendent of Financial Institutions, to try and intercede with the bank.

Despite the fact that Donald MacPherson had been a respected official in the federal government office that supervises and regulates banks, despite the fact that he knew bank presidents by their first names, the Bank of Montreal held its course. MacPherson had written a letter to the then-Chairman and Chief Executive Officer of the Bank of Montreal, Matthew Barrett. It said, in part:

> Dear Matt. I am writing to ask you to intervene in the most bizarre case of indifference and perhaps incompetence that I have ever been involved with, including my long years at the OSFI. In the most dramatic terms, the cases involved the destruction of an honest and hardworking individual over a period of more than ten years. There are also suggestions of deceit, the disregarding of court orders and extremely bad customer management practices on the part of the long series of Bank of Montreal employees.
>
> Hans Steel, indebted to the bank, was placed in receivership in 1982, with Clarkson Gordon, now Ernst &Young, as the receivers. At the time, Mr. Terbeek was given every indication that the liquidation of the company would satisfy all creditors, including the bank.

The rest we know. When we went to the Bank of Montreal in 1995, we faced the same arguments that Terbeek had been facing for many years. Producer John Soroka was as annoying as he could be and still maintain contact with the bank. Soroka had been arguing that, after all was said and done, Terbeek had no real assets, and reminded the bank about the old line that says you can't get blood out of a stone.

Then a new official was assigned this troublesome file and the giant bank started to move, ever so slowly, toward a settlement. Finally, a letter was sent to Terbeek from the Bank of Montreal. The best part of the letter, for Terbeek, said this: "Further to your recent discussions, we confirm that Bank of Montreal is prepared to abandon further pursuit of this indebtedness subject to verification of your insolvency as substantiated by Statutory Declaration of your worldwide Assets, Liabilities, and Income and verified by our internal investigation."

It didn't take long for the Bank to verify that Terbeek's "worldwide assets" were zilch. The Bank of Montreal proclaimed that "further pursuit of this matter would be inappropriate" and blew away the Terbeeks' $332,000 bank debt.

Bob Souchuk's small business in Windsor, Ontario, was a great success. But Bob's health could not have been worse. One day in 1994, his doctor told him he had liver cancer, but no operation was possible. The doctor told him he had six, maybe nine months to live, so he'd better get his life in order.

Bob, a self-made man who had built his own business out of not much more than brain power, sweat, and labour, was not going to go that easily. He told his doctor he wanted a second opinion. He was told that was a waste of time.

"You say you want a second opinion and he says, 'Don't bother, it's not necessary'?" I asked.

"That's right. That's exactly what he said. I was more mad than upset. My wife was crying because of the news. But I was more irritated at the system," said Bob, who later admitted that irritation was a great motivator.

He started researching the type of cancer he had and found out an operation was possible in the United States. So back Bob went to his doctor. The doctor admitted he knew an operation was possible even in London, Ontario, but told Bob the waiting list was too long. The doctor did agree to try and get Bob on the waiting list.

Five weeks later, an increasingly nervous Bob Souchuk discovered his doctor had not even called the London surgeon. Souchuk made a note to himself to get a new doctor, should he survive his current ordeal, drove across the bridge to the United States, and had the life-saving operation in Detroit.

It cost him $80,000 out of his own pocket. But he was alive. Bob came to us because he thought we should know about this gaping hole in the health safety net.

It took three tries before the Ontario Health Ministry agreed to pay for the operation. The first time, the application for financial assistance was refused because there was no real proof that the operation had to be done without further delay.

The rule says, in the best of cold health bureaucratese, that it must be proven "that delay in receiving this service in Ontario would result in medically significant irreversible tissue damage." Bob Souchuk and I grimly agreed that death was certainly irreversible tissue damage.

The second refusal said the U.S. operation was "experimental," and therefore not eligible for coverage. The third time around, a Health Ministry Appeal Board agreed the operation was not experimental and a Health Ministry spokesperson, glad we would not be around to bug her anymore about this case said, "The Ontario Health Insurance Plan will pay 100 percent of the medically necessary services, in terms of whatever bills come in from the hospital and from the physicians." Bob Souchuk was reimbursed more than $80,000.

While $80,000 might be a typical price to pay for a surgical procedure in the Unites States, that amount of money is a bit high for a home telephone bill in Canada.

Sinnathamby Sivakumar had a telephone bill that usually cost him $150 a month. That amount allowed for the occasional call back to his native Sri Lanka.

Imagine the pandemonium that broke out one day when the telephone bill came from Bell and it was 144 pages long, for a grand total of $73,687.45. The bill detailed five thousand calls to adult chat lines. It took some time to explain to the family exactly what these chat lines were all about. The family certainly hadn't made them.

We discovered the calls had been made from a separate apartment downstairs, where a tenant had lived for a few months. When the tenant left behind his unpaid bill, Bell just lumped the bill onto the Sivakumars'. And just as quickly, Bell removed the charges for the family when we explained what had happened, and the fact the tenant in the basement apartment was just that, and not a member of the Sivakumar family.

But it didn't end there. The chat line service provider, Interactive Media Corporation, wanted to sue the Sivakumars for the $73,687.45. Bell assured us they would talk to the company and tell them the family was not responsible for the calls. The huge bill disappeared and the Sivakumars reverted to the more comfortable $150 a month telephone bill.

Incidentally, the guy in the basement wasn't just some yokel out for a good time. He was a scammer. He would call these "976" numbers and be given a personal identification number. At that point, his account would be billed $10. Then the PIN could be used later, from any phone, to access $10 worth of adult chat. So our tenant could walk about with these PINs and sell them in bars and pool halls at much less than the retail price. To him, it was all profit. No way he was going to pay the telephone bill after he skipped out.

Michelle Marion of Prince George, British Columbia, thought the worst of her life was over in 1992, when she survived a near-fatal traffic accident.

The simple fact she had survived was a miracle. Doctors had told her mother that Michelle had a 25 percent chance of pulling through. Well, she did, even though the accident left her partially disabled. It also left her with an insurance settlement of $250,000. Marion invested it with Investors Group. And that's where she met her investment counsellor, Todd Weigel. Then her luck went south again.

Todd Weigel and his wife, Luzmarie Rivera, were friendly. Marion didn't see it right away, but they were too friendly. Marion and her boyfriend and the Weigels went places together. Once they went to Whistler, where they had a great time, and Todd Weigel paid. They all became friends. Friends suspend critical judgment and trust each other.

And so it was that Marion saw nothing suspicious in Weigel's insistence he could make a lot more money for her, if she took her money out of Investors Group and invested it with him, personally, in a company he owned called Ramot Industries. She did, collapsing her investments with Investors Group a little at a time. It became a routine thing to do. Marion's dividend cheques, $1500 a month, kept coming — although at that point, they were being paid by Weigel. So what could be wrong?

The routine became bizarre when Luzmarie Rivera asked to borrow $50,000 from Marion so the Weigels could build a house. Marion even agreed to that. After all, they were friends, and Todd Weigel worked for Investors Group. At the end of several months, Marion had handed over more than $230,000 to the Weigels. Then the ship hit the sand.

Marion discovered that Weigel had left Investors Group just about the same time her dividend cheques stopped coming. Suddenly, it was over. Todd Weigel was gone, nowhere to be found, and Marion's money was gone, too. Weigel had promised to double Michelle Marion's money. All he did was make it disappear.

Through the Internet, one of the newer tools in our Hawk Utility Belts, we found Todd Weigel in a new business venture in Vancouver. He was a smoker, so he was easy to grab as he stood outside his office and puffed away with his smoking staff. We were just a few feet away in a dark-windowed van. I yanked the sliding door open and there we were, all around Weigel as his staff quickly melted away.

"Goldhawk. *CTV News.* Will you talk to me?" I asked a startled Weigel. "Will you talk to me about Michelle Marion in Prince George?"

"Michelle Marion," said Weigel, as if the words were unfamiliar to him.

"You know Michelle Marion."

"Oh, yeah."

"Of course you do. You've got her $230,000. Remember that?"

"No. No comment."

"Is she ever going to get her money back? Can't you at least answer that for us?"

"No comment," said Weigel for a final time, as he disappeared into his office.

When they heard the story and then checked out what we had told them, Investors Group officials, from head office in Winnipeg, reacted quickly. They immediately started paying her monthly $1500 "dividend" cheque until a longer-term solution could be worked out. And it was. Michelle Marion's nest egg was restored.

Marie Moore of Salmon Arm, BC, had the great misfortune to get caught up in the middle of a medical equipment argument. Marie was diagnosed with a brain tumour and travelled to Toronto where she underwent surgery to have it removed. As a matter of routine and safety, not all of the tumour was removed, because part of it was too close to a major artery in the brain.

That was in September of 1994. By 1996, the tumour was starting to grow again. Her neurosurgeon told her the best way to have it removed was with a machine called a gamma knife. The procedure is called stereotactic radiosurgery. The tumour is killed off by gamma rays. Marie's neurosurgeon said it was the only machine accurate enough to do this kind of precision procedure.

Then came all the honking and tweeting from various medical practitioners, doctors, health bureaucrats, and other associated whiners, moaners, flaks, and policy wonks who say "No" for a living. We soon discovered we had stepped into the middle of a war between those who loved and cherished the accuracy and dependability of the gamma knife (not available in Canada) and those who loved the linear accelerator, which was readily available in Canada, but was not the kind of precision tool needed to zap brain tumours afflicting patients such as our Marie Moore.

We helped Moore wade through several layers of appeal, both in British Columbia and in Ontario. We were always there to needle and prod all the players, reminding them that Moore's condition was worsening, and that her severe headaches and numbness had returned with a vengeance.

Then it happened. The Health System twitched like a beached whale and out popped a decision. Marie Moore could have the operation in the United States and the BC Health Ministry would pay. But by then, Moore had already had the gamma knife procedure in the U.S., with financial help from her kind neighbours and fellow citizens in Salmon Arm. Marie was able to pay them back when she got a cheque from the government for $34,948.50.

When Chris Brazeau called me from Pembroke, in Northern Ontario, she was looking out her kitchen window and describing for me what she saw. That was her problem. She was looking at a new fibre board plant that had been built in her part of Pembroke. The plant was hundreds of yards away from her home.

But its presence was felt in her neighbourhood twenty-four hours a day, seven days a week. The plant spewed wood particles. Sometimes they floated through the air like snow. They stuck to everything. You could wash your car three times a day and still it would be dirty by the next morning.

And when the wind was in the right direction, which it usually was, Chris Brazeau and her husband Steve could smell formaldehyde. It made one of their daughters ill. When the plant spewed heavily, parents would order their kids inside, worried what long-term exposure to this treated sawdust-like material used in particle board or fibre board might do.

Inside the computer-controlled, state-of-the-art MacMillan Bloedel plant, we found sympathy for the plant's nearest six neighbours. Workers knew the plant was making life miserable for a few families. They also knew how vital the jobs in the plant were to the local, always fragile economy.

Plant Manager Barry Whitelaw was determined to get his new facility working properly and just as determined to satisfy the neighbours. True enough, the new plant was malfunctioning. Plant designers and builders were working overtime to improve the pollution-control devices. Whitelaw was convinced he could make the plant work efficiently. It wasn't supposed to spew particles of anything. He estimated it would cost another $2 million and take several months to fix the emissions.

Why not just buy out the neighbours and let them move away to keep peace in the Pembroke family in the shorter term? That was our suggestion. It was dismissed. A buyout was not being considered, we were told. It had been raining wood particles almost steadily from the time the plant opened eighteen months earlier, and the

171

residents would just have to wait a few more months — or maybe a year, at most.

Then it happened. It was as if a dam had broken somewhere. Graham Whitelaw sent a letter to the six closest families:

> After giving this matter considerable thought, the Company has decided to offer a package to address the concerns raised in our meeting last week and previously raised with the Company.
>
> The package will consist of either a buyout of your home immediately, at a purchase price to be determined by fair market appraisal, or, an option that may be exercised by you at any time until early 1999. The option would allow you to require MacMillan Bloedel to purchase your home, again at a value to be determined by a fair market appraisal, at any time that you wish between now and early 1999.

Whitelaw also offered the families $5,000 each for out-of pocket legal and moving expenses. The settlement was worth about $750,000. It was the first time we had ever heard of a forestry company buying out its neighbours after complaints about pollution problems.

Complaints about insurance were legion at *Goldhawk Fights Back*. Each of the four of us, even though we were only journalists, carried twenty-five or thirty cases at a time, just as lawyers or social workers might. And in each caseload, you would find several insurance issues. Sometimes they involved a basic misunderstanding of insurance — what it covers and, more importantly, what it does not cover. And sometimes we encountered insurance companies with leaden butts. Drag out the claim. Make the process last a long time. Maybe the customer will give up and go away. Many did.

One insurance problem stands out in front of the pack. It's a story that demonstrates the much-acclaimed but seldom-attained pinnacle of good faith in the marketplace: A promise is a promise.

Evelyn Fantin and the man she was living with back in 1987 agreed that Fantin would take out a life insurance policy on him that would also be a savings-vehicle for her, paying off in her old age. The policy seemed a bit too good to be true, so she made sure she got the branch manager at the Standard Life office in Windsor, Ontario, to spell out all the benefits in a letter. This was the good part:

> The combination of the Protection and Guaranteed Investment Program provides not only savings for retirement but also considerable flexibility in the future. The two combination programs are as follows: $250,000 protection paid up at age 65, with cash accumulation amounting to $284,074. You can take this money in a lump sum or it will also provide $2,840.74 per month for a lifetime pension.

That's what it said. So that's what Fantin believed. Fantin soon became estranged from the man she had been living with, but the policy carried on. And Fantin, a single mother of two, paid her $278 premium every month, without fail, even during those months when money was tight. This was Fantin's nest egg, and nothing was going to deter her from making sure that $284,074 would be there when her friend turned 65 in 2009.

Then Fantin met a retired insurance salesman. He had a look at the policy and the letter and said, indeed, it was way too good to be true. Fantin could not believe what she was being told. She had been so careful to get that payout promise. She checked with several people at Standard Life and the sad truth came out. The policy in 2009 would be worth about $98,000, just a little more than a third of what she had expected.

She wrote letters of complaint to Standard Life and then to the Life Underwriters Association. It forwarded her letter to the Ontario Insurance Commission. And the commission forwarded her letter back to Standard Life. That little bit of buck passing took two years.

We went to Standard Life's ombudsman in Montreal. Maurice Marchand was sympathetic but definite in his assessment of that golden letter from the branch manager. Marchand said the $284,000 amount was dead wrong. "That's why the letter is concise and vague in some aspects, and confusing," said Marchand, who appeared to be running out of adjectives.

I offered my own quote from the letter: "'You can take this money in a lump sum or it will also provide $2,840.74 per month for a lifetime pension.' That part's not confusing."

"From the client's perspective, it certainly isn't," said Marchand.

The Fantin case went back into the Standard Life appeal hopper one more time. Officials drafted an offer. But the president of Standard Life rejected it as inadequate.

Then came a much better offer. Fantin got an amendment to her policy that guaranteed a value of $284,000 in 2009. Standard stopped short of offering Fantin the choice of a $2,840 per month pension for life. They did the math on that one. Fantin will be fifty-eight in 2009. At age seventy-five, Standard Life would have paid out well over half a million dollars on that policy.

But Fantin won big time on the policy itself. The company will inject an extra $186,000 into her policy by 2009, making it worth $284,000. To Standard Life, a promise was a promise.

No amount of money can replace a father or mother, a husband or wife, a sister or brother. But money can buy, or at least rent, some comfort and security. Money is usually the only hard and fast proof we've got that something unfair, unjust, unkind, unexpected, unethical, immoral, or illegal happened.

No one is quite sure what happened inside the Federal Government's Mulock Building, at Jarvis and Dundas streets in Toronto. We did discover this: At least twenty of the men and women who worked there from 1975 to 1990 died of cancer. The total included three Royal Canadian Mounted Police officers.

The three men had worked together in the same small office in the building. All three of them died of the same rare brain cancer within eighteen months of each other. It was all too outrageous to be a coincidence. It took years for us to demonstrate for the federal government that the polluted air in the old building triggered the cancer that killed them.

It meant that lifetime pensions were granted to each of the three widows. The pensions will average out at $500,000 each over the next twenty years or so. It was a huge victory for the widows, after they had all been told the deaths were not linked in any way, but nothing changed the cruel fact that three strong, healthy cops in their late 40s or early 50s were killed by their jobs.

8.

Bring the Dog

In our nine-year battle against the CTV suits, their minions, the bad guys, and the bureaucratic bozos, we still found the time to wonder about what it was that we did, and what we needed to do the job well. Sure, we helped people get what they deserve, but that was more of a book title than a job description.

We were often asked if we were investigative journalists or consumer journalists. We said no to both. The mention of "investigative journalist" drove me nuts and usually provoked a small performance whenever I heard it. What was the alternative? Did any of us actually want to be non-investigative journalists? Wasn't a journalist, by her very description, supposed to be investigative? I mean, what else is there? I had come to the conclusion that there were really only two kinds of journalists: investigative and decorative. Since I was definitely not decorative, I must be investigative by default.

Any good, experienced, working journalist can dig out the facts, follow a money trail, tell a tough story. All that is needed is the one thing many editors will not allow their reporters to have — time. You can't catch a bad guy in a day. You can't get the goods on a politician during normal working hours. It might take a week. Maybe longer. Maybe never. That's the investment in time, the gamble that news organizations must make if they want to turn their own reporters into "investigative" reporters.

It's much easier to build a consumer reporter out of spare parts found in any television newsroom. Consumer reporters are, more often than not, shoppers. They tell you what to buy. A recent consumer television report in Toronto compared the relative merits of toasters. There was one notable model that came equipped with see-through sides so you could watch your bread get brown. No need to wait for the toast to pop up in our instant gratification world. Watch the toasting process as it happens.

The reporter did note, as his voice became grave with concern, that not all toast was toasted evenly and that the toaster's record with bagels was "spotty." The story ended with the consumer reporter offering the opinion that a see-through toaster, priced at $90, might not be "worth the dough."

So what does a good investigative reporter, by default, need? What tools are essential? At *Goldhawk Fights Back,* we always felt we were armed, mainly, with attitude, guts, and strong bladders. Wardrobe wasn't a problem.

But we did need (or at least went through) a lot of communications equipment. Cellphones needed to be able to withstand a scuffle in a back alley, a bounce off a brick wall, a drop from a good height, and come with enough spare batteries to keep us talking for at least twenty-four hours in one stretch. The same went for walkie-talkies and for wireless microphones.

The thing that gave us the most trouble, in the early days, was a hidden camera. Actually, we didn't have a hidden camera. We could have bought a sneaky-cam kit, built into a snazzy briefcase, for $40,000, but the mere mention of that kind of money in a single equipment expenditure made our financial comptroller's socks roll up and down.

We wondered about whether or not it was a wise purchase anyway. How could we take a snazzy briefcase into a draught room in Outlook, Saskatchewan? Wouldn't a briefcase look a little out of place on my lap bouncing along in a pickup truck through the desert wasteland of the Blood Indian Reserve in Alberta? How could any of us play the part of a gullible investor, standing there with a snazzy briefcase while some Oil Can Harry gives us the once-over, scanning for those out to con a conner?

We needed flexible, cheap equipment. So I made it myself. Step by step. Trial and error. We tried to make all the dumb mistakes early to get them out of the way. I assembled our sneaky-cam gear part by part.

We got a good, tiny microphone, which I fit into the clip end of a fine-line magic marker. It could be worn in a shirt pocket, a lapel pocket, or clipped into the outside pocket of any bag or purse.

The camera was nothing more than a chip or two embedded in a square plastic box about the size of a pocket-sized box of wooden matches. The lens was a tiny peephole in the middle of the box that automatically focussed a color image. The trick was to make it invisible in a piece of clothing.

We tried anchoring it to the inside of a large-knit sweater by a piece of yarn that inevitably got into the picture. And what good is a large-knit sweater in August?

I then attached the camera to a flat silver pin that Laurie could wear on her shirt or jacket. The camera peephole saw through the tiny lattice work of a trellis embossed on the pin, with a man leaning nonchalantly against it. It could have been Humphrey Bogart. It was a weird pin, to be sure. But everybody looked at it. We collected dozens of "I really like your pin" comments from staring women in elevators. The men stared, too. All of our hidden camera subjects were caught looking right into the camera.

But the Humphrey Bogart kit had its problems. The pin, with its camera backing on the inside of the jacket or shirt, was heavy, and kept slipping out of place.

The accompanying battery packs and digital recording deck equipment were strapped on to Laurie, creating suspicious bulges. We had tried wireless gear, where the camera sends a video signal to a nearby receiver, but it was always our experience that the signal would cut out momentarily, just as we were about to discover who killed Aunt Nelly.

And to get a picture, Laurie had to be pointed in the right direction. Conversations, we were soon reminded, seldom took place with both people standing and facing each other directly. We got a lot of sound in those days, accompanied by shots of furniture and the occasional hand moving through the frame for emphasis. Finally, we gave up on body packs and went back to cases.

I installed the gear in a small, nondescript bag, and we took it to Montreal to bag the fortune teller lady who removed curses for a price. I had read a sad letter from a woman I will call Anna, about her mother. Her mother had been having problems with Anna's alcoholic, unemployed father. Her mother went to the parish priest for help. He said to pray and then pray some more. Her mother then saw an advertisement in an Italian community newspaper. Translated from Italian, it said: "Signora Lidiana speaks Italian. Helps to resolve problems of love, marriage and any other concerns. She will show you results. Removes the Evil Eye and curses. Satisfaction from the first moment."

Anna's mom went for an appointment. It cost her $40. The next appointment cost $140. Then came the third visit. Anna wrote in her letter to me:

> By the third visit, Lidiana only let my mother in her home because she said I was too young to understand the situation. So I waited in the car while my mother divulged more information about her situation. About an hour later, I see my mother horrified, terrified, shaking, telling me that an evil curse had been placed on my father...she asked my mother to go home and take an egg and do certain things with it.

Anna's mother had been told to take an egg from her refrigerator, wash it, and put it in a shoebox under her bed for one week. Then she was to bring the egg to Signora Lidiana. The signora broke the egg, revealing some kind of black, hairy looking thing inside. Anna's mother was instantly horrified and convinced of the existence of the curse. After all, the egg had come from her own home. It cost $8,000 to remove the curse, payable in cash to the signora. Interestingly enough, $8,000 was exactly what Anna's mother had in her savings account. It must have been revealed to Lidiana in those long, private conversations.

When Anna found out what had happened, she went to a lawyer and called us at the same time. The result was that Lidiana sent $5,500 in cash, in a paper bag, to the lawyer's office. The lawyer took out $600 for his own trouble and gave Anna's mom the remaining $4,900.

The bug-in-the-egg scam is an old one, but it usually works. It's so horrifying. When Lidiana was handed the egg from a client's home, she also had, tucked between her fingers, a wad of brown bread, wrapped tightly in the middle by black thread. When Lidiana broke the egg with a finger, she pushed the "bug" into the centre of the yolk. I tried it in the office several times. It was a simple trick to master. The results were impressive, especially if you didn't know what was going on — or if you had been told somebody put a curse on your family.

We wanted to make the egg trick famous and put our own TV curse on Signora Lidiana. How many other elderly people had been impressed enough by the egg trick to hand over money?

Normally, Laurie would be the one to go in alone on these missions, with the crew and me monitoring from hiding, outside. My well-known television face was a dead giveaway for this kind of gumshoe work. But we knew that Signora Lidiana usually had several people in her house, including at least one or two large, menacing men who would doubtless come in handy in case there were any misbehaving clients. So I made the decision to go in with her. Our crew would not be in Montreal until the next day.

I bought some hair gel and gave myself Ernie Eves hair, slicked down so tightly I would have remained well-groomed in a wind tunnel. Then I put on some Henry Kissinger glasses and practiced carrying myself as if I were a nerdy, non-threatening Caspar Milquetoast. We practiced Laurie's cover story several times. Signora Lidiana was far from a fool. It would have to be good.

Laurie's boyfriend had been killed in a tragic accident. He was a coast to coast itinerant drug salesman and one dark, stormy, icy night, his expensive SUV slid off the Trans-Canada Highway just east of Thunder Bay, and he was killed. Laurie just couldn't get over the fact that he was gone. I was the commiserating mutual friend. Laurie called and made a tearful appointment.

A huge hulk answered the door of the dump where Lidiana told us to come. He led us, without a word, to a bedroom on the other side of a large, central room that was filled with incongruous, expensive leather furniture. Little Lidiana was waiting for us at the doorway into her room. Smiling, she let us inside. There were no chairs.

Lidiana sat on the bed, in the middle, and gestured for us to sit on each side of her. I was carrying the sneaky-cam in the bag, and placed it on the floor near my feet, with the lens pointing up toward Lidiana. It looked perfect. Laurie began her story in a low wail. She had been worried she might peak in grief a little early, so she was starting out slowly.

I just played it dumb and sympathetic. Every once in a while, I would grunt in agreement. The surroundings were bizarre. Every inch of flat surface, including much of the floor, was covered in candles and religious statues.

There were a lot of Blessed Virgin Marys, some small as a Pekingese, some large as a German Shepherd. There were a lot of Jesus statues too, and countless other, unidentified saints. The furniture was best described as heavy European. *Maybe it was from Transylvania*, I remember thinking, as Laurie wailed on, with a concerned, nodding Lidiana seemingly hanging on every word.

The wallpaper could have easily been seventy-five years old, the parts of it I could see in between the religious pictures and dozens of crucifixes. Probably twenty or thirty candles were burning, the smell of hot beeswax heavy in the air. *Hell*, I thought, *pulling a bug out of an egg in here would be a real attention-grabber.*

I looked down at the silent bag, hoping it was recording, although I started to get worried that Laurie was running long. All we had on tape was her performance; Lidiana had said little so far. Laurie was in full flight now, sobbing uncontrollably. Lidiana put a comforting arm around Laurie as she wrapped up her sad tale, now truly out of breath from a stellar lament. Lidiana began her soft, soothing pitch. She could help, she was sure. More visits would be needed.

She told us the story of how her own husband had died of a heart attack, and how before he died, a pacemaker had been installed by doctors.

"And you know," she said, looking at me, "they put that pacemaker right in here," raising her hand and clamping it down hard on my leg, just above my knee.

"In there?" I asked, incredulously as I heard Laurie snort and then wrench it into another loud wail.

"Yes," said Lidiana, as if she were revealing a horrible medical secret for the first time. Then she turned back to comfort a newly-agitated Laurie who was sobbing in staccato bursts now, doing her best not to laugh, her hands covering her face. I kept shaking my head in amazement, trying to force a kind of dumbfoundedness into my voice that I hoped would cover up any mirth trying to leak out.

Lidiana was keen to make another appointment for Laurie. We did and left, morosely, with deep thanks to Lidiana who charged us the usual $40 first-time rate. As soon as we were back to the car, we checked the sneaky-cam. It hadn't worked. The angle was all wrong. All we had was a sideways shot of the Blessed Virgin Mary. The bag was too floppy. There was a bit of useable audio.

We put the story on the air and immediately heard from two daughters who told much the same story as Anna. In all three cases, the elderly mothers had held onto their deep belief that a curse had been at work in their lives. If nothing else, the story demonstrated for them — and others who might be roped in by Lidiana — that the bad egg was just a cheap trick with an expensive price tag.

Getting the sneaky-cam gear to work was becoming an obsession. One day, I saw it as I was walking by a luggage store — a small, gender-neutral case you might sling over your shoulder to carry a wallet, or notes, or even your lunch. It had a lot of outside pockets — big ones for newspapers, small ones for a pen, pencil, or a certain wired-for-sound fine-line marker.

Now I was inspired. I bought a small digital video camera with a connection that would also record a video signal from another camera. I fitted the digital camera tightly into a rigid plastic case and fitted it with plugs that would connect the digital camera inside with the chip camera, microphone, and battery packs hidden elsewhere in the bag.

The chip camera was sewn permanently into an outside pocket. The pinhole lens was fastened to the centre of a brass grommet in the middle of the pocket, allowing it to see. To make sure the grommet looked like nothing more than a fashion statement, I fastened other grommets all over the bag, in a uniform design. Then I painted the grommets black to match the bag's nylon covering. I left two pockets in the bag as they were, so the bag operator could actually use it for practical purposes, further obscuring, I hoped, the bag's true purpose.

It worked like a charm. The bag got dropped, bumped, plunked down on counter tops, and nothing ever came loose. It was tough and dependable. And in an emergency, the digital camera could be removed from the bag and unplugged from its bag wiring in just a few seconds, giving us an extra camera when the big one just wasn't around.

The little camera could also see in the dark. We could shoot a licence plate or a document in total darkness, and the resulting green picture would be illuminated by infrared lights on the camera. The lens would allow us to focus in to a specific paragraph, or even a few words, on a page.

The case had a little dog embossed on the label. So that's what we called it — The Dog. "Better bring The Dog on this one," we would remind ourselves. One day we took The Dog hunting in Barrie, Ontario. We were after con artists, as usual.

Five senior citizens in Barrie had invested about $85,000 in an off-shore investment scheme that promised to give them a remarkable 30 percent return on their money. As if. A few interest payments were made, then the money sort of disappeared. Eighty-nine-year-old Alex Carrigan was hurt the most. He invested $50,000. It was all the money he had — his retirement savings from working as a bus driver in Glasgow, Scotland for more than thirty years.

Carrigan had seen an ad in his favourite local newspaper, called *Seniors Plus*. "The *Seniors Plus* paper was for seniors, you know, trying to help them as best they can," Carrigan told me. "I thought, I can't do any wrong here — going and putting my money in here."

Carrigan called the newspaper, and Publisher Wally Moran dropped by Carrigan's apartment to tell him about the investment. It was called, according to Moran, a Guaranteed Insurance Investment Certificate. Carrigan's investments and profits would be guaranteed under this scheme, according to a story Moran wrote, praising the program, in his own newspaper. An appointment was made for the next day.

Carrigan went to the *Seniors Plus* newspaper office where Moran introduced him to Philip James Peacock, a man who normally sold top-soil and used cars in Barrie. Carrigan gave Peacock $50,000 to invest. He made the cheques out to Peacock personally, a mistake to be sure. Carrigan got a couple of dividend payments — in cash. Peacock would just drop it off in a paper bag. Carrigan asked him why he didn't send a cheque, and Peacock told him they didn't deal in cheques.

The money trail wandered all over the place. Peacock said he gave the money to Ian Stanley Anderson, a so-called offshore investor involved with a company called Highland Financial Corporation that operated internationally. Then Anderson told me that Peacock just kept the money himself. The bottom line was uncomplicated — the $85,000, including Carrigan's $50,000, was gone.

So we went looking for refunds. We dropped in on Peacock's top-soil outlet. He hid in the back room when he saw the camera crew through his front window.

Laurie and I sauntered into the store, Laurie carrying The Dog, looped carelessly over one shoulder. I engaged Peacock in conversation as she put The Dog down on the counter, leaning on it as if it were just another piece of junk she was required to carry around in her line of work.

As Peacock and I chatted, he moved to a chair, so Laurie realigned The Dog to follow the action. Peacock insisted the money had gone to Anderson and that this whole affair had caused him quite a bit of stress. He allowed that he felt sorry for the five investors, one of whom had died after handing over his money.

"I'm dealing with his wife," said Peacock. "And I've been doing that since Christmas. He died right around Christmas. I've had a hell of a time. Brings tears to your eyes, when you think about it," added a dry-eyed Peacock.

We tracked Ian Anderson down to a beautiful cottage in Central Ontario. Crew and all, we marched on the front door, The Dog in tow. Anderson, a large, pear-shaped man, opened the door and waved off the camera crew. He would talk to us inside, but the crew would have to wait on the porch. Fair enough.

In we went. Anderson breezily dismissed this whole brouhaha as if it were almost too trivial for him to deal with — oh he of the millions and millions, or so he said. This sure wasn't much of a news story, he said. *Well, it might not feel like a big news story now,* I said to myself. *Just wait until we stick it in your ear.*

With The Dog rolling, Anderson went all magnanimous on us, explaining that he did not have the money, did not really know where it went, and that probably Peacock had it. Anderson admitted that all this publicity was a bad thing.

"I'll give you back the $85,000 or I'll put up the $85,000 to stop this," he said.

That's the promise that went on television, but no money ever flowed from Anderson. Soon, Police in Barrie were interested in the case. After an investigation, they charged Peacock and Anderson with an assortment of twenty-eight offences, including fraud. But by then, Anderson had moved to Prince Edward Island. Barrie Police were not sure of his location on the Island. They were reluctant to send officers to PEI on what could have been a wild goose chase.

That didn't stop us. We went to PEI, located and recorded two residence addresses, a place of business (he was about to begin operating a limousine service in Charlottetown), and tracked down a full description, including plate number, for his black SUV.

Then we tracked down Anderson himself, as he sat idling in a supermarket parking lot, near Murray Harbour North. No Dog this time. We parked at the other end of the lot. I bailed out quickly and began a fast walk to the SUV. Jennifer and the crew approached from a different angle, keeping the equipment low to the ground so Anderson could not spot us coming. Suddenly, I popped up at his open window; a second later, the crew was there too.

"You lost?" asked Anderson, always the cool guy.

"No. Are you?"

"No. I'm home. Please take that (camera) out of my face."

"It's not in your face."

"Yes, it is."

"I'm sorry. We're not turning it off."

Anderson rolled up the window and drove off. The next time we saw him, a few weeks later, he was in police custody back in Toronto. He had only rude comments for us that time.

Anderson and Peacock pleaded guilty to fraud and were convicted. Alex Carrigan's family hired a lawyer and sued Anderson, Peacock, and Publisher Moran. Peacock had already paid some money back to Carrigan, the result of a restitution order during the criminal trial. Ian Anderson was bankrupt for a second time, this time owing creditors more than $1 million, so there was no blood in that stone. And Moran, not charged criminally, had forever declared himself both innocent and penniless.

In the civil trial, Mr. Justice Peter Howden of the Ontario Superior Court, ordered Walter James Moran to pay $88,000 in damages to the Carrigan family. Moran said at the time that he was appealing the award but remained broke.

In his judgment, Justice Howden said of Moran and *Seniors Plus*:

> This is not simply a case of a newspaper merely taking an advertisement and being careless about the facts. In this case, Moran actively participated in the fraudulent scheme in using his and his publication's position of trust with elderly readers by falsely representing the scheme, meeting the prospects, encouraging them to pay into the scheme, acting as the continuing contact person thereafter, being present for the pitch to obtain the money, seeking to personally and corporately profit from it, and later trying to cover by denying to the plaintiff's son and daughter-in-law that he ever knew much about it at all.
>
> Detective Carson (Barrie Police) stated that the only reason that Mr. Moran was not charged with fraud, in addition to Peacock and Anderson was that the prosecution needed a witness with knowledge of the whole scheme and that was Moran. Detective Carson had recommended to the prosecutor that he be charged.

Our contact with Moran throughout this story was a hit-and-miss affair. In the beginning, he would never submit to an interview. He refused several times to even talk to us on the telephone. When we went to his newspaper office, he called the Barrie Police, who threatened to ticket us for illegal parking. Later, when we sat outside his house in Orillia, he called the Orillia Police, who showed up, shook their heads, and left. We shook our heads and left, too, thinking we had seen the last of Wally Moran.

About two years later, in April of 2001, we were back in Barrie, listening to the details of yet another fine investment opportunity for seniors. At least it sounded fine and looked fine as an advertisement in the *Seniors Plus* newspaper. The ad read:

> Ask yourself the following question: Can you afford to lose the money you have invested in equity mutual funds or in the stock market? Would your lifestyle, your security, your peace of mind be affected if you did lose your invested funds? Of course it would.
>
> There isn't room in this ad to give you the details but if you wish to receive more information on getting a much better return on your money and with excellent security, I would ask that you contact me at the address below to set up an appointment and get this information for yourself.

And who is this "me" in the ad? Wally Moran, of course.

John Banning of Barrie was one of thirty investors Moran had found for his latest investment scheme. In partnership with International Realty and Financial Consultants, Moran was promoting mortgage investment opportunities in a run-down section of Canton, Ohio.

The idea was that a renovator would take out a high-interest mortgage on an abandoned dump of a house, fix it all up, sell it, and pay off his mortgage, like real fast. The problem for John Banning was that the renovator just walked away from his mortgage. The Bannings were the proud owners of a dump of little value. Canton city officials told us that a lot of houses in that industrial neighbourhood were mortgaged with Canadian money. Officials were worried some of the houses would have to be demolished, they were in such bad shape. And Canton officials had no faith in many of the renovators who had bought some of the abandoned houses, no faith they would be able to fix them up well enough to pass current building standards.

Sure, it was possible to make good money with these mortgages that were being shilled by Moran. But they hardly lived up to the "better return on your money and… excellent security" standards in the ad.

John and Margaret Banning were deeply worried about their financial loss. Then John Banning died, leaving behind Margaret, who was deaf, to fend for herself the best she could. With the help of the legendary founder of the Rumball Centre for the Deaf in Toronto, Reverend Bob Rumball, we heard about the details of the investment deal with Moran.

Margaret Banning had hired a lawyer to deal with the Canton property mess. We went to look for answers from a man who seldom gave us many, Wally Moran.

We had absolutely no faith that Moran would agree to talk, especially on camera. So we waited near his office, hoping he might go for a walk. He did. He was not happy to see us. He immediately called the police on his cellphone. I told Moran I wanted to talk about the Banning situation. I told him that I had been talking to Margaret Banning about the investment that went south. Moran snorted. He wanted to know how I talked to Margaret Banning, since she was deaf. I just shook my head. Such sensitivity. It was overpowering. Then he said to me, with a wry smile, "Why don't you talk to John Banning?"

"That's very funny," I said. "He's dead."

"I know," said Moran, "he's a friend of mine — was a friend of mine."

Moran had written a letter to a lawyer in town, who was chasing him to pay the $88,000 in damages awarded to the Carrigan family. In the letter, Moran was again proclaiming his innocence in the Peacock/Anderson scam. Moran wrote, "Why would I deal in a penny-ante scam like Peacock's?" In another part of the letter he says, "Just by way of making my point, my readers have nearly $2 million invested currently in U.S.-based mortgages returning 18 percent plus closing penalties. Not a penny of those funds are (sic) at risk. I've had as much as $120,000 U.S. in my pocket at one time."

And yet, there was never any money to compensate the Bannings. And the Carrigans are still waiting for their $88,000, as well. In a later interview with Moran, I asked him about the money.

"Why haven't you made any money?" I asked. "Why do you wind up penniless, if you're so smart?"

"Great question," said Moran with a smile. "I'll decline to answer it."

9.

Banking on Insurance

For many of us, insurance is a fickle creature. It never seems to be the right kind. It's hard to know what it covers and what it doesn't cover. It has a bad habit of not being there when we need it most. Even if we can find the policy, it's impossible to wade through all the legal gibberish and babble to know what it means. If we buy the insurance through a bank, and we buy a lot of insurance there, we're only dealing with the monkey, not the guy hand-cranking the music box. Then to round out our long list of peeves, if we make a claim on our car insurance or our house insurance, the premiums just go up, anyway.

We do need, however, to make a few concessions to the insurance weenies. There are some immutable truths about insurance. Insurance is an exact science. Either you're covered or, more likely, you're not. Just because you paid insurance for years without a claim means nothing. It gets you sweet bugger-all. Insurance is protection. When it expires, you buy more. Insurance is a business that strives for big profits. Insurance is logical, fact-based, and riddled with numerical tables. There is little art or compassion in the efficiency-driven world of insurance. Additionally, there is no crying in insurance — well, there is, but nobody really listens, despite all the patented insincerities voiced by people who are hired to say "No" as frequently as they can. I say all these things in fairness to the insurance industry before sticking a fork in its ample rear end.

Nancy and Frank Wettlaufer got a bank loan at the Bank of Nova Scotia in 1995. The loans officer strongly recommended that the loan be life insured, for their own protection. As Nancy said to me, months later, "They said, 'You should really take out life insurance. It does cost you a little bit extra, but in the event something should happen to one of you, then one person doesn't have to pay (the loan) on their own.'"

When the Wettlaufers signed their loan and insurance forms at the bank, there was the usual "pre-existing condition qualification" box to be checked off. Essentially, the Wettlaufers verified that neither of them, in the last twelve months, had visited a doctor to take tests or receive treatment for "cancer, leukemia, AIDS, lung disease, liver disease or heart disease." At the time, Frank Wettlaufer mentioned that he had been to his doctor a few days earlier to be told he had pneumonia, and the doctor put him on antibiotics. That produced no reaction from the loans officer, as Nancy recalled to me later, so the whole process was completed.

But the pneumonia did not go away. Later, chest X-rays revealed a tumour. A diagnosis of cancer was confirmed in a biopsy on September 15th, 1995, a month and a half after the Wettlaufers got their loan.

Both Frank and Nancy were upbeat, even after the diagnosis. Frank was confident he could beat the disease with treatment, but his condition worsened. He died on May 4, 1996. A few weeks later, Nancy went to the bank to fill out a claim form for the life insurance on the loan.

The reaction from Canada Life was almost lightning-like. Within a day or two, a letter was sent to Nancy to tell her the company would be checking out the circumstances of Frank's death with his doctor.

Two weeks later, a second letter rejected Nancy's claim. No benefits were payable, said the letter, because Frank had been treated for lung cancer before he signed the loan. Wettlaufer's visit to the doctor and the diagnosis of pneumonia was being considered by Canada Life as a treatment for lung cancer, even though lung cancer was not diagnosed until six weeks later. In conversations we had with Canada Life, we were told that Frank Wettlaufer should have somehow known he had cancer.

An internal Canada Life report details the conversation an angry Nancy Wettlaufer had had with Canada Life officials. Note in particular the ass-covering parts and obvious company handling methods being employed to properly process Nancy Wettlaufer. The parenthetical remarks are mine:

Mr. Wettlaufer did see his doctor on July 31, 1995 (a few days before the loan was signed) as indicated by Mrs. Wettlaufer. However, in addition to prescribing an antibiotic, the doctor was sufficiently concerned by the symptoms exhibited by Mr. Wettlaufer that a chest X-ray was done August 2, 1995. The findings from that chest X-ray led to a second X-ray on August 14, 1995 and further testing resulted in a formal diagnosis of cancer by the end of August, 1995. (But the biopsy results, indicating a positive for cancer were not known until two weeks later).

Although the formal diagnosis did not occur until after the loan was written, the investigation that led to the diagnosis started on July 31, 1995, four days prior to the date of the loan. We therefore maintain our decision to decline the claim based on the pre-existing condition exclusion.

On June 11, 1996, Olivia (from Canada Life) spoke to Mrs. Wettlaufer after the claims examiner was unable to satisfy Mrs. Wettlaufer's concern about the claims decision. Olivia explained to Mrs. Wettlaufer how the pre-existing condition exclusion works, but Mrs. Wettlaufer was upset and not prepared to accept the explanation.

In the course of the conversation Mrs. Wettlaufer indicated that she would see a lawyer and would go the Bank to let them know "what Canada Life was doing to her." Olivia explained that she was free to seek legal counsel and voice her concerns to the bank, standard procedure in this type of conversation, but unless the information that the doctor gave us was incorrect or incomplete, we would not be able to reverse our decision. This seemed to upset Mrs. Wettlaufer further. Olivia did not cut off further conversation, nor did she hang up. She simply restated the Canada Life position and let Mrs.

Wettlaufer know that there was nothing further
Canada Life could do, given the medical history.

When we first went to Canada Life, we were turned down flat. We
were told that Frank Wettlaufer had a pre-existing medical condition
that disqualified the claim, despite the fact the Wettlaufers knew nothing about it, and the doctor, who may have had his suspicions that he
kept to himself, didn't really know about it until several weeks later.

We suggested that maybe the words "and anything else of a medical nature that might be construed as suspicious, curious, or even
thought-provoking" should be added to the pre-existing condition
clause. Canada Life did not see the humour in the suggestion. We said
we were going ahead to tell this story on television, even though we
were not able to assist Nancy Wettlaufer.

A few days after that, we got a letter from Canada Life, which said
that the Wettlaufer case had been reviewed by the company's internal
review process. "This is our internal review charged with determining
whether decisions on contested claims have been correctly determined, are fair, and so forth," wrote a company spokesperson.

"We have concluded that the claim should be paid. It was felt that
both the timing of the events surrounding Mr. Wettlaufer's diagnosis
and the wording of the pre-existing clause were factors that could be
open to interpretation to the benefit of the policy holder. A cheque has
been forwarded to Mrs. Wettlaufer."

Reg and Jean Seaborne of St. Catharines, Ontario, knew all about insurance. They studied policies before buying them. They usually knew
exactly how they were protected, and by whom. For them, the most
important kind of insurance protection they could buy was insurance on
their mortgage, the single biggest debt most of us will ever have.

Before they renewed their mortgage with the Royal Bank of
Canada, the Seabornes had always had both life insurance and disability insurance. It was, for Reg and Jean, an important safeguard for both
of them, in case something happened. So the mortgage was renewed in
1991, same conditions, same bank branch, same loans officer as the

previous mortgage. Everything was in place once again. All the documents appeared to be in order.

Then the worst thing happened. Reg had a nervous breakdown. It triggered a heart attack. He was disabled. After the initial concerns for Reg's health were addressed, Jean went to the Royal Bank to make arrangements to claim against their disability insurance. It wasn't there. The Royal told the Seabornes that no disability insurance had been offered in 1991. They only had life insurance.

The Seabornes, always careful with this kind of thing, could not believe it. They had not been told. If they had been told, they would have bought some disability insurance elsewhere. Nothing is worse that believing you are insured when you are not.

Suddenly, the Seabornes were in deep financial trouble. They knew they couldn't pay their $166,000 mortgage. They had been left unprotected and faced with the prospect of selling their home. The stress just made things much tougher for Reg. His condition deepened as the "For Sale" sign went up on their front lawn. Everything was seeping away — their financial independence and, to Reg, his dignity.

The Royal Bank was selling insurance on its mortgage as a sideline. That's usually the way it works. The insurance is brought into the deal by a loans officer who works for a bank, not an insurance company. The loans officer, understandably, knows all about mortgages, and maybe not all that much about insurance. You just check the right boxes and move on to sign the mortgage.

Since all other conditions had been the same as the last mortgage, the Seabornes made a dangerous assumption about how they were covered, ably abetted by bank officials who said nothing to the Seabornes. Sure, disability insurance was not available. A Royal customer could have read that information in a pamphlet. But nobody, say the Seabornes, told them.

So that's the argument we took to the Royal Bank. David Moorcroft, the vice-president of public affairs, did concede there might be room for confusion, but still insisted that if you looked at all the mortgage documents, you would come to the conclusion that there was no disability insurance. It was shaky, soggy ground for either side of the argument. Moorcroft did promise the bank would try to work out a solution.

First, the Royal went to Prudential Life Insurance Company of America to see if Reg Seaborne's claim would have been accepted if he had had disability insurance. Prudential said yes, it was an acceptable claim. So the Royal went halfway with the Seabornes. It reduced the $166,000 mortgage to $58,000 and adjusted the monthly payments accordingly. Clarity cost the Royal $58,000, but it meant the "For Sale" sign came off the front yard at the Seabornes.

Pamela Webb of Toronto promised herself she would not drop the battle she was having with an insurance company. On November 8, 1994, she wrote me this eloquently passionate letter:

> I do not know where else to turn with this. I even had to stop for a while because I thought I would have a nervous breakdown. But I cannot let this drop.
>
> My husband David worked for Atlantic Packaging as a tractor-trailer driver for seventeen years. David suffered two heart attacks in those seventeen years, and after his second heart attack, because of the damage done to his heart, he was told he could never work again and he had to have a quadruple bypass. They weren't sure his heart would start again after that but, thank God, he pulled through.
>
> So my husband was getting a disability pension from the Federal Government and a long-term disability pension from Great West Life, through his work. Then in October, 1992, we got a letter from Great West Life stating they thought he was capable of working, at a sedentary job, so he would not get any more long-term benefits.
>
> My husband did not have an illness that got better with time, and stress is one of the things you must avoid with a heart condition. We were appealing this decision with Great West. And then we had to move to a cheaper apartment on June 30, 1993. My

husband of twenty-five years died of a heart attack that night.

I phoned Great-West Life and told them that because of the stress they put my husband through he had died, and I took up his appeal. I was told, three times, the disability insurance had been denied because they thought he was capable of working. And by denying his appeal, they can also deny paying his life insurance.

I am forty-two years old, and I feel as though my life stopped on June 30, 1993. I owe his sisters for his funeral, and to this day, he still does not have a headstone.

I didn't understand why Great-West had also denied the life insurance claim, until I read David Webb's Group Benefit Plan. Under the Life Insurance for Employees section, it said, "Application for an individual conversion policy must be made within thirty-one days after termination of insurance." It sounded harmless enough, but what it meant was this: Great-West had cancelled Webb's disability payments. It meant that Webb had only thirty-one days to apply for a conversion policy, an individual life insurance policy for which he would have had to pay the premiums.

All well and good and fair, but nobody told the Webb family about this little clause. The system must have been making the assumption that in cases such as this, workers were glued to their policy benefit plan booklet, having read and understood every word.

Normally with insurance, there is a legal duty to inform a customer when the insurance has been cancelled. This rule of law applies to any kind of insurance — car, house, or life.

But that rule, we discovered, was complicated — and perhaps nullified — by the fact that this was a group insurance plan, where those individual insurance rules do not necessarily apply. We were told by a law professor familiar with insurance issues that the insurance company has no duty to inform those insured if the policy is a group policy. And the group insurance policy company usually considers the employer to be its customer, not the employees. The law in this area, we were told, is "murky."

Murky or not, we asked Great-West Life to review the case. It did, and sent this note to the Webb family: "Although Great-West Life has no liability for this claim, we are prepared to consider a settlement on compassionate grounds." The settlement was $21,000, plus interest to the time of David Webb's death.

Daughter Darlene said to me, "I wanted them to consider my father a person. Not just a number, a policy number. And a lot of the money will be used to put a stone on his grave and to finish paying for the funeral."

When Gary and Jackie Yuill, of Listowel, Ontario, came to us, they were still in mourning over the loss of their daughter. A bright, promising architecture student, Jennifer Yuill died of a sudden, severe asthma attack in the summer of 1997. Jennifer had two student loans. One was life insured, the other was not. The local branch of the Bank of Nova Scotia, where the uninsured loan had been taken out, at first told Jennifer's parents that the loan would not have to be repaid. Then the branch found out the money *would* have to be repaid. After all, Gary Yuill had co-signed the loan. The Yuills didn't have a spare $9,000 lying around.

The news that the Yuills would have to pay was delivered in a bankly kind of way, draped in a flag of glad tidings. This is how Jackie Yuill described her conversation with a local bank official: "She wanted us to re-mortgage our house with them. Take all our loans. They would take everything over for us. And we would borrow X number of dollars to pay off Jennifer's loan," said Jackie.

"So that was her gentle way of saying you were going to have to pay?"

"Yeah. After she had talked to somebody in head office."

"So, here was the bank saying, 'Boy do we have a deal for you. We'll let you re-mortgage your house so you can pay off this loan.'"

"Yeah," said Jackie, with a sad, little laugh.

Our first question for the Bank of Nova Scotia was why this loan hadn't come with some life insurance, and the BNS just told us they hadn't considered it necessary for this kind of loan, but that they might consider offering it in the future.

Of course, nothing prevents any of us from buying enough life insurance on our own to cover all our debts. That just makes good sense, and we shouldn't rely on banks to tell us that.

In any event, since no life insurance was offered, we asked the Bank of Nova Scotia if it could review this situation. Back came a letter to the Yuills, from a senior vice-president at the BNS:

> I have recently been made aware of the circumstances surrounding the student loan extended to your daughter and her subsequent death. As a mother of two cherished children, I extend my greatest condolences to your and your family on your personal loss.
>
> Regarding the Scotia Student Loan, our Collections Manager has recommended that we fully write off this account, for a net loss of $9,621.29 based on your financial circumstances and for sympathetic reasons.

Zhana and Alfred Zolotovitsky also suffered the worst tragedy parents can endure: the death of a child. In 1994, in Surrey, British Columbia, Larisa Zolotovitsky had been struck and killed by a car as she crossed a dark stretch of road on her way home. A police report noted that no charges were laid against the driver. The Royal Canadian Mounted Police officer noted that the scene of the accident was "completely dark, with no street lighting," and that Larisa Zolotovitsky was "dressed completely in black, which would make it impossible to be seen by a car until it was too late."

Larisa's parents flew from their Toronto home to Vancouver, to bring their daughter's body back for cremation and burial. In addition to the gaping hole left in their lives, the death of their daughter cost the Zolotovitskys more than $13,000.

The Insurance Corporation of British Columbia, the public auto insurer, sent the Zolotovitskys the standard $2,000 death benefit. It was such a pitiful amount, it simply added to the Zolotovitskys' grief. How could a life be worth only $2,000? But officials at ICBC told the Zolotovitskys that even if they took ICBC to court, damages would amount to very little. Larisa did not support her parents either financially or physically. She lived thousands of kilometres away in Vancouver. While their daughter's loss was immeasurable in their own eyes, in the cold, categorical eyes of the law, Larisa's life carried a minimal dollar value.

We asked ICBC if there were any circumstances under which a little more money could be paid, at least to help overcome travel, funeral, and burial expenses. ICBC claims-officials told us they had already decided to pay an additional $3,000. Now they would double that to $6,000 as a final offer.

That meant, in total, $8,000 of the Zolotovitsky's expenses would be paid. I still felt it was an astronomically inadequate amount of money for a life. But then again, it was money simply being used to finance a death.

After the story aired, I got a note from a woman in Hudson, Quebec. She had included a letter to be forwarded to the Zolotovitskys. It said:

> I was moved by your story on *Canada AM* this morning. This cheque will not ease your pain over your daughter's untimely death, but it will help with one or two related expenses. My husband was killed by a drunk driver in Vancouver, and because he was the breadwinner, I was awarded a large settlement from ICBC. The system should be fairer because your daughter's life was precious, too.

Enclosed was a cheque for $1,000.

In the insurance regulatory jungle, while death might carry a cheap price tag, disability can cost millions. On June 5, 1990, a motorcycle collided with a car at the corner of Burris and Buckingham in Burnaby, British Columbia.

Two lives were ruined that day. Darren Gervais, twenty-one, was disabled for life. Muriel Yewdale, eighty-two, was thrust into poverty, losing everything she had to pay off a $4.3 million dollar lawsuit. In what became a five-year legal battle, there were no winners, except for some of the lawyers.

Yewdale had been attempting a left hand turn when Gervais' motorcycle slammed into the front fender of her Cadillac. Yewdale said she hadn't even seen the motorcycle before the collision. Gervais had no memory of the accident at all.

Two days after the collision, Yewdale was rushed to hospital, complaining of chest pains. She had developed a heart condition. It led to triple-bypass heart surgery. The family blamed it on the stress caused by the accident.

Lawyers for Gervais sued Yewdale for damages in the Supreme Court of British Columbia. She was found 100 percent responsible for the accident. Judgment was granted against Yewdale for more than $4.3 million. The widow had $1 million in liability coverage on her car insurance. That was taken, leaving Yewdale on the hook for $3.3 million, personally.

She declared bankruptcy. All her assets were sold. She lost the title to her home, where she had lived for the past fifty years. She lost the two acres of land around her home, where she had planted every tree. She had nothing left to call her own except some furniture and her paintings of favourite spots in her two-acre garden.

Her family came to us for help in 1993. Maybe we could persuade the bankruptcy trustee and the new owner of the Yewdale estate to let her stay in her home for awhile as the rest of the property was divided up into separate building lots.

Mrs. Yewdale, using a cane, met me at what had been her home and property. We walked through many of the gardens she had planted, past groves of huge trees. She was feeling somewhat hopeful about the future, but talked about the terrible months after the accident and her own brush with death.

"I didn't know if it was worth living, or if I should die, rather than go through all of this. Night after night. No sleep. In the morning, face the grey, rainy days and say, 'What am I doing here on earth?' You know, there is supposed to be peace in heaven," said the tiny, fragile widow.

For what it was worth or what it could accomplish, both the bankruptcy trustee and the developer who had bought the Yewdale property were sympathetic. In the short term, we were assured that Mrs. Yewdale would be allowed to stay in the house, even as bulldozers cut her garden into house lots.

The legal action had continued all along. The $4.3 million judgment was appealed. The judgment was upheld. Then Yewdale and family members hired another lawyer to go after her original lawyers — lawyers who represented the insurance company, Insurance Corporation of British Columbia, and a lawyer representing the personal interests of Muriel Yewdale herself.

The new lawyer, Douglas Lahay, told the court in his opening remarks, speaking on behalf of Yewdale, the plaintiff, "With respect to the issue of damages, it will be the plaintiff's position that if she had been properly advised, a settlement before trial would and could have been achieved. The plaintiff will show how she could have contributed to a settlement without even the need to sell her home."

The court found in favour of Yewdale and awarded her more than $300,000. The evidence had shown that an early offer from Gervais' lawyers, to settle out of court, would have cost Mrs. Yewdale a little less than $1 million. Mrs. Yewdale could have sold part of her land and kept her home. But there was what could best be called a "breakdown in communications" between all the lawyers and Mrs. Yewdale.

"I think Mrs. Yewdale can breathe a sigh of relief now," Lahay said to me after the judgment. Indeed, she could. She had enough money to rent her former home, on the promise from the developer that she could stay there for the rest of her life, which she did.

If you drive by that neighbourhood in Burnaby today, you will see nothing of the Yewdale estate. Six new homes sit on the property where the old Yewdale mansion and massive garden once defined the neighbourhood. It took only one tragic accident, just down the street, to change all that forever.

And to anyone who thinks that a million dollars worth of liability insurance sounds like enough, have a chat with your insurance broker. And remember Mrs. Yewdale.

Alfred and Darlene MacWilliams and their two sons, in the long-distance trucking business on Prince Edward Island, had a run-in with liability insurance that almost sunk their little company.

It all started when son Sterling discovered what he considered a minor oil leak in the engine of the rig he was driving, on a run between Lethbridge and Calgary. So he did what any good trucker would do. He shut it down and called his dad, back on the Island.

"I didn't think it was serious," Alfred told me later. "It was an oil leak. You have them all the time. So, I had it towed in to get it fixed."

But it was no ordinary oil leak. It was a major engine job. The shop in Calgary charged $14,000, and on top of that, Alfred and Darlene shipped $10,000 worth of engine parts to the shop to be used in the repair.

So, $24,000 later, money Alfred had borrowed from the bank, Sterling was on his way. The engine died in Fergus Falls, Montana, where he had gone to pick up another load. The shop there said the truck needed a new engine. Shop mechanics just shook their heads over the botched repair job that had been done by the mechanics who worked on the engine in Calgary.

The new engine cost $32,000, but Alfred and Darlene were tapped out. The bank would not loan them any more money. Alfred complained to the shop in Calgary, who told him he should make a claim against their insurance. After all, they were supposedly protected against this kind of disaster.

Alfred made the claim. But the truck, capable of making $1,000 a day, sat idle in the Fergus Falls shop for the next forty-eight days because the bill remained unpaid. That drastic drop in revenue caused big problems back on the Island. The Bank was threatening to repossess another truck because the MacWilliamses had fallen behind in the payments. It was all a trucking house of cards and it was about to fall down. With the other truck gone, the business would surely die.

Then, at the last minute, Royal & SunAlliance paid the $32,000 repair bill and Sterling got back on the road again. But the bank back on PEI still wanted its money, or it would take another truck.

We went to Royal & SunAlliance to see what was holding up the additional $50,000 claim for the forty-eight or so days of lost business. Alfred MacWilliams was adamant that he had sent Royal & SunAlliance all the information they had requested. In fact, MacWilliams told us he sent in the material several times, after the same material had been requested several times. It appeared as though it was tire-spinning time at Royal & SunAlliance.

We called Royal & SunAlliance and they got back to us in a day. The adjustor wanted to sit down with the MacWilliamses and work out a settlement. The cheque for $50,000 arrived from Royal & SunAlliance on a Monday morning, just hours before the bank had promised to send its repo men to the MacWilliams' farm to scoop a truck. Talk about heading them off at the pass, this was it.

Sometimes insurance issues involve relatively small amounts of money that still mean a world of difference to people who have little or no money in the first place.

Brian McFarlane lived a modest life in a small trailer — really small. The day I went to visit, we sat in the only sittable place, at the dinette, room for two across from each other. Under my chair was a fully functional litter box. It was a hot day. There was no breeze. McFarlane apologized for the feline funkiness of his trailer. The cat, Tiger, had belonged to his "best friend in the world," fifty-five-year-old Rose Marie Lavoie, who had died in a fire. Tiger had been in her apartment when the fire happened, but somehow he survived.

On the day of the fire, March 29, 1996, McFarlane had been in Lavoie's apartment, but left to look for a job. Lavoie, who suffered from epilepsy, apparently was smoking a cigarette during a seizure and it set fire to the apartment.

McFarlane was devastated by the loss, beating himself up because he had not been there to help. It would have saved her life. "I was going out to look for a job. I left earlier. I'd say about a half hour later than when it happened. I would say I was the last person to see her alive."

McFarlane was horrified, and fixated on the damage the fire caused. "The intensity of the heat in that place. I had a clock in the hall cupboard. It was plastic and it melted. And the TV and all the stuff. It just melted around her."

McFarlane knew that Lavoie had a small $7,800 life insurance policy. He checked with Norwich Union and found out that he was the beneficiary. Norwich Union asked him to supply a death certificate and a birth certificate. He did, in July of 1996. Then he waited. And waited. The company kept telling McFarlane it was having trouble establishing that this was an accidental death, where Norwich Union would pay triple indemnity, $23,400.

Finally, in January of 1997, Brian McFarlane came to us. Norwich Union told us the same story. They were having trouble establishing that the death was accidental. Norwich Union suggested maybe we could get a copy of the fire report and send it on to them.

Well, we did. The fire report fro the Ontario Minister of the Solicitor General was, at least we thought, as simple journalists, conclusive. It said, in the "Summary Section" of the document:

> The deceased was paralyzed on her right side. It was not unusual for her to have up to four seizures weekly. The deceased had careless smoking habits and whenever she had a seizure, her "Life Line" usually activated, causing emergency vehicles and personnel to attend. There was a tremendous pressure on the deceased by numerous persons close to her to attend a home care facility.
>
> The cause of death was carbon monoxide poisoning, indicating the deceased was alive for a portion of the fire.
>
> The lighter found on the couch and the smoker's materials found around the body all indicate the fire was caused by careless smoking.

Then there was an addendum to the report, written five days after we had requested a copy, that emphasizes for any doubting insurance company, that the fire and the death were accidental. The addendum said, "There was no flammable liquid present at the fire scene. The pathologist report did not indicate anything out of the ordinary. As a result of these findings, there is nothing to indicate this fire was anything other than accidental."

We sent the report to Norwich Union. It was the proof and categorical language they had wanted, so they said. McFarlane got a cheque for $24,373.69.

So McFarlane, down on his luck, with no money and no job, had a little positive push to help him get on with his life. McFarlane looked at the cheque and Tiger, The Cat Who Wouldn't Die. He told me that he could now believe that all things were possible.

Therese Ayotte and her husband, Victor, of Sudbury, Ontario, did some one-stop shopping back in July of 1995, when they signed a mortgage. The mortgage was with National Bank and the life and disability insurance covering the mortgage was handled by National Bank Life Insurance Company.

Then Victor, healthy, strapping, and vigorous his whole life, developed liver disease. It lead to a liver transplant, but the transplant did not go well. During his dying days, if there was one thing that comforted Victor, it was that insurance. NBLIC had been, as fully expected, making disability payments during his long illness. They would be automatically changed to a death benefit when he was gone.

Victor Ayotte died in September, 1997. Then the runaround began. Therese Ayotte, still in mourning, now had to worry that she would not be able to keep up mortgage payments on her home. That was why the Ayottes had bought the life insurance in the first place — to save a surviving spouse from that ordeal.

By the time Therese Ayotte had come to us, she had been waiting almost a year and a half for the life insurance to be paid out. And she was in deep financial trouble. She had been allowed to defer her mortgage payments to National Bank, while the NBLIC made up its mind about the life insurance claim, although why the claim should be a problem, Therese never knew.

She was once told by somebody at NB that NBLIC might have been concerned about a reported visit to a chiropractor in 1994. That's the first absurdity we tried to chase down when we got involved. We called NB at its national headquarters in Montreal, and were told that NBLIC was not concerned about any visit to a chiropractor, but that NBLIC was having trouble getting medical records from the Ontario Health Insurance Plan, a whole province away from Montreal.

NB promised us that NBLIC would work twice as hard now to get this claim settled. During that time of hard working, Therese got a call from NB (a different official from the one we had contacted) to pressure Therese about the mortgage, wondering when the payments would resume.

We couldn't believe it. NB was literally across the hall from NBLIC, in the same headquarters building in Montreal. Did they need an introduction? Were they out of inter-office memo paper? We called again to complain and the nagging stopped.

NBLIC finally paid out, after a twenty-month delay. Therese was sent a notice from NBLIC that her mortgage at NB, $155,974.20, had been retired.

When we went to Montreal, Jocelin Dumas of the National Bank spoke publicly for NBLIC. "We know it's unusual in this case. And we've done really all we thought can be possible to get this information. But that's the time it took," said Dumas.

"I would assume that most of your cases do not take twenty months to resolve."

"I can assure you of that."

While Victor Ayotte of Sudbury, Ontario, went to his death believing he was leaving behind financial security for his family, Vic Vanstrepen of Port Coquitlam, British Columbia, despaired in his dying days when he discovered the life insurance he thought he had did not exist.

Vanstrepen, sixty-three, died on December 31, 2000, beaten by brain cancer and by a bank that said he had no life insurance. Vanstrepen's daughter Connie spoke for the family. "It took a major, major toll on his outlook on getting better. He was so focussed on trying to find out what went wrong. They were just giving him the runaround. And he would cry."

Added Vanstrepen's widow, Leona, "He couldn't believe it. He was just too devastated. And then when he tried to fight it himself, he said, 'I'm too sick, I can't do this.'"

When the Vanstrepens got a new mortgage on their home, they checked the boxes they had routinely checked in past mortgages, including boxes that disclosed both Vic and Leona had diabetes. The mortgage papers all went through, and the Vanstrepens could tell that each month the bank was deducting $95 to cover life insurance premiums for both of them.

Later, when Vic became ill and was told he would not live much longer, both he and his daughter Connie began getting Vic's papers in order. A call to the Bank of Montreal devastated them both. The Bank had no record of any life insurance. The insurance deductions had been made by mistake.

Customer Service weenies swung into action and refunded all the premiums the Vanstrepens had paid for the last eight months and, for good measure, put an extra $250 in the family's account, hoping that would top-up bank goodwill in the Vanstrepen household.

The reality was, Leona Vanstrepen on her own would not be able to pay down the $66,000 mortgage. She would lose the family home.

We tried to figure out what had happened to the insurance form. The answer was simple. It had been lost. Somewhere between the Bank of Montreal and Sun Life, the application had disappeared, even though insurance deductions had begun as if the insurance had been in place.

The Bank of Montreal then re-submitted the insurance application, only to have it turned down because of the diabetes. But if the Vanstrepens had known that eight months earlier, they would have been able to find life insurance elsewhere.

That was not to say that Vic Vanstrepen was in poor health. He wasn't. He felt great. He did have a routine operation for kidney stones, and during the operation he had suffered a slight stroke. On further examination, doctors found the brain tumour.

In the end, the Bank of Montreal and Sun Life Assurance made good on the mistake. They split the loss and paid off the $66,000 mortgage.

Back in 1945, when he was twenty and about to get married, Ronald Cameron decided he'd better do the sensible thing and get himself some life insurance. He bought it from Manufacturers' Life. He paid the first year's premiums in advance, a pricey $67. Over the years, the premiums would be paid up full on the life insurance, which then would remain in force for the rest of Ronald Cameron's life.

But for a time, Cameron, who was seventy-five years old in 2000 and living in Red Deer, Alberta, had been getting all these letters from the newly-termed Manulife Financial. Cameron could not decipher what they meant so he just tossed them in a drawer. His wife had died years earlier. She was the one who looked after that kind of stuff.

We got a call from Cameron's daughter, Diane, who lived in New Mexico but had been visiting her dad. She had figured out that her father's life insurance was now worth a total of $141.56. According to the letters, Cameron had taken out a loan on his life insurance in 1977 for $1152 and never paid it back into the insurance account. So the insurance had just been eating away at its own value, making automatic loan repayments for twenty-three years.

When it was all explained to Cameron, he just scoffed. He said it never happened. "Show me my signature on that loan," he told his daughter. But Manulife could show no signature and no loan documents. All it had, on microfiche, was a notation that the loan had been made against the insurance.

Finally, Manulife conceded to us it did not have enough proof the loan had been made, so the company wrote it off. Cameron's policy was then worth $4, 327.86. Not all the money in the world, to be sure, but it was Cameron's money, back where it belonged.

One of Manulife's weaker excuses about the whole case was that it had lost track of Cameron somewhere in the mid-90s. Cameron thought that was a hot one. He had been living in the same little house in downtown Red Deer since 1974.

Insurance is a source of great comfort for many people. Just knowing it's there offers a feeling of security. That's how Yvette Lacelle, the grandmother of thirteen, always felt. Yvette, who lived in Cambridge, Ontario, died of cancer following a brief illness.

Back in 1984, Lacelle had bought this special cancer insurance that paid for treatment of cancer and then paid out $10,000 if the policyholder died from cancer. It was Lacelle's little nest egg. She wanted it to go to her grandchildren when she was gone — something for them to remember both Grandma and Grandpa.

But when Yvette Lacelle died, the family found out the truth. There was no death benefit. In 1990, Lacelle had been sold a "new, improved" cancer policy that was "bigger and better" than the old policy. But nobody realized that the death benefit had been dropped in that policy in favour of more hospital coverage.

We went to Mark Sylvia, the President of Hartford Life. His company had bought out the insurance company that had sold the policy to Lacelle.

Said Sylvia, "The change in coverage benefited most clients. In her case, the particular client died quite quickly without a lot of hospitalization, and so wasn't able to use the new benefit."

Why was the old death benefit dropped? "It was so expensive for the small amount of coverage it offered that they (AFLAC Insurance) felt people were better off to go out and buy a separate life insurance policy where they could get significantly more coverage for the same premium," said Sylvia.

Well, it all made good insurance sense to us, but none of it helped Lacelle's policy. I said something like that to Sylvia, who told me he had already decided to pay out on the policy "because of the client's circumstances."

And so now there is a little bit of money in a family nest egg that will buy graduation and wedding gifts for thirteen grandchildren who will remember the kindness of Yvette and Raoul Lacelle.

10.

Unforgettable

So much of what happened at *Goldhawk Fights Back* was unforgettable. The injustice and unfairness; the outrage; the cold cruelty and the amazing kindness; the unbelievable life situations; as always, the humour; the people themselves who pulled us, with little effort since we were willing participants, right into their lives.

I remember as if it were yesterday the Christmas party that *Goldhawk Fights Back* threw for its clients at CBC, back in 1982. Producer Trudie Richards and I had what we thought was the idea of the century. We would bring together all the clients we had helped at *GFB* during that year, at a Christmas party to be held in "The Kremlin," the nickname for the old CBC Regional Headquarters building on Jarvis St. in Toronto.

Management types were cool to the idea. That was usually the pattern. Richards and I had to heat them up with our usual whining, cajoling, and shouting. Management reluctantly agreed, warning us that CBC security guards would be posted, just in case a few of the more troublesome clients we had might find something worth stealing.

The party was wonderful. The guests knew each other by their problems. They had seen each other on television and needed no introduction. It was a room full of famous people eager to talk to each other and celebrate their victories over the heartless and inattentive system.

One little girl brought me a *Goldhawk Fights Back* drawing and presented it proudly. It was a picture of a hawk with a little, pink, dripping thing in its mouth. Each week, we gave a "Razzberry of the Week" award to some deserving public personality blockhead. I dropped a dripping raspberry on a letter to the proud recipient.

"So what is that in the hawk's mouth," I asked. "The Razzberry?" The little girl shook her head.

"Oh no, Mr. Goldhawk," said the father. "It is the flesh of the bureaucrat."

"Ah. Well, there you have it," I said, with no more questions to ask.

At the end of the evening, *CBC Newshour* host Fraser Kelly and I were trying to stuff John Kellerman's wheelchair into the back of a cab. John was already in the back seat, entertaining the driver. Kellerman had first come to us about the telephone company that wouldn't allow him enough time to dial his call with his cerebral-palsy-disabled fingers. John was unsinkable. He had once run for mayor of Toronto.

Other guests were streaming by the cab, bidding farewell to us and to each other. They waved at John. There was much laughter — including laughter at the inability of the two us to get the folded wheelchair properly positioned in the trunk.

"Goldhawk, I tell you," said Fraser, pausing in his labours with a big grin on his face, "this is what journalism is all about."

For cruelty, however, nothing was more memorable than the heartless bastards at Procan in Montreal — a mail-order house that sold cheap junk for big prices in the hope you would get an even bigger prize that never came.

Ellen Ennett was eighty-two and suffering from multiple sclerosis when the mail-order jackals found her. She was living in a convalescent hospital where she spent most of her days in a wheelchair. Somehow, the marketers got her name, address, and room number at the hospital, and her telephone number.

By the time we rescued Ellen, having been called in by her daughter Chyrel, it was too late. In her room, Ennett was surrounded by some of the cheap junk she had bought on her way to depleting her $9,000 savings account. Several companies had been active in getting her money. The most successful was Procan. It had sold her, for example, four dozen cheap plastic coffee mugs for $2,628.01. Each mug was stamped with this large, garish lettering, "Compliments of Ellen Ennett." There they sat in the corner, the box half-opened.

The marketers pestered her on the telephone all the time, promising she would win a car. She always thought it would be nice to give it to her daughter. They talked her into ordering all manner of stuff, including an alleged diamond and sapphire tennis watch.

One day, even after she had told them she had no more money, two goons from Montreal came to the hospital, intent on taking Ellen Ennett to her bank, where she could withdraw cash and pay some supposedly overdue bill from the marketers.

They walked boldly into her room and wheeled her out, down the elevator and out past several nursing stations where personnel were too busy looking after patients in the hospital to worry about one who was being kidnapped.

When they got out front, the goons noticed that Ennett's wheelchair would not fit into their van, so they decided to wheel her to her bank, several blocks away. But that soon became too much like work, so the pair abandoned her on the sidewalk. She was rescued later, unhurt, by hospital staff who had been called by police. We managed to get some of her money back.

We met Bill Quinn in hospital, too. After eighteen years working for Canadian National Railways, his health was ruined. A year earlier, doctors were telling Quinn and his wife, Hannah, that his lungs were contaminated with heavy metals. He had a choice: He could have a lung transplant, or he could just wait to die. A constant supply of oxygen was the only thing keeping him alive.

Bill had always been an upbeat kind of guy, but this was getting him down. "It's really, really hard," he told me. "My whole life is just a shambles."

For the last several years of his life, Quinn had worked in the locomotive engine repair shop. He was a pipefitter, often surrounded by powerful chemical solvents used to clean engine parts. Doctors found in his lungs, among other things, asbestos, cadmium, aluminum silicates, titanium, and chromium.

Ken Wheeler, a partner at Workers' Initiative, an advocacy service in Winnipeg where Quinn lived and worked, summed up for the Manitoba Workers' Compensation Board Quinn's working conditions:

> In the period immediately preceding his illness he was repairing hoods and sanders immediately adjacent to the area where locomotives were cleaned with caustic soda. There was also an open drain running through Bill's work area. This drain amounted to a chemical cocktail, with various acids, caustic sodas, and cleaning compounds flowing into it on a frequent basis.
>
> During much of Bill's working day, he was lying on the floor, with his head a matter of a foot or so above this drain. In addition, caustic soda from the cleaning booth next to him came over or under the curtain separating the two areas. On several occasions, he attended the nurse because of a burning sensation in his throat. As a member of the Workplace Health and Safety Committee, Bill raised these problems a number of times, but nothing was done to solve them.

With a lot of prodding from us, and from Wheeler, Quinn finally won his case. The last time we saw him alive was in a London, Ontario, hospital, where he had just received a new lung.

A month after that, Wheeler, arguing before the Workers' Compensation Board, won a final appeal. It established that Quinn's illness was linked to his job. That meant a pension for Quinn and protection for his family. Also, it would set an important precedent in similar cases that would come before the WCB. The victory was a little more solid proof that your job can kill you.

After his victory, Wheeler said to me: "My heart was full. My eyes were full of tears. We won."

There would be more tears from Hannah and her kids on December 27, 1996. Quinn's body rejected the new lung, and he died.

I will always remember the nods and sheepish grins as we walked in rolling on CAW Local 676, in St. Catharines, Ontario. We were there to strike a blow for workers' rights — but the bad guy in the piece was the Local itself.

For twenty-three years, the Local's only staff member was Helen Pierce. She did it all, through thick and thin, through strike and settlement, and now it was time for her to retire on a pension cheque of $63 a month. For years, Helen had tried to join a union of office workers, but nobody wanted to represent a Local of one.

So now the Local leaders were shucking and darning about the surprising and unexpected unfairness of it all. After some Goldhawk-induced pressure from the office of CAW President Buzz Hargrove, Local 676 topped up her retirement fund by a one-time payment of $30,000. That didn't bring Pierce's pension even close to a CAW pension for a worker of the same seniority, but then again, she was never paid what union guys earned on the shop floor, either. Solidarity forever, unless you work for a union.

Kelly Randall is a second-generation logger who grew up in Campbell River, British Columbia. As a kid, he got tough moving from logging camp to logging camp. He was once a Golden Gloves boxer. Then he turned to country music — a singer/songwriter. Back in 1996, Randall was mailing his latest CD, *Smokin' Gun*, out to radio stations across the country.

Some radio stations complained they never got the CD. Others said they got it all right, but the CD was either scorched or out-and-out melted. Randall went stomping off to Canada Post to complain, only to find out that a mail truck in Northern Ontario, carrying his CDs, had been involved in a traffic accident. The truck caught fire and somebody died in the accident.

Suddenly, Randall felt bad. Here he was complaining about his CDs, when a driver had died in the accident. Randall wanted to know more, but Canada Post said there were privacy issues involved, and would say nothing.

So Randall came to us. He wanted us to play detective and find out what had happened. We did. The driver who died was a twenty-year-old man who had been driving a pickup that drove head-on into the mail truck. He had fallen asleep at the wheel at 4:15 in the morning.

The dead man was Anthony Wemigwans from the First Nation community of Wikwemikong on Manitoulin Island, in Georgian Bay. He left behind his wife, Lisa, and his two-year-old son, Brett.

Randall wanted to compose a song. He did, on a CD entitled *Tony's Gift*. The song imagined a teenaged Brett singing to his father in the spirit world. It was a kind and gentle gesture that touched everybody in Wikwemikong.

It is impossible to forget the love that kept Carmen and Markus McCauley going in Windsor, Ontario, in 1998. Markus was totally paralyzed by multiple sclerosis when Carmen called us to help.

We managed to ensure a supply of life-giving oxygen for Markus at no cost to the McCauleys. The oxygen supply company and the Ontario Government had been locked in a battle over the cost of the oxygen.

In a move designed to get the Ontario Health Ministry off its ass, the company, Vitalaire, had been billing the cost, $700 a month, to the McCauleys. The McCauleys couldn't afford it. We got a guarantee, in writing, that Vitalaire would never come after Carmen and Markus to collect on those invoices.

Markus communicated by blinking his eyes. No blinks meant no. One blink meant yes. I said to Markus, "You have quite a fighter here in Carmen, don't you?" Markus blinked once, before the question was barely out of my mouth.

"Well, that was a quick yes," I laughed, as Markus blinked again.

"He trained me," Carmen chimed in.

I think it's fair to say that Wayne Cave hated his former wife Elizabeth. He tried to kill her. He stabbed her eight times, but she survived. Elizabeth's male companion, Michael Braham, was stabbed thirty-eight times. He died. Cave held one of his own sons hostage at knifepoint, trying to fend off the police. Finally, they overpowered Cave. His son was unhurt.

Cave is serving a life sentence in prison, but he was still attacking Elizabeth and her family from behind bars. He wrote poison pen letters to everybody — government agencies, including the local school board, the Children's Aid Society, and the company where Elizabeth's brother worked. He alleged drug use and sexual abuse. He also made countless harassing collect telephone calls.

Elizabeth wanted it stopped. It felt to her as if she were serving the life sentence right along with Cave. We got it stopped. Prison officials clamped down, even though earlier they had told Elizabeth that it was a free country and Cave could write or say anything he wanted.

The young victims in this story, Matthew, who was eight at the time, and Stephen, who was ten, suffered no physical scars from the ordeal. But their mother will always worry about the savage violence those young eyes saw.

Thirteen years later, in 2003, the Ontario Government Throne Speech carried this somewhat encouraging promise: "Your government will support crime victims and fight crime by implementing call-monitoring and call-blocking services in provincial jails to prevent inmates from harassing victims or their families."

Back in 1944, during the war, a young boy who had lied about his age to get into the army died in an army training exercise on Prince Edward Island. Claude Brooks had been travelling in convoy when the jeep he was riding in suddenly veered off a bridge. Claude and two others were killed.

Their names, all these years, had been listed among the war dead in Canada. But Claude's name was never included on the Royal Canadian Legion monument in his home town of Wellington.

The excuses were that Claude was in the Reserves because he was so young, he was not in a war zone, and he was not involved in military action when he died.

Tanton Wedge, a veteran himself, was outraged when he realized young Brooks' name was not on the war memorial. In a letter to me, he wrote:

The names of servicemen killed in wartime, whether as a result of enemy action or misadventure during training, have always been placed on war memorials. And besides, the Gulf of St. Lawrence was a war zone, so much so that the Canadian Government closed it down to shipping in 1943 due to heavy losses in merchant ships. German U-boats also sank, among others, HMCS *Chedabucto*, HMCS *Charlottetown*, and HMCS *Shawinigan*.

Several thousand lives were lost in this war zone as a result of enemy action taking place off the coast of PEI. So the people objecting to the placing of Claude Brooks' name on the local monument because his death was not in a war zone, are nuts.

We took that message back to the local legion hall, but they just trotted out the same old excuses and hinted vaguely that they might discuss it at the next legion meeting. When they didn't, we went to the provincial association and then to legion headquarters in Ottawa.

We were told, in no uncertain terms, that the Royal Canadian Legion Policy on service (just to skewer another local excuse) says that everybody is treated in the same way. There is no discrimination according to service. So it doesn't matter if somebody served in the Reserves, they are treated equally.

Word seemed to trickle down. The Wellington Branch of the Royal Canadian Legion said yes. And as our camera rolled to record the carving of Claude Brooks' name on the war memorial, Claude's younger brother, Grant, watched in silence, a tear in his eye.

"His name is here. It's in stone, now," Grant said to me. "I was thinking, as I watched, *If only my mother and father could see it.* I was thinking of them."

In 1994, inmates at the Kingston Penitentiary asked us to investigate two recent deaths, within four days of each other, inside those notorious old walls. One inmate, Tex Gentles, had died after having been subdued by guards; another inmate, Darren Stapleton, hanged himself with his own belt.

Both cons were members of a prison committee investigating violence inside the toughest prison in Canada, holding some of our most dangerous criminals.

The two surviving members of the committee, Rudy Martens and Ted Johnson, now had raw and graphic proof of their concerns about violence — much of it triggered, they said, by overcrowding. At that point, of the five hundred inmates at Kingston, half of them were double-bunked in cells that measured 6' by 8'.

Martens and Johnson had some ideas to make the prison a bit more livable. With our help, they got through to Warden Ken Payne. But none of that would change the fact that Kingston Pen is a hopeless place where little is accomplished.

"What's this prison doing? What's it turning out? It's turning out monsters," said Martens.

"When your faith in government is taken away and then you are led out onto the street, it is hard to be a law-abiding citizen," said Johnson.

"All this is meant as pure punishment? There is no rehabilitation?" I asked Martens.

"No. When the guys get out of here, they are truly dangerous."

"So this is a factory, turning out bigger and better criminals?"

"Yeah."

I put the bigger and better criminals question to Warden Payne, as we walked the huge exercise yard.

"I think that's probably a fair assessment. I think we could all agree with that," said Payne.

"You've had an opportunity to talk to Rudy Martens about some of his concerns and recommendations, haven't you?" I asked.

"Not so much talk as giving him approval to go ahead with some things. I read the paper and there's the fact you are here today to follow it up. Most of the points he makes are right on the pulse."

A few days after the story ran we got a note from Martens which said that the publicity was having a positive effect:

I believe that the recruitment of new staff, policy regarding native prisoners, and most of all a politeness by the tyrants, was caused by your reporting. Inmates have been coming up to Ted Johnson and myself every day with suggestions for programs and ways to take positive control of their lives. Many prisoners are beginning to put aside their misery.

But then a few days after that, Martens was badly beaten by several inmates who just figured that he was getting too big for his britches. It's a prison thing.

It was a cold and snowy night in January, 1998, when we landed at Edmonton International about 9 p.m. I rented a huge SUV land-yacht to help us bash through the ice and snow to Vermilion, about three hundred kilometres away. Nancy Feenstra was waiting for us. We had rescued $30,000 of $37,500 she had handed over to Montreal telemarketers.

They were like sharks. Money grubbers from eight different fly-by-night companies were engaging in a feeding frenzy. All the companies worked together, using the same big lie: Nancy had won $186,000. The cheque was waiting — all she had to do was pay the investment charges, carrying charges, and insurance charges. Each payment of $2500 sent by Nancy also netted her some piece of junk smaller prize — not exactly paintings on velvet, but not far from it, either.

Nancy made fifteen payments. She drained her bank account. Borrowed more money. The bank wound up repossessing her car. Nancy remained focussed on that $186,000 cheque, allegedly from the Chase Manhattan Bank. At one point, one of the greaseball telemarketers told her to get dressed up because a courier with a big cheque was coming to her tiny town. Nancy recorded that conversation as she heard the guy say that they were "hiring a photographer from the Vermilion area. The photographer will be there at twelve, and he will take a picture of you holding the cheque."

Nancy was left holding the bag. She felt foolish. She felt awful. When she started telling them she had no more money to send to get her big cheque, the crooks became abusive: "I said, 'We know you can come up with the money.' We checked your bank and you were approved. That's what I'm telling you, so don't keep telling me you can't come up with the money. Nancy, please. Don't be such an idiot. My God. Don't be so stupid. Are you an idiot? Are you a total moron?"

Nancy was just one of thousands of telemarketer victims that year — telemarketers who stole roughly $45 million from Canadians in 1998 alone. Nancy, despite the soul-destroying verbal assaults, was lucky. We retrieved $30,000 from a company called Consumers Group, just before it was raided by the RCMP.

When we left Nancy later that night to blast our way back to Edmonton, she said to me, "I wonder what ever happened to that $186,000 cheque?"

I met the larger-than-life Roy Sugai on the Blood Indian Reserve in the southern desert land of Alberta — the land of the legendary chief who ruled the Blood tribe back in the 1870s, Chief Shot-on-Both-Sides. Even today, the historic and colourfully descriptive last names persist: Many Fingers, Crosschild, First Rider, Good Striker.

In 1997, Sugai and his wife, Georgia Niokos, were trying to start a bulk fuel business. We helped him get a $20,000 federal grant that had earlier been denied because of a technicality.

We were on the Reserve to convince the Blood Indian Council to grant Sugai a business licence. Eventually it would come, but that day we were on the trail looking for Band officials, driving for hours on dusty trails and half-trails. We wanted to locate the Chief, but found out later he had just come back from San Francisco and then headed off to Las Vegas.

When we had started out on the day-long fruitless search, leaving Sugai's land and trailer behind, one of Sugai's dogs kept pace with the pickup for kilometres, running on my side of the truck and occasionally looking at me.

I motioned to the dog and Sugai laughed. "Oh, he's just showin' off for company."

Not all of our memories were locked away in our forty-five large file-folder drawers. Not all of it was stored on our more than two thousand Betacam tapes. Some of what we were and who we met and what we did was just hanging on our walls, or crammed into shelves. Our walls were covered in Thank You notes, interspersed with words of alleged wisdom, a few threats, and points of view that seemed appropriate to our crusading brand of journalism.

Then there was the address section, with its many theories on who I was. We got: Deal Goldhawk, Gold Huck Fight Back, Goldsmith Fights Back, Daly Goldhawk, Mr. Gold Hack, "Goldhawk Fights Back" (Dale Carnegie), Golshawk Speaks Out, Goldwater Fights Back, Dr. Goldhawk, Dale Golhowk, The People's Helper, Dale Gold Holdhawk, Air Your Beef, Goldhawk Flashback Memory, Goldman Fights Back, Mr. Gold Hork — Fight Back, Goldhawk Fright Back, The Obusman, Goodheart Fights Back, Goldfarb Fights Back, Mr. Larry Goldhawk, Goldhawk Bites Back, Mr. Whole Talk, Goldhawk Chickens Out, Dalehawk, Dale Goldhawk: Mercy Lawyer, Dr. Garry Goldhawk (Attorney), and the inexplicable Goldhawk Fight Stock.

The mailing address was CTV Network Headquarters in a Toronto suburb called Agincourt. Our viewers thought better. They called it Agent Court, Agenda Court, Asian Court, and my personal favourite, Aging Court.

The wall somehow kept us grounded, connected to Canadians. After all, everything on the wall came from them — the thanks, the threats, the conspiracy theories, the encouragement, the praise, and the candid thoughts and opinions of thousands.

Visitors to the office stared intently at the wall. Some were amused, some amazed. There were those who never understood why the wall was there, or why it had any value.

Then there were the little gifts: a plastic bird in a little white cage, ornamental plates and wooden platters, handmade ties, various knick-knacks and souvenirs from assorted towns and cities, and a wooden beer mug large enough to hold a six-pack. Somebody sent me a short-sleeved checkered shirt. To the mock horror of my staff, I wore in on TV one night, complete with an abandoned tie I had found hanging on a coat rack at the *Goldhawk Fights Back* Used Furniture Depot.

When nobody was around, I would read some of the stuff on the wall, relishing a moment in time I never wanted to forget. New material was added to the wall all the time. Nothing was ever taken down. Sometimes you had to dig down to find the good stuff. Here are a few samples:

Dear Goldhawk: The cheque was in the mail. Who would have believed it, eh? The day after the broadcast, I was attending a seminar and two gentlemen came up to meet me because they had seen me on television. One gentleman and I are discussing a new computer system for his business. And the other fellow has asked me out on a date. Thanks and thanks again, Taylore."

"Mr. Goldhawk, in today's increasingly mean-spirited and bottom line only society, you are a breath of fresh air. With such weak political leadership at the provincial and federal levels of government, I am sure that your services will, unfortunately, be needed, more often in the future. Yours Truly, Michael Briggs."

"Ordinary Canadians sometimes need a little help in their dealings with government. It is ironic that those who are supposed to be looking out for our welfare are often the ones we need to be protected from in their obsession to save money. John McNulty, Halifax."

"I have seen some of the cases you have solved by embarrassing different companies into taking another look at themselves. It sure would be great if only the public would let you know how many other cases never got to you, just because the people mentioned your name. We appreciate you. Thomas Jacobs."

"You people are truly fabulous, insane workaholics." (Anonymous.)

"Don't despair. You are appreciated. Virginia Armitage."

"You're still the greatest and you're getting better. I like your style and I like the way the Network allows you the freedom to do your thing. Take care of yourself. Stephen Olink."

"Dear Homosexual Sympathizer Goldhawk: Homosexual breaks the order and balance of nature."

"Dale, you will probably not appear on *Fashion File*, with your inimitable style of sport coat and blue jeans but you have my resounding support. You are a national treasure, blue jeans and all. If Lloyd Robertson is the jewel in CTV's crown, you are its diamond in the rough. Keep up the rough stuff. Wayne."

"Dear Goldhawk: The girls at Riverview are having sex for one cigarette. Think on this. They say you can't walk near the bushes, there is so much activity going on. Hope you can do something. Nellie"

Then there was this narrative from a woman talking about what happened to her husband one night. She relates it in a matter of fact tone, as if this kind of thing happened every night: "The man pulled out a knife, cut my husband (Paul) on the shoulder and took off running. Paul was then handed a gun by someone and he fired a few shots at the man who was by now, across the street in a parkade. The man finally went down; the other guys left." (Name withheld.)

"Dear Sir: It is my understanding my sources tell me, that you know God. I am his son and I have proof. Sincerely, Robert."

"Then, on August 16, 1977, Elvis died. Then I buried him and that's how I got Graceland. God Bless. Room 29."

"Dear Goldhawk: I am in Kingston Pen and was asleep as you walked past my cell a few weeks ago. I must warn you that if you put too much heat on these guys you will make yourself a target for hypnotism. I have wanted to warn you since I saw you confront the satanic Kim Campbell about those brainwashing experiments in Montreal. All for now, Dale. Stu."

"I was moved by the compassion and sensitivity that you showed. In this day of increasing violence and decreasing compassion, this particular story showed the humanity that is still alive in us today. Sincerely yours, Manny Sciberras."

On the wall, in a spot of its own, is a single sheet of legal-size paper. It's a photocopy of the last page of an appeal to a Workers' Compensation Board Panel. The appeal for benefits was denied.

The paper was turned into a suicide note. Beside the typewritten words, "The appeal is denied" are the words "LIFE DENIED" printed by hand. The note continues, "No one had any prior knowledge of what I had planned for the shotgun. I acted solely on my own. Goodbye. Love, Rick."

The paper is splattered with photocopied blood. Rick's family wanted me to have it, to remind me how bureaucratic decisions have the inadvertent power to destroy lives.

11.

Making a Difference

In the beginning, we worried a lot about whether or not we were making a difference. We knew we were comforting the afflicted and afflicting the comfortable, but were we really helping people get what they deserve? Was our participation making any difference in the lives of the men and women who came to us for help?

Producer Marlene McArdle did most of the worrying for us on that front. When she first joined *Goldhawk Fights Back*, after I had grabbed her away from CBC, she had a little trouble getting accustomed to our manic, head-banging style. She also found it tough to believe that a journalist could make a direct difference in somebody's life.

As she started solving problems, she would often say of our involvement, "It's probably just a coincidence, but..." Every time she won a case after that, we would all joke that it was a mere coincidence. Over the years, we figured that our involvement turned the tide in almost all of the cases we fought. We were never 100 percent responsible for a victory and we were never 0 percent responsible, either. Having said that, most of the cases probably had us 70 or 80 percent responsible for a successful outcome.

The truth of the matter was that we treated all victories the same. We downplayed them. We made it seem as if victory was a foregone conclusion. We expected to win, so when victory came, it was no big deal. We even announced our defeats, if the issue touched enough people and was important enough for Canadians to know about so it wouldn't happen to them.

The Desk at CTV, when it thought about us at all, complained that we needed more fanfare. Don't slip a good victory past the goal posts without making a big deal out of it, I was told. But I seldom did what I was told.

Over the years, I think we developed a reputation as honest brokers. Both sides in a dispute could deal with us. We were tough, but we were fair. Our first priority was solving problems and fighting for change. Putting it on television came later. Turning *Goldhawk Fights Back* into a team that honked and snorted at every victory would soon turn off the contacts we needed to get things done. Besides, we had much more affinity and affection for whistle-blowing than blowing our own horn.

It's no stretch of the imagination to say that we were heavily involved in John Gibson's life, in Bowmanville, Ontario. Gibson, in 1996, bought a specially equipped van from Care Transportation International. Gibson has multiple sclerosis, and needed the van to get around. It had a power lift for his wheelchair and hand controls for driving. Gibson bought it from looking at a picture. When the thing arrived, it was a junker. Gibson drove it once, declared it unsafe and unreliable, and parked it in his driveway. He demanded his $9,000 back from Care Transportation.

That's when the saga began. Care Transportation would not take the van back, but did say it would take over Gibson's monthly payments to the bank while it looked for a new buyer for the van.

Every month for the next four years, this is what happened: Care Transportation would neglect to make the van payment, the bank would call Gibson, Gibson would call Marlene McArdle or me, and we would make a reminder call to Care, whereupon the payment would be made.

Finally, after four years, Gibson's landlord complained the dead van was sinking into the asphalt of Gibson's driveway. He had to scrape together $2,000 to pay off the remainder of the loan. The van was towed away.

Said Gibson after the long ordeal, "I used to be in customer service when I was healthy enough to hold down a job. I can't believe how lousy the customer service was with this company. In the past, in the marketplace, your word was your bond. Maybe a handshake. These days in the marketplace, you need to walk around with a lawyer strapped to your ass for protection."

We often found ourselves on the medical beat. We convinced the Ontario Health Ministry to fund a $5,000 a month drug to extend the life of eighty-one-year-old Tom McNevin of Toronto.

We searched the world for a discontinued drug called Proloid, to help the suffering of the very few, including Joan Gilchrist of Vancouver, who could not tolerate a newer version of the drug.

We helped widower Bob Porter, of Caledon, Ontario, get some answers in the tragic death of his wife, Dawn. She had died alone in a house fire while the rest of the family was out. There were many unanswered questions in the death, among them why it took the fire department twenty-two minutes to arrive at the fire, only to find the house fully engulfed in flames.

Porter could not put his wife's death behind him until he had some answers. We asked for and got an inquest into Dawn Porter's death. The jury recommendations were all focussed on improving the 911 emergency telephone system in Peel Region, west of Toronto. It gave Bob Porter and his three children some comfort in their grief and offered finality to that time in their lives.

We engaged the services of both an Ontario coroner and a British Columbia coroner in a case involving the death of Sam Anderson, a seventy-five-year-old retired contractor in Deep Bay, British Columbia.

Anderson's pickup truck had been hit, head-on, by an out of control vehicle. His injuries were severe. He had to be cut out of his truck with the jaws of life. His eyes had been torn from their sockets by the force of the impact. He was blind. Near the end, Sam told his wife Helen that he didn't want to live.

Six weeks after the accident, Anderson died in hospital. Cause of death was listed as "Natural." An earlier heart condition was blamed for his death. It meant Helen could have no accident claim for the death of her husband. Despite the fact she hired a lawyer and debated the issue with the Insurance Corporation of British Columbia for five long years, nothing changed. Claim denied.

We went a different way. We presented all the medical evidence to an Ontario coroner and asked him, in theory, what his determination for cause of death would have been. He said "Accidental." Then we took that theoretical evidence to the Office of the Chief Coroner in Burnaby, BC, and asked them to take another look, based on the professional opinion we had from Ontario.

That office could have rejected our buttinsky approach, but it didn't. Dr. S.J. Carlyle, the director of forensic sciences, wrote in his re-examination:

> It is unfortunate that the initial Judgment of Inquiry omitted specific identification of the traumatic injuries sustained by Mr. Anderson in the accident ... It is true that his coronary artery disease was a long-standing, pre-existing condition, but the stresses of the accident have specifically destabilized his cardiac status contributing to death. Consequently, I would recommend that the classification of this event be regarded as accidental.

The battle was finally over.

When sixty-five-year-old John Vanderkemp called me from his Powell River, British Columbia, apartment in a seniors' residence, he hardly knew where to start. Vanderkemp had a bad heart. He was also recovering from a recent stroke. And the owners of the home, the local Kiwanis Club, had banned his electric wheelchair from the hallways and public areas of the home.

Once, Vanderkemp broke the rule as he made a mad dash for the mailboxes. For that he received a written threat, slipped under his door, that he would be kicked out of the home if he did it again.

Vanderkemp was under extreme stress from his banishment, and now his threatened eviction. Where would he go? But Vanderkemp was a fighter. He relished the fact that we were taking on his case.

The seniors' home made the excuse that Vanderkemp was a hazard in his electric wheelchair. He sometimes ran into walls. He could pose a danger to other residents. But Vanderkemp was too disabled to use a manual wheelchair, and flatly refused to have somebody push him around like an invalid. All we knew was that the wheelchair ban was a blatant violation of the British Columbia Human Rights Code.

In the middle of the fight, Vanderkemp fell in his apartment, breaking his hip. From his hospital bed he talked to us about continuing the fight as soon as he got out. But two days later, he died of a massive heart attack, brought on, said the doctors, by his battle and his fall.

With help from his sons, we continued with the fight and had the ban on electric wheelchairs lifted in the seniors' home. It's what John Vanderkemp would have wanted.

Brad Jolley's family in Nanaimo, British Columbia, came to me back in 1997. Brad Jolley, twenty-five, was dead from a shotgun wound to the chest. The RCMP conducted a quick investigation of the blood-spattered bedroom where Jolley had been found, and within minutes had decided it was a suicide.

On top of their overbearing grief at his sudden death, family members were outraged the RCMP would neatly conclude it was suicide. But the RCMP were adamant. One officer even showed me how he believed Jolley, in a kneeling position, held a sawed-off shotgun against his chest, braced the stock against the floor, and pulled the trigger.

That theory is challenged by a lot of conflicting evidence at the scene, gathered by the family and a private investigator the family hired.

Jolley kept the shotgun in his house, showing it off to friends from time to time. It was never loaded. On the morning of his death, his bed was made. The dishes were done. His lunch was in the truck, so he obviously returned to the house for something. Said his brother, Kevin,

"Making his lunch, taking it out to his truck, being fully dressed for work, and getting there and deciding, *I just can't take this. I'm going to kill myself today.* I don't buy it."

There were other problems with the RCMP suicide theory. There had been no history of attempted suicide; Jolly had no problems, either financial or domestic; two shells were loaded into the gun, but only one was fired; there was no shotgun contact wound on Jolley's chest — an expert said the gun had been fired from a few feet away; and there were no powder burns on Jolley's hands, when there should have been.

Had somebody been in the room with Jolley that morning? Had two of them been fooling around with the shotgun when it went off? Was Jolley murdered?

We asked the District Coroner to investigate. Coroner Jack Harding contradicted the police finding of suicide. He wrote:

> The occurrence of foul play does not have much support in this instance. It is unlikely and unreasonable to suppose that someone could have entered his locked residence and shot him with his own gun considering the circumstances in which he was found.
>
> A suicide note was not found and there was nothing in his immediate behaviour to suggest he wanted to take his own life. There were no defining factors to classify this tragic happening as a death due to suicide.
>
> A possibility exists that his gun could have accidentally discharged while he was examining it, although friends have indicated that the gun was always left unloaded.
>
> Regretfully, I am unable to conclude this Judgment of Inquiry with an absolute determination of the classification of death. The sad and untimely happening is therefore classified as undetermined.

"Undetermined" is only used in BC in 5 percent of the cases examined by the Coroner's Office. But at least for the family, the cause was no longer suicide.

In November of 2002, I wrote a *Goldhawk Fights Back* column for the Canadian Community Newspaper Association that gave a wedgie to Standard Life for a series of recent earnest television commercials. In a financial world where commercial malfeasance and white-collar crime seems more the rule than the exception, Standard Life was showing little snippets, supposedly from Standard Life employees, attesting to their sincerity and love of all customers.

One guy with a Scottish accent said, "I'll treat your money as if it were my own money."

"Huh? Hey, pal, you'll treat my money as if it were my money. Period," I wrote in my column.

A few months later, although the commercial stayed mainly the same, the Scottish guy was given a new line: "I'll treat you the same way you want to be treated." Always a good policy to fall back on the golden rule. Can't go wrong there.

When you see or bump into something that rubs you the wrong way, do not take a back seat. Revel in a wide-open democracy that still allows us to dissent. Say "No" when they try to get away with something. Don't put up with a system that screws people.

Never go quietly.

Epilogue

When *Goldhawk Fights Back* was invented back in 1981, nobody had the faintest idea how it would work — or if it would work. I was front-and-centre in that group. Years earlier, in 1969, I had been dipped in crusading journalism at the *Toronto Telegram*. My mentor was Frank Drea, a crusty, crabby, wrinkled (weren't we all), journalist with a finely honed sense of outrage and a hidden heart of gold.

We had a staff of six at "ACTION LINE." We cranked out solutions to problems and put them in a front page column in the *Tely* every day. Crusading journalism, with Drea at the helm, worked just fine. No problem was too big or too small for us. Any ox could be gored.

Drea even taught me how to drink cheap LCBO Cognac (his favourite) for breakfast, while we sat in his car on the roof parking lot at the *Tely* building, now the *Globe and Mail* building. It made the cafeteria coffee, if not tastier, racier.

But television was a different place. It was somewhat more respectable, or so it thought. Rules about content and deportment were everywhere. There was no handbook on how crusading journalism, or its more modern handle, "advocacy journalism," should and could work.

So, armed with my experiences of the past, remembering my days with Drea, who by then had gone off to slay new dragons as a cabinet minister in Premier Bill Davis's Ontario Tory government, I made it up. First at CBC, then at CTV. I had superb teams at both places. Special people who believed you had to roll up your sleeves to do this kind of work.

Without even knowing it at first, we were developing our own set of rules and tactical strategies. When we tried something and it worked, we used it again. If it didn't work, we set it aside for a time when it might work. We never gave up. We prided ourselves on being relentless.

I think it's fair to say we made every mistake it was possible to make. We sure had the time and opportunity. Everything got tested in the cold, hard world. Out of it all, out of the whole adventure, came the lessons that we learned about how to get what we wanted for our clients. Finally, we had our own handbook:

1. Set a goal. When you embark on a project, make that goal, in your own mind, attainable. Just asking or demanding that a bureaucrat, a politician, or a large corporation do something dulls your mission. It makes it easier for them to say that nothing can be done. it also means you are asking for the world. Not only are you demanding action, you are asking the other side to do all the heavy thinking to come up with a solution. What's your contribution to the negotiations, except for outrage?

2. Plan your attack. Know all there is to know about your opponent. Know as much as you can about the issues involved. Don't leave yourself open for a history lesson on the issues by your opponent. It puts her in the driver's seat, gives her the momentum.

3. Open a file. Keep it up to date. Record everything that happens. Record phone conversations, if necessary, just for your own use and knowledge. If the issues are complicated, transcribe the phone conversations. It's remarkable how much additional information and insight you can gain from seeing the conversation in writing.

4. Start at the bottom. Work your way up the ladder quickly, if you need to do that. Never be accused of trying to go over somebody's head or shortcutting the company or government "process." Make sure the head you are talking to says "No" before you go over that head to the next level. When you are told "No" at Level A, consider it your approval to go to Level B.

5. Defer to the superior knowledge of your opponent. Then politely, but firmly, tell him he's wrong. Do it in a way that gives him wiggle room. Don't argue if he says he's right. Just let it hang in the air and carry on.

6. Slip your proposed solution in the back door. Make him think it was his idea. Reinforce the notion as he mulls over the solution. Slowly agree that he might have a point.

7. Never get angry. Be controlled, but forceful when necessary. Don't let him think he's got you at his mercy, but remember that anger is just loss of control — not much of a precision instrument for success.

8. Never back him into a corner. Even a rabbit will bite you when you do that. Don't deliver ultimatums. Ultimatums are negotiation stoppers. And if you deliver one, you might be forced to carry out the threat.

9. Resist unnecessary delays. Governments and businesses like nothing better than to drag out disputes for years, hoping you will become discouraged. Do as much as you can to move the process along quickly. Once negotiations stall, you are in trouble.

10. Speak plainly. Resist the temptation to be eloquent. You might be sacrificing comprehension as the price. Make sure both of you understand each other. If you veer off the track because you failed to ask a question or said you understood when you did not, you are also in trouble.

And one final note for the bad guys. You know who you are. Stop making the same mistakes when you meet the media. You only make matters worse for you and better for the likes of me.

Here is your top ten list of the biggest mistakes you can make when confronted by a Goldhawk-type reporter:

10. Never return telephone calls. Pretend the hack on the other end of the line does not exist. He will give up and go away, eventually.

9. When the reporter does get through to you, in a moment of ill-advised inspiration, you say "No comment." Translation: "I have something to hide but it is none of your business."

8. You underestimate the reporter. You lie with impunity. She winds up knowing everything about your little scam. So you wind up looking like a petty crook instead of the big time con artist you really are.

7. You overestimate the reporter. You give him all kinds of useful, pertinent, detailed information about your company, knowing you are on the side of truth and light and he gets it all wrong and makes you look like the original Oil Can Harry.

6. You remember that expensive media training course you once took where the training weenie told you to stay on-message. No matter what the tough question, return to your message which might be, for example, "Al's donuts will not make you fat." All you do is annoy the reporter and he will find a way to get you.

5. Get angry and rise to the bait. Congratulations. You have just bumped up your embarrassing little story to the top of the show in the nightly news because you displayed emotion — the great engine of television news. Time to re-read mistake number 8.

4. Tell sloppy lies that can easily be shot down, even by a reporter who has trouble finding his pants in the morning.

3. When all else fails in the interview you foolishly agreed to do, threaten to sue. That just makes the aggressive reporters more suspicious. The dumb ones don't understand the libel laws, anyway.

2. Call security and have the television crew thrown out of your building. You have now moved your story into the headlines for